Contents

Contents

For Robert

Introduction

ISLAMIST TERRORISTS made me write this book.

The fear of the 'enemy within', a constant of life in the West since the attacks of 9/11, was pushed to a new high in 2016 by the rise of Islamic State in Syria and Iraq (ISIS), coinciding, as it did, with an unprecedented wave of migrants and refugees into Europe from elsewhere, and to which the violence in the Middle East also greatly contributed. I didn't want my country's borders closed to Muslims, à la Donald Trump in America. I did not believe that the many could, or should, be held accountable for the actions of a few. But like Trump – and to use his election campaign phrase – I did want to figure out what the hell was going on.

By mid 2016, an estimated 850 Britons were said to have left the country to join ISIS, many of them following the fashion of adding the suffix 'al-Britani' to the jihadist's traditional nom-de-guerre; and around half of them were reported to have returned from the warzone.[1] The threat of Islamist terrorist attack here is not imaginary. As the deaths and injuries wrought around the Palace of Westminster in March 2017 proved, Britain is not immune to the ISIS-inspired horrors visited on Brussels or Paris or Nice in 2015 and 2016. The government's official terror-threat level has been fixed at 'severe' – the second highest category, meaning an attack is 'highly likely' – for almost three years.

The fact remains, though, that the number killed by Islamist terrorists on home soil is minute. In the decade preceding the

Westminster attack, their victims numbered precisely one, the unfortunate Royal Fusilier Lee Rigby, beheaded in a Woolwich street in 2013. In those terms, Islamist terrorism presents no existential threat to our way of life, any more than the much worse bombing campaign mounted by the IRA in the 1970s and 1980s did.

Where, then, does our fear come from – and how frightened should we really be? Counter-terrorism has become big business since the rise of al-Qaida in the 1990s, a self-perpetuating industry whose effects on society, its cohesion and its happiness are demonstrably corrosive. Constant vigilance breeds suspicion and division. It may be a necessary evil, but could more be done to mitigate it, and if so, what?

Paradoxically, it doesn't help that, for reasons of operational security, the government tells the public very little about how it assesses the terrorist threat. For instance, at the end of 2015, Prime Minister David Cameron revealed that in the previous year the security services had foiled seven ISIS-inspired terror plots in Britain, but gave no details of what the public was supposed to have been spared. Did he mean seven potential 9/11s? Or was he talking about some teenager caught sending a dangerous-sounding email or buying an oversized knife? Terrorism works in the mind. In the absence of real data, we tend to imagine the worst.

That is why, in 2016, I set out to try to make my own assessment of the Islamist threat, and the public and official responses to it, and to examine the cost to society, the impact that the demon of terrorism has on us all. I wanted to learn more about why so many young Muslims were abandoning their lives in the West for a warzone; to discover what could be missing from their lives that they thought ISIS could replace; and to investigate what, if anything, their local communities could do about it.

The scope of my inquiry soon grew wider than these security questions, however. It puzzled and troubled me that Islam, a religion practised by a quarter of the world's population, should be so maligned in its British manifestation. In a speech in 2011, Baroness

Sayeeda Warsi, one of Britain's most senior Muslim politicians, famously observed that hostility towards Muslims had become socially acceptable even among the educated classes. As she put it, Islamophobia – a neologism that has now passed into common usage – had 'passed the dinner table test'. Discrimination against Muslims has since gone even more mainstream with the emergence of a new, rightwing populism in the West, above all in America.

In Britain, as across the Atlantic, Islam remains widely mis-understood by the non-Muslim majority. I did not start out as a stranger to the religion myself. As a foreign correspondent and author, I have been writing about troubled Muslim-majority countries for twenty-five years, including ones on President Trump's controversial refugee ban list. But I was also aware that I didn't know as much as I perhaps should about Islam in my own country, and I looked forward to filling that gap and to finding out what it really means to be a Muslim in modern Britain. What compromises must a devout Muslim make in order to succeed as a citizen in a society as increasingly secular as ours?

What I found was a community boiling with resentment at the way they are being treated, above all the way they are collectively blamed for the proportionally tiny number of violent extremists among them. The mood in too many places I visited, from Birmingham and Bradford to Luton and London, is tinged by fear, paranoia, anger and confusion. British Muslims feel under assault from mul-tiple directions at once: from the tabloid (and not so tabloid) press, from Nigel Farage's UKIP party, from a resurgent far right and, perhaps most worryingly of all, from the government itself.

Under the Counter-Terrorism and Security Act of 2015, Britain's public sector employees, all half million of them, are now obliged to refer to the authorities anyone undermining what the Home Office calls 'fundamental British values', on the grounds that they could be vulnerable to radicalization; and in the first year of the Act's operation, some 7,500 people were indeed referred, most of them Muslims, and nearly half of them children. The government wants British Muslims to integrate better into wider society, a sensible enough ambition, given how prevalent their culture and religion have become. Its counter-terrorism policies, however, are in danger of producing the opposite effect, a deep new wedge between Muslims and the rest of us.

This is not something British society can afford, if only because Muslims are not the insignificant religious minority they once were in this country. Through a combination of migration and a higher birth rate, the number of Muslims has more than doubled since 2001 to over 3 million, accounting for 5 per cent of the population. In some cities and towns like Leicester or Blackburn where Muslims are most concentrated, the proportion is as high as 25 per cent. The rise of Islam is, arguably, the most dramatic change to the make-up of British society in modern times – and the process is not over yet. In 2015, for the first time, the most popular name for newborn boys in Britain was Mohammed, or one of its variant spellings. One in twelve British schoolchildren is now a Muslim; one in four British Muslims is under 10 years old. If the trend continues there will be 5.5 million of them by 2030, more than the entire population of Scotland. Whatever happens, there can be no doubt that Islam is a part of all our futures now.[2]

I spent hundreds of hours talking to Muslims in shops, mosques, schools, community centres, on the street and in their homes, in towns and cities from Cardiff to Inverness, and the more I heard and saw, the more convinced I became that it is not just counter-productive but profoundly unfair to go on viewing them through the distorting prism of national security. Far from being secret enemies of the state, the Muslims I interviewed repeatedly insisted, unprompted, that not only was Britain a great country in which to live, but also that they felt and were proud to be British. Opinion polls consistently find the same thing. One much-cited poll, conducted for the think tank Demos in 2011, found that 83 per cent of Muslims were 'proud to be a British citizen', which was actually 4 per cent more than for the population as a whole.[3]

With attitudes towards Muslims so ugly in the country, I anticipated that many might be reluctant to open up to a nosy, non-Muslim Anglo-Saxon like me, yet in the event only a very few were. Instead I was greeted almost everywhere with friendly curiosity, kindness and the traditional hospitality that I have come to associate with Islam abroad. I was constantly struck by the values that, for all the undoubted problems, still powerfully underpin British Muslim communities and how similar, ironically, these are to those of old-fashioned Toryism: the importance of family, respect for authority, probity, a strong sense of community, a belief in self-sacrifice and hard work. British Muslims are also more generous with their charity giving than any other sector of society and they do not restrict themselves to Muslim causes. In the month of Ramadan in 2016, according to the Charity Commission, they raised around £100 million, the equivalent of £38 a second.[4]

My eyes were not closed to the problems of British Islam. As I soon discovered, many nominally Muslim communities are blighted by crime, often drug-related, committed by youths far beyond the influence of the mosques. Public opinion remains rightly outraged by the sex-grooming gang phenomenon first exposed in Rotherham in 2014. More than 12,500 British Muslims are in jail: almost 15 per cent of all prisoners and three times the proportion of Muslims in the country as a whole. It is also true that some traditional Muslim values – disapproval of homosexuality, for example – are badly out of kilter with modern mores. The views of some conservative Muslims do sometimes make the political goal of social integration look harder to achieve.

But I had no wish to join the critics' chorus. Islam's drawbacks and incompatibilities have been repeated ad nauseam. I set out with the unapologetic intention of giving voice instead to the drowned-out counter-arguments, to hear what might be good and useful about the way it is practised in Britain. Our happiness as a nation does depend, finally, on the prospects for co-existence.

What I learned is that many of the most problematically conservative beliefs are cultural in origin, not Islamic – which usually means the culture of south Asia because, thanks to Britain's imperial past, three-quarters of the country's Muslims are of that heritage. For example, the practice of intermarriage, honour killings, perhaps even backward attitudes towards women in general, are all often exclusively ascribed to the religion rather than to old cultural traditions, and this has unfairly given British Islam a bad name. In any case, those traditions are most likely to be upheld by the first generation of Asian migrants, who mostly arrived here in the 1950s and 1960s. With every passing generation – and British Asian Muslims are now entering their fourth – the customs of home are perceptibly fading. Not as fast as the reformers would like, no doubt, but, lost in the maelstrom of criticism from within and without the community, and despite all the setbacks and challenges, I found plenty of evidence of adaptation and change.

British Muslims are not just capable of integrating. Sadiq Khan, a Pakistani bus driver's son from Tooting and one of a record thirteen Muslim MPs, was elected Mayor of London in 2016. He wasn't the first Muslim to reach high political office, nor even the first child of an immigrant bus driver to do so.

'From one son of a Pakistani bus driver to another, congratulations,' tweeted the Business Secretary, Sajid Javid.

'From this daughter of a Pakistani bus driver to a son of a Pakistani bus driver, congratulations,' echoed Baroness Warsi.

'Bus drivers,' observed *The Times* writer Tim Montgomerie, 'are clearly the new Etonians.'

This book is all about the extraordinary societal change behind that joke, and which made Khan's election not just possible but statistically probable, since one in eight Londoners is now Muslim. His rise to power is as symbolically potent, in its way, as Obama's election as the first black US President in 2008.

Khan is a Muslim Dick Whittington, a British version of the American Dream.

Public life is stuffed with other Muslim role models, from millionaire entrepreneurs like the *Dragons' Den* star James Caan, to high-profile journalists like the *Today* programme's Mishal Husain. There are Olympic champions like the runner Mo Farah or the boxer Amir Khan, as well as over two dozen Premier League footballers. There are singers like One Direction's Zayn Malik, entertainers like *Citizen Khan's* Adil Ray, even a celebrity chef, Nadiya Hussain, the 2015 victor of *The Great British Bake Off*. Just as suggestively, the Royal Navy has for the last eleven years had a Muslim Rear-Admiral, Amjad Hussain. What is not to like about a roll call as star-studded as this? In fact, who could possibly argue that Britain would be better off without such people, who so demonstrably enhance the life and culture of the country? As someone wittily suggested on Twitter, what Britain needs is Mo Farah and Less Farage – especially in these times when even Mo Farah, as a holder of dual British and Somali citizenship, briefly faced exclusion from the US by an executive order of Donald Trump.[5]

My encounter with British Islam was a revelation on several levels. It was, first, a voyage of geographical discovery. I consider myself well travelled in the country of my birth, but my year on the road took me to many towns and cities that I had never been to before. It was an experience as exotic, in its way, as any of my past journalistic forays into Yemen or Somalia or Afghanistan, and it was marvellous to find such a thing on my doorstep, accessible for the price of a few train tickets. It was like looking at a picture I thought I knew through new glasses and finding detail and nuance in it that I never suspected existed. I did not expect it, but my perception of physical Britain and, through that, the wider question of what it means to be British, were both drastically altered.

Another consequence that surprised me was how angry I became with the government. I used to think that critics of the

Conservative government's austerity programme were essentially whingers. In the middle-class Edinburgh enclave that I call home, the sorest effect of the cutbacks was the closure of a council-run swimming pool that my children liked, and if this was what it took to balance the Chancellor of the Exchequer's books, I thought the country could live with that. Even the poorest people on benefits seem to have a telly. Poverty is relative, it isn't the nineteenth century any more and nobody is dying of rickets. But my visits to some of the poorest urban environments in Britain shook me out of my complacency.

Cuts to public spending in these places, I learned, are often not dramatic or even, necessarily, immediately felt. The effects, rather, are insidious. I visited mosques that have taken over the running of food banks because the local council can no longer afford to. I met policemen whose forces lack the manpower to send community bobbies into schools to form the relationships that ensure that Muslim children stay out of trouble in the future. I met Muslim migrants struggling to learn English in part because the government has cut spending on English language classes, even as it publicly insists that proficiency in English should be a condition of British citizenship. In many urban Muslim communities, especially in the post-industrial north, cutbacks like these reinforce the old perception that London, down in the rich southeast, is not just out of touch but also that it doesn't really care – and that is another serious obstacle to the social cohesion that the government calls a priority.

The third surprise was that it brought me closer to the religion itself. From my time in Afghanistan, particularly, I was predisposed to admire aspects of it, especially its spiritual qualities. A well-sung *adhan*, the Muslim call to prayer, still puts the hairs up on the back of my neck in a way I have seldom experienced in church. Like the Afghans', the daily lives of a great many British Muslims seem governed by *taqwa* – the nearest translation is 'God-consciousness' – in a way that has almost entirely

8

disappeared from my own Christian culture. And although I am not a very religious person, I also know that I am not alone in sometimes envying what the Muslims have. Even the former Archbishop of Canterbury, Rowan Williams, has worried in the past about the lack of spirituality in our national life.

This gentler side of Islam is seldom mentioned in the shrill debate over extremism, integration and immigration. I was not in any way looking for it at the outset of my project, but as the months went by and the more time I spent in the company of Muslims, the more attuned I found myself becoming to the Islamic way of thinking. I grew comfortable in mosques and soon looked forward to visiting them. I began to think that religious conservatives sometimes had a point when they railed against Western decadence and self-centredness. I even found myself agreeing with movements and campaign groups that were labelled 'extremist' by officialdom. I consciously allowed myself to be drawn in, eager to discover how close to Islam I could come without taking the plunge of actually converting. In the summer of 2016, much to the amusement of my young children, I fasted for the entire month of Ramadan, one of the five pillars of Islam.

I did all this partly out of private curiosity, but also out of a conviction that if Britain, as a society, wants Muslims to integrate, the rest of us will have to meet them half way – because the process cannot possibly succeed if it is treated as a one-way street. Governments have worried for years that mono-ethnic (and mono-religious) enclaves in our inner cities can become breeding grounds for extremist ideas, but as I discovered, these enclaves are only partly created by ethnic groups choosing to cluster together. The phenomenon of 'white flight', as Anglo-Saxon natives stereotypically get fed up with the smell of curry, sell up and move out, is a major factor too.

'Politicians and policymakers need to encourage white British residents to remain in diverse areas; to choose, rather than avoid, diverse areas when they do relocate,' said the noted expert on social cohesion Professor Ted Cantle. 'We've never sold the idea that mixed communities are more exciting places to live, with more going on.'[6] Professor Cantle's words echo a famous verse in the Koran, which says that human diversity is a gift from God – and who is to say that it is not?

> Mankind! We created you from a male and female,
> and made you into peoples and tribes
> so that you might come to know each other.[7]

Interaction with British Muslims was, for me, more than 'exciting'. I found it culturally and spiritually enriching. The more I saw of Muslims, furthermore, the less alien they and their religion seemed to me and the more apparent our commonalities became – and I found this strangely reassuring, a calming antidote to the uncertainty and fear of our troubled times. At the same time I was also, as a writer, frankly overwhelmed by the breadth of British Islam. The year of research I gave myself turned out to be not nearly enough to explore it all, or even to move far beyond its Sunni south Asian iterations that form the centreground. Readers will therefore find almost nothing in this book about, for instance, the country's half million-strong Shia community, or the small but influential Ahmadiyya. A comprehensive survey would probably require separate sections on the country's communities of – to name just a few – Turks, Iraqis, Iranians, Syrians, Palestinians, Arabs, Afghans, Somalis, Moroccans, Nigerians and Indonesians.

But I make no apologies for these gaps. Britain's ethnic and religious variety has confounded many better authors than me. Our cities are famous melting pots of the world: London, obviously, but what about Manchester, a city of 500,000 and another magnet for migrants, where as many as 200 languages are spoken and four in ten young people are bilingual? Some

300 languages can be heard in London but, in proportion to its size, Manchester claims to be the most culturally diverse city on the planet.

Of course such diversity does not thrill everybody. The speed of the rise of Islam, in particular, has convinced many Westerners that it is time for a pause. In January 2017, a poll conducted for the London-based think tank Chatham House found that on average 55 per cent of citizens of ten European countries agreed with the proposition that 'all further migration from mainly Muslim countries should be stopped', a finding gleefully re-tweeted by Donald Trump. The percentage of those agreeing in Britain was among the lowest of the countries polled but, at 47 per cent, the difference was still marginal.[8] So it could be that Brexit Britain will yet choose a different path, closing its doors to more migrants and turning its back on the old national tradition of live-and-let-live.

But somehow I doubt it. There is a reason that the far right has never established itself in this country as it historically has elsewhere in Europe. Our tolerance of others, so often cited by politicians as a 'fundamental British value', is indeed a genuine and deep-seated characteristic naturally arising from our long history of cohabiting with different peoples and cultures. The British remain a mongrel race at heart, adaptable and phlegmatic, with a keen eye for cant and no patience for racists. Britons, moreover, have a happy knack for puncturing inter-racial tension with humour – as evidenced, perhaps, by the 'Urban Clearway' road-sign I once saw in Slough that some enterprising graffiti artist had prefixed with a 'T'. This kind of casual, irreverent racism can easily be misunderstood but it is seldom malicious in intent. There is often a big difference between words and actions.

Some time ago, long before UKIP, the EU referendum and the rise of Trump, I found myself chatting to a fishmonger in east London, a proper gorblimey Cockney type whose father and grandfather had run the business before him and whose spectacular window display had drawn my eye. I complimented him on this and remarked that I had never seen some of the exotically coloured fish on sale.

'Them's red tilapia,' he said. 'Very popular with the darkies.'

He was a specialist in jellied eels – a local delicacy, he said, that 'the bloomin' towel-heads won't touch. They won't eat any fish without scales. Don't ask me why.'

He said that the most popular fish among his Muslim customers were bream and carp – and he was stocking piles of them. He observed that, because of immigration, his neighbourhood had changed beyond all recognition since he was a boy. But I detected no sense of resentment, nor racism, despite his language. The newcomers were valued customers and indeed essential to the survival of the family business. They had different tastes and the fishmonger had simply adapted.

That is the side of the British character to which a government anxious for integration ought to be appealing. But is it? The authorities seem instead to be playing to baser instincts, pursuing policies based not on national traditions of compassion and tolerance but on vindictiveness, suspicion and fear. The authorities' handling of Mohammed Ahmed and Yusuf Sarwar, two 21-year-old ISIS recruits who absconded from their parents' homes in Birmingham in 2014, is a case in a point. The wannabe jihadis knew so little of the religion they intended to fight for that, before their departure to Syria, they packed a copy of a cheat notes book called *Islam for Dummies*. Once they got there they soon grew disillusioned with the war and signalled to their parents that they wanted to come home. The nearest ISIS permitted Yusuf Sarwar to get to the front line was as an ambulance driver, picking up dead bodies from the battlefield. He and Ahmed were not Islamist terrorist material but naive young men who had made a very stupid mistake.

Yusuf Sarwar's mother, Majida, went to the police, who told her that her son – whose grandfather had fought in the British army – would be leniently treated if she encouraged him to return. Instead he was arrested, tried and sentenced to twelve years and eight months in prison.

'This is not justice,' a tearful Majida told reporters. 'What kind of justice is this? They said I was doing the right thing, that when my son came back they would try to help, but this terrible sentence – all they have done is to set me against my son.'

Yusuf's punishment was not just ethically uncomfortable, it was also tactically obtuse, because genuine terrorists will never be caught without the cooperation of the communities from which they spring.

'The police say "mothers come forward", you can trust us, we will help. But now they will see what happened to my son. What kind of person would go to the police if they think their son will get twelve years in prison?'[9]

With all the undoubted problems confronting our astonishingly multicultural society, living in an ever more crowded land, Britons face a stark choice: to insist that people think and behave alike, or to find new ways of living with our differences. Some of those differences may be unpalatable but, in the end, the diversity for which our cities are globally famed is surely something to celebrate and defend, not fear and destroy. Patience, understanding, humanity, humour: they are all qualities in short supply in Trumpland. But they need not be here – and I know which version of al-Britannia I prefer.

1

Britain First

Dewsbury, West Yorkshire

IT FEELS, THE PHOTOGRAPHER next to me agrees, like the barricade at Rorke's Drift just before the first attack in *Zulu*. The waiting police have been joshing each other to ease the tension, stamping their feet against the cold, but they fall silent as the chanting begins up the hill and out of sight in the station car park, their helmets swivelling in unison towards the source, breath rising in the raw winter air.

A sergeant chivvies his men into a straighter line. There are hundreds of them in Dewsbury today, a glittering wall of hi-vis jackets lining both sides of the narrow road down into town. Some have been bussed in from as far away as Newcastle, a hundred miles to the northeast. There is a long history of street violence here and the council has taken no chances.

The chanting gets louder, a well-drilled call and response routine full of menace. At last a wobbling motorcycle crests the hill, its flashing blue light bouncing off another phalanx of day-glo policemen, who are forced to bunch up by the narrowness of the street until their shoulders are touching. With their black gloves clasped before them, they advance towards us as slowly and as poker-faced as undertakers. The little press pack fans out into a thin line across the bottom of the hill and opens up on this irresistible target with volleys of shutter clicks.

Behind and above them waves a mighty forest of flags. The red-and-white of St George predominates, although there is a

Saltire in there too, and a red Welsh dragon. *Britain First*, the marchers call themselves. The flags are a good trick. There are only a couple of hundred marchers but they seem far more numerous, like the vanguard of some mediaeval crusade. They are, perhaps, Britain's most active far-right organization, who like to boast of their 1.3 million Facebook 'Likes' – and they are regular visitors to this unfortunate West Yorkshire town. In the middle of the front row is their leader, Paul Golding, a heavy-set man from Swanley in Kent, who once threatened to defile the site of a new mosque in Dudley by burying a pig under it. His blond hair is closely cropped and he is dressed like a respectable businessman in a smart dark overcoat, a white shirt and blue tie.

'Britain First!' he shouts into a megaphone.

His followers pump their fists. 'Fighting back!'

His sidekick, the flame-haired Jayda Fransen, is easily recognizable from the movement's many online videos. She is brash and opinionated with a talent for outrageous publicity stunts, a talisman for Britain First's mostly male members who call her 'our very own Boadicea'. Their agenda is not sophisticated. Britain, they say, is a Christian country for Christian people, and they are intent on reversing what they perceive to be the creeping Islamization of the country. The message is well reinforced today by Jayda, who is literally shouldering a large white wooden cross. She starred in one of their most viewed YouTube videos in which she led a 'Christian patrol', complete with an army Land Rover, down Brick Lane in the heart of east London's Bangladeshi community, distributing ugly leaflets and confronting women in veils with veiled threats.

'ISIS scum!' yells Golding.

'Off our streets!' they roar.

'Paedo scum!'

'Off our streets!'

The photographers point and click, point and click, holding

their ground as the cavalcade descends. A number of white working-class clichés are on show now – the unsubtle tattoos, the shaven heads, the beer bellies and bulldog necks. I zoom in with my camera on a pair of tall Doc Martens boots painted in the colours of the union flag. As the front line reaches us I race ahead to get another view, down into the pedestrian zone between shops all firmly shuttered for the morning. Knots of Asian men stand about, hunched in their hooded parkas against the cold, closely watched by yet more police. They are the reason for the march today – representatives of the community that Britain First says has taken over and ruined this ancient English town of 60,000.

It isn't hard to see why Britain First might think that. Few communities in Britain have undergone such dramatic demographic change since the 1960s when the first Asian workers arrived to work in Dewsbury's famous woollen mills. Today the town contains twenty-six mosques, and whole suburbs, notably Ravensthorpe to the west and Savile Town to the south, are almost entirely populated by Asians.

The uniforms of all the armies in the world were once made in this corner of Yorkshire, according to local lore. The town is thus literally a part of the fabric of the nation. Dewsbury was the centre of the 'Shoddy and Mungo' industry, an early nineteenth-century method of recycling old rags or rejected inferior cloth into new wool. The landmark Machell Brothers' Shoddy and Mungo mill, although long since converted into flats, retains its sign in foot-high letters a hundred feet wide. The sign describes the raw materials: mungo was Yorkshire for 'mustn't go', while shoddy has since entered the English language.

Dewsbury presents other impeccable English credentials, including very early Christian ones. A Saxon minster church stands on the banks of the River Calder on the spot where, according to legend, St Paulinus, the first Bishop of York, preached in the early seventh century. So the crosses brandished by Jayda Fransen and the others do have a kind of resonance here – as does their demonstration itself, in fact, because Dewsbury is no stranger to working-class protest. During the Industrial Revolution, the town was a noted centre of Luddite and then Chartist agitation.

Since the 1960s, however, once proud and prosperous Dewsbury has declined and become notorious not just for racial discord, poverty and drug-related crime, but terrorism. And it seems that everyone in Britain, not just the far right, blames the Muslims for that. The town is perhaps the classic symbol of all that has gone wrong with Muslim immigration. A Britain First march in such a place seemed an excellent starting point for my research, therefore. I hoped that an understanding of what has happened to Dewsbury, and how, would start to unlock for me many of the mysteries of al-Britannia.

The undisputed hotspot for terrorists is the suburb of Savile Town, the onetime home of Mohammad Sidique Khan who led the 7/7 suicide attacks on London Transport in July 2005. Two ISIS recruits also came from here, including Britain's youngest suicide bomber, 17-year-old Talha Asmal, who blew himself up in northern Iraq in June 2015 under the nom-de-guerre Abu Yusuf al-Britani. Asmal was accompanied to Iraq by his best friend, Hassan Munshi, also 17; Hassan's older brother, Hammad, became Britain's youngest convicted terrorist following his arrest in 2006, aged 15, on his way home from school with a pocket full of ball bearings, and notes on martyrdom and explosives manuals hidden under his bed.[1]

It is not from Asians that the trouble comes today, though, but from two white demonstrators, one of them a teenager with spiky blue hair, who try to push through the cordon as the march turns the street corner. They have broken away from today's counter-demonstration by the leftwing organization Unite Against Fascism, whom the police have corralled in the town square. The pair are easily halted and bundled backwards into an empty doorway, the blue-haired boy squeaking, 'Who protects the fascists? *Police* protect the fascists!'

The press photograph the police photographer who takes their mugshots. The marchers grin and whip out their smart phones to film the scene as they pass. It is an odd surveillance-society moment. About the only people not taking photographs are the two under arrest, who can't because their arms are behind their backs.

It starts to rain as the rest of us eventually disgorge into the main square. The police fan out into a giant horseshoe shape and the demonstrators head for a stage set up by the front steps of an immense, ornate town hall, the most conspicuous symbol of Dewsbury's wealthy past. I dodge out just in time and take up position under a colonnade by the post office.

The speeches are predictably aggressive. Paul Golding tells the crowd that he is 'a realist, not a racist', but then he says that the Koran exhorts Muslims to cut the heads off non-Muslims and reminds us that in Rotherham they have gang-raped 1,400 of 'our girls': reason enough, he insists, to ban Islamic culture from the UK.

'No more mosques!' he cries, and the audience echoes him: 'No more mosques!'

Jayda Fransen goes further. She says that the whole of Islam is a violent jihad and that the Muslim god is actually Satan.

'These Muslims will not integrate,' she says. 'They want to take over. But you know what? I've had enough of no-go zones, of being called a slapper because I wear the clothes I like, of halal food on the shelves of my supermarket. But we don't eat halal in Great Britain. Enough! No more! No more mosques!'

There are several distorted references to Christian tradition. Jesus, she says, had the right idea when he drove the money-changers from the Temple of Jerusalem. His table-turning, indeed, was a kind of extremism. 'And you know what? Great Britain is *our* temple – and if we have to defend it, so be it.'

Jayda is interrupted at one point by the clanging of a bell high above her. 'Ah, you hear that?' she says. 'Ain't it lovely? A Christian sound in our *Christian* country.'

The audience look briefly puzzled – the sound is from the town hall clock, not a church – but such details aren't important; the crowd still adore their Boadicea, who finishes her speech, no less bizarrely, by leading them in the Lord's Prayer. The Christian principle of loving thy neighbour as thyself is at no point mentioned.

The wind blasts the square and the rain, the policeman's friend, turns to hail. All edges and surfaces, the town hall, the flags, the policemen's caps and helmets, are suddenly softened by a granular white shroud. The crowd, underdressed and already cold, hunker further into their collars. I shelter beneath the colonnade next to an elderly Asian with a beard like a crescent moon, who introduces himself as a local councillor and the town's postmaster. He clicks his tongue and rolls his eyes at the inconvenience of it all. Tomorrow, he frets, is the last day for self-assessment tax returns and the forced closure of his post office could cause some of his customers to miss the deadline and incur penalties, or even to lose their jobs.

'These people won't leave us alone,' he says, pointing his chin at the bedraggled demonstrators. 'Dewsbury has been struggling. Half the shops are empty. No one wants to invest here because of our reputation – because these people keep coming back.'

It is no weather for a riot and the sodden demonstrators are soon being shepherded back to the train station. I stand with a gaggle of Asians who watch them go with slow, exaggerated waves of the hand and ironic smiles.

'Bye-bye,' says one of them pleasantly. 'I hope you find employment soon.'

Separated by policemen, the marchers can only scowl. I photograph a marcher in a tatty denim jacket who stares me down and gives me the finger, which makes all the Asians laugh. They are used to the far-right coming to their town and have learned how to scorn them. Unlike the postmaster, they prefer to shrug off the disruption, and having listened to the speeches I can see why, to them, Britain First seems more absurd than threatening. The counter-demonstration at the far end of the square, although much thinned out by the weather, is still going: a faint chant from a small marquee decorated with balloons saying *We are Dewsbury*. The atmosphere perceptibly lightens as the marchers go. Britain First's retreat feels like a battle won.

*

My first impression of Dewsbury, formed on an earlier visit in the winter of 2015, was not a happy one. I see now that I arrived with a set of prejudices that the journalist in me secretly wanted confirmed. The stories I had heard were just so good. Dewsbury was one of a handful of British towns that the banned extremist organization Muslims Against Crusades once proposed turning into an autonomous Islamic Emirate, entirely governed by sharia law. Savile Town, enclosed on three sides by the River Calder, sounded like it was already close to fulfilling that ideal. At the 2011 census, just fourteen of the suburb's 4,500 residents declared themselves white. My favourite story, although I was never able to stand up, concerned a local primary school that had arranged a fun day out for its pupils in the nearby Yorkshire Dales. The organizers were baffled when, one by one, the parents refused permission for their children to take part. It eventually emerged that they were worried that if their young offspring left town they would realize they were not, after all, living in a Muslim-majority nation.

My guide that sunny winter morning was Danny Lockwood, the founder of a local newspaper, *The Press*. As the author of an excoriating social history called *The Islamic Republic of Dewsbury*, he had played the tour guide many times before. He led me on a stroll around the famous town centre street market, with its photogenic sweetie stalls and butchers' shops selling 'mucky fat', the local term for lard. Originally for clothiers, the market has remained in operation for almost seven hundred years, apart from the seventeenth century when it was closed due to plague – and it still draws tourists. Dewsbury was even mentioned by the Beatles in their 1967 film, *Magical Mystery Tour*, in which one of the magicians announces: 'The bus is ten miles north on the Dewsbury road and they're having a lovely time!'

Danny was a big, bluff man, a former semi-professional rugby player in his late fifties who seemed to know everyone, and we made slow progress as he stopped to gossip with the stall-keepers. It all seemed very homely, very Yorkshire. But then he pointed out the many empty shops and the untenanted Victorian glass and iron arcade. The big retailers like Marks & Spencer pulled out years ago, leaving behind clusters of charity shops and cash converters. The town's five cinemas had all closed. Even McDonald's had given up and was now a cheap discount store whose proprietors were once caught selling amyl nitrate over the counter. A prominent high street pub lay derelict: 'Not enough drinkers these days,' said Danny. 'We used to have twenty-five pubs. There are only three left.' In a back street 200 yards from the market we passed a bleached blonde prostitute in skin-tight jeans and a fake fur jacket, then an ancient man creeping along on a zimmer frame.

'That's Fred the soldier, that is. He still likes to wear his medals. He's getting on now, is Fred.'

You could see why Danny, who was born and raised in Dewsbury, might have a gripe. The town centre was hollowed out and had gone to seed. A white population was still clinging on, but it was ageing and would soon be dead and gone. Dewsbury's future, he acknowledged, was Muslim. Forty per cent of all residents under eighteen, he said, were Asian. It wasn't just about the pubs. Everywhere we went he pointed out once proud local institutions that had either closed or been converted to new, Muslim uses. A big Victorian church in the town centre had become a mosque, as had the old Liberal Club. Even the former pork abattoir had been turned into an Islamic Centre. ('We had a good laugh about that one,' Danny said.) Meanwhile, developers had converted one or two abandoned mills into blocks of des-res flats, but they were mostly still empty, because who would want to move to Dewsbury? In an estate agent's window there were houses for sale for under £30,000.

It didn't help that the town's civic pride had been stripped away in the 1970s by a reorganization of local government, when the police station was closed and the magistrate's court was moved to Huddersfield. Old-timers like Danny were still bitter about that, but there was no doubting who and what he mostly blamed for the town's decline. This was a man who had just ghostwritten the autobiography of Tommy Robinson, the Luton-born founder of the English Defence League, of which Britain First is a spin-off.

Dewsbury's story, I knew, was not unique but followed a kind of template replicated in towns and cities across England's post-industrial northwest. The fortunes of these places over the last half century were mixed. All have had problems learning to live with their burgeoning Muslim communities, but perhaps none have got it so spectacularly wrong as Dewsbury, the national epitome of a race-relations disaster.

Danny explained how it happened as he drove me towards Savile Town. The first generation of Asians who arrived in the late 1950s were welcome. The heavy woollen industry was enjoying a post-war boom and mill workers were in short supply. But when the mills closed down in the slump of the 1970s, thousands were thrown out of work. The white middle classes began to move out, leaving behind an unemployed underclass dependent on benefits, furious at the Asians who were perceived to have taken their jobs. The National Front demonstrated in Dewsbury beneath banners reading 'Send them back' as long ago as 1975.

But the Asian incomers didn't or couldn't go home. They brought their wives over and started families – often big families – and began to find work elsewhere. 'White flight' led to a glut of houses for sale, which depressed property prices, allowing the new residents to snap up the empty terraced homes. Savile Town became an enclave of Indians from Gujarat, and Ravensthorpe a slice of Pakistan. Many of the former mill workers found legitimate employment – the town is still a major centre of bed and mattress manufacture – but from the 1980s a significant number of their young turned to petty crime, car theft and then to drug-dealing, exploiting links with the subcontinent's heroin trade. They found a willing market in the region's impoverished white underclass. Dewsbury was plunged into a spiral of related crime and violence from which it had yet to recover.

'You see this?' said Danny, as we drove down a long road crowded with small Asian restaurants and fast-food joints. 'I've counted and there are twenty of them. The funny thing is, there are never any customers. That's because they're front businesses. The restaurant trade is great for money laundering.'

The town's drug problem naturally did nothing to improve race relations. The whites and the Asians blamed each other for the social collapse and retreated further into their respective ghettos. We went through the suburb of Thornhill, which Danny said was 95 per cent white.

'There might as well be razor wire in between,' he said.

Matters worsened in 1989 when, in protest at the publication of Salman Rushdie's *The Satanic Verses*, Asian youths from Savile Town sacked the Scarborough pub. The landlord and his regulars, most of whom had been enjoying a quiet game of cards when the mob arrived, were forced to barricade themselves upstairs as the bar was destroyed in an orgy of broken glass and the cars parked outside were torched. A police helicopter watched it all from overhead yet there were never any arrests, which further infuriated the indigenous whites.

Police inaction was a theme to which Danny returned again and again.

'Savile Town has become a place where policemen tread very lightly – and rarely – where elected white councillors can be attacked by Muslim rivals in broad daylight, and where the kingpins of the drugs trade thrive largely without fear of sanction,' he wrote in *The Islamic Republic of Dewsbury*.

There was, he insisted, 'one law for us and another for them'. The authorities, he explained, preferred to let the Muslim communities police themselves, not, as they often claimed, in a spirit of mutual tolerance and respect for a different culture – the principle underpinning the whole idea of 'multiculturalism' – but because to arrest an Asian miscreant was often too much hassle. This was the unintended consequence of the Race Relations Act of 1976. If an Asian youth was stopped by a white policeman for, say, speeding, and the youth turned around and accused him of racism – which the youths almost routinely did – then the officer would automatically be suspended while the counter-charge was investigated, a process that could take weeks.

I later interviewed a retired local police inspector, Phil Tolson, who confirmed what Danny had said.

'He's quite right,' he told me. 'It's no good having two sets of standards. But the complaints were so voluble. I think we were scared.'

Born just after the war in the Flatts, a long-demolished slum of tiny, unplumbed back-to-backs, Phil was the embodiment of old Dewsbury, who spoke in a mellow Yorkshire burr redolent of a gentler and more courteous time. I met him in the café of the Sainsbury's superstore on the edge of the town centre, a new magnet for the town's white old-timers. An elderly gent greeted him cheerily as he tottered past to another table.

'He used to be a demon fast bowler,' Phil observed dryly when he was out of earshot.

A lady customer asked us to watch her handbag while she went to buy a newspaper.

'She wouldn't have done that if she were a Muslim.'

When he joined the force in 1973, he conceded, policing in Dewsbury was rough around the edges.

'Domestic-violence cases were dealt with by fists, not paperwork. There were a lot of ex-military on the force and they were tough – strict. It was common for people to appear before the magistrate with a bloody nose. It was a bit sharia, actually.'

The Asian community, he said, gave them little trouble in those days. Racism, he acknowledged, was an issue for West Yorkshire police, but he insisted that it was never the Asians but the black communities up in Leeds and Huddersfield who were the worst victims of it.

'The Asians seemed to fit the stereotype. You know: head down, hard-working, careful with their money, fond of a barter.'

Even so, he detected a certain laziness among the police towards Asians, a tendency to fob off their complaints.

'I ran a forum for cab drivers in Wakefield for a spell. The drivers were all Asian and got a lot of abuse from white drunks in their cabs, and they complained that the police never did anything about it.'

The old ways of policing Dewsbury began to disappear when the town's force was regionalized, and changed for good with the development of 'race relations culture' in the 1980s. Investigating a complaint about Asians, he said, often just wasn't worth the paperwork. The whole community would hear about it, and then the elders, and then someone would formally protest or petition for a retraction of the charge. He remembered how, in the 1980s, a white reveller was strung up from a Savile Town lamppost and almost killed. And yet the prosecution case was less than vigorous and eventually faded away, mainly for lack of witnesses. Just as tellingly, in the tense aftermath of 9/11, he sent a liaison officer to a mosque in Savile Town to advise its committee how to secure their premises against hot-headed reprisal attacks.

'He came back to the station spitting about some Asian cabbie who'd pulled up and started jeering about how the Muslims were going to "get their gold back" from us Western thieves. My constable wanted to file a report, but I prevented him. Now, if it had been the other way round, a white cabbie having a go at one of my officers, there definitely would have been a report. So Danny's right: I'm guilty! But I don't regret it. It was my job to keep things smooth between communities and police involvement often just inflamed things.'

His attitude to the community he had helped police for twenty-seven years was complex. He respected the Asian work ethic and actually admired the transformation of Savile Town, which he said used to be 'a shit hole'. He counted local Pakistanis among his friends, and once even holidayed with a Dewsbury family in their district of origin just outside Islamabad. He was full of scorn for a recent initiative, announced by the prime minister, to force Muslim women to learn English or face deportation, a policy that he said was 'not thought through'.

His preferred prescription for better community relations sounded sensible.

'There are two sets of values at work and that's bound to cause clashes. We need to come to an accommodation – a merger. Some people are so prejudiced. They say things like they don't like the smell of curry on their street, and that's silly. Most Brits are very tolerant in my experience. But the compromise has to come from both directions. The community here has produced terrorists, remember. People round here say, you never hear them apologize.'

On the other hand he had also encountered the worst of Asian culture in the course of his long career, and this had inevitably coloured his views and stretched his patience.

'I saw a terrible honour killing in Bradford in 1982. A husband set fire to his wife with paraffin because she wanted a divorce. She was melted to the settee. It took her five days to die.'

He recounted another case in Bradford where Asian police officers were suspected of colluding with the contract killers hired by a father to hunt down his 18-year-old daughter who had run away.

'Asians on the force: that's when equality can go too far. You don't put a wolf in charge of the sheep.'

Phil's attitude to the immigrant generation was, perhaps, typical of a certain older native Englishman: the kind who considers himself tolerant of racial difference, and who would be appalled at any suggestion he was not, but who nevertheless harbours all sorts of prejudices and misconceptions. Although he didn't preface any of his sentences with that classic telltale 'I'm not racist, but', it wouldn't have been so surprising if he had. At his local Boots, he told me at one point, a newly employed pharmacist was serving her customers in a full niqab, prompting some white locals – though not him – to boycott the shop in favour of one around the corner.

'It's seen as provocative. It's her right, but she doesn't have to wear a niqab. People think it harbours extremism, that she maybe knows bombers. There's just this feeling that white sensitivities have been abandoned by a liberal elite. And when people like me start to feel a bit pushed, I just think the world is in trouble.'

It turned out that Phil was an example of the white flight that had hollowed out Dewsbury town centre, and had moved home long ago to white-dominated Mirfield, the next-door town.

'My wife couldn't bear it any more. She said the town centre had become alien.'

28

He added that there was 'Asian creep' even in Mirfield, where the council were building 700 new homes that everyone understood would end up being occupied by Asians.

'To be honest, we're thinking about moving further out again.'

*

Danny and I crossed the bridge over the Calder into Savile Town, with Danny explaining how the suburb was notorious for postal vote fraud, which had, naturally, never been properly investigated. The democratic process, according to him, was routinely subverted in West Yorkshire by Muslim block-voting, a hidden clan loyalty system known as *biradari* politics. Danny had once been sued for libel by Shahid Malik, the former Labour MP for Dewsbury who became Britain's first Muslim minister in 2007, over a letter in *The Press* that Malik interpreted as implying that he had rigged a council election by playing the race card, perhaps even by orchestrating a polling station mob. The jury's verdict was hung and the two sides settled out of court before the case went to appeal.

After such a build-up, Savile Town's neat terraced houses looked disappointingly ordinary. There were no white faces, but, in truth, few faces to be seen at all around its grid of quiet streets. I had assumed that Danny, locally reviled for all the mean things he had written about the place over the years, would choose not to stop the car and might even insist on keeping all the doors locked. So it was a surprise when he pulled over by a small supermarket and popped out to buy a crate of mangoes.

'I always get these when I come down here,' he said, winking. 'The wife loves them, and they're cheap.'

Housewives in saris milled about the fruit and veg on display, two old men with beards pottered past, but none gave Danny a second glance. I was perplexed: race relations around here didn't look too bad at all.

But back in the car we turned into South Street, which was dominated at the far end by the tall green dome and minaret of an enormous mosque: the Markaz, the British headquarters of the Islamic faith renewal movement the Tablighi Jamaat, an off-shoot of the Deobandi movement. The entrance was blocked by stout metal gates guarded by a sentry post hung with signs prohibiting unauthorized persons, trespassers, photography. I took a photograph. This was not how mosques were supposed to be. It was without doubt the most forbidding mosque that I had ever seen, in any country.

The security arrangements, I learned, had not always been there, but had grown up in response to the hostile world outside. The Markaz had been a magnet for far-right demonstrators for years. And yet to Danny, the gates and Keep Out notices were typical of what he considered Savile Town's haughty disregard for white indigenous feeling. He recalled how, in 1994, some 50,000 pilgrims descended on the Markaz overnight for an *ijtema*, a vast open-air Islamic conference for which the Tablighi Jamaat are famous in their native India. The flood plain by the river was turned into a forest of tents and the Savile Road, the only route in and out of town from the south, was closed to traffic for days. Yet neither the police, nor the council, nor even *The Press* had any inkling that an ijtema was to take place. Communication between the communities did not exist.

We drove on towards Savile Town sports ground, where Dewsbury Cricket Club once hosted county matches and Danny used to play rugby. We got out to look at the old pitch, a magnificent natural amphitheatre with long views over the town centre, now an unkempt football ground surrounded by banks of tall weeds and grass. He told how the presence of white sportsmen, and particularly of white sportswomen, became increasingly unpopular in Savile Town during the 1980s. Youths shouted abuse at the ladies' hockey team on their way to, from and during matches. Then the cricket pavilion and stands mysteriously burned down. The police advised that the ladies' presence was 'provocative', and persuaded them to hold their matches elsewhere.

Danny and his rugby mates hung on for longer, but the pressure eventually became too much even for them. He recalled how they would arrive on match days to find the pitch littered with broken glass, some of it deliberately buried along the try lines where players dive across the turf. Like a forensics team on a murder hunt, the two teams were obliged to crawl the length of the pitch in a line before each match could start, extracting glass from the grass. The grounds were finally abandoned and, later, sold to the Markazi Mosque, 'in the interest of community relations', for the nominal sum of £1.

Our tour finished in a quiet cul-de-sac on a housing estate just beyond Savile Town in an area called Lees Holm, the address from which Mohammad Sidique Khan left to blow himself up in London in 2005. There was little to distinguish the house, a red-brick semi with a fanlight front door and box hedging around it, from a million others in Britain. Its ordinariness was its scariest feature, testament to the impossibility of spotting the enemy within. Sidique Khan was a graduate of Leeds Metropolitan University who worked as a primary school mentor, whose colleagues later recalled a quiet man who never spoke of his religious or political beliefs. His mother-in-law Farida Patel, a council liaison officer at a school in Dewsbury, had twice been invited to Buckingham Palace to meet the Queen in recognition of her community work and was said to be 'devastated' by her son-in-law's actions. No one had had a clue about his views, let alone his plans.

There was a transit van parked outside advertising a recreational 4x4 business. I wondered what it would be like to live in such a house, in the very kitchen where Sidique Khan perhaps mixed his peroxide-based explosives. Danny used to live on this estate and we stopped to chat to a lady he knew: 'Hello, pet, how's things?' She lived just a few doors up from where the bomber once lived but said she had never known him. The first she knew about any terrorism was on the morning after the attack when she drew her curtains to find the street choked with journalists and outside broadcast vehicles. Sidique Khan and his three co-conspirators had just killed fifty-two people and injured almost eight hundred others, in Britain's first and deadliest Islamist suicide attack. For many in Britain, Dewsbury's reputation as 'the town that dares not speak its name' was as good as sealed.

As well as ghost-writing Tommy Robinson's autobiography, Danny had just updated and republished *The Islamic Republic of Dewsbury* with the new subtitle *Requiem*. Phil Tolson the policeman, for all that he saw much good in the Muslim community, was just as gloomy about the future.

'It's too late for Dewsbury. The only lesson is, we mustn't let it happen again.'

*

There is, of course, another version of Danny Lockwood's tale of race relations doom. I heard it first in Cocoa's, a hot-chocolate bar naturally popular with teetotal Muslims, on the day of the Britain First demonstration after the marchers had left. The counter-demo in the town square was over, cut short by a blast of icy air that upended the little garden marquee protecting their sound equipment, and the assorted elders and activists in charge had retired to Cocoa's to thaw out over a post-mortem of the day. A party of women in full niqab at a corner table tutted at the freezing draught let in each time the door opened. The place was soon packed and steamy with the smell of sodden clothes.

I was the only white man in the shop but I felt no animosity here, only friendly curiosity, which again surprised me. The town's reputation had taken such a battering over the years, from the press, from the far right, even from Muslim communities in other cities and towns, that its residents have developed a thick carapace designed to repel inquisitive outsiders like me. But in the triumphant afterglow of their counter-demonstration, and perhaps because I too had braved the day's sleet and hail, I found them willing to talk.

Mohammed Afsar, a retired textiles worker, and Mohammed Pandor, a mufti from Batley who runs an organization of Islamic scholars called the Peace Institute, and whom I would get to know well in later months, were robust in their town's defence.

'I've been to the north, the south, the east and the west,' said Mufti Pandor, 'and I promise you: Dewsbury is a good and loving place.'

When I recounted Danny Lockwood's story of glass in the rugby pitch, Afsar outright refuted it.

'But I ran the Savile Town Community Centre. I even played on that pitch! And I've never heard that story before.'

Savile Town's evil reputation, he insisted, was greatly overblown for such a small place.

'There are only ten streets in Savile Town, with about one extended family living in each street.'

Yes, it was a mono-ethnic enclave, but that was not the fault of the residents, who as Muslims naturally flocked towards each other and towards their mosque. If anyone was at fault it was the original white owners, who had taken advantage of good prices for rotten properties. No one had forced them to move out.

'It is a shame because we are all brothers,' Afsar said.

He described a recent community meeting where a white local had stood and recounted how he had moved home four times in order to escape the takeover of his neighbourhood.

'The fifth time, however, he decided to stay – and you know what? He said he was amazed at how kind his new neighbours were, how well they looked after him. Too much is decided by misperceptions.'

I asked about postal vote fraud, biradari politics, the allegations against Shahid Malik MP ten years ago.

'Shahid isn't that kind of person,' Afsar said. 'People round here cried when he lost in 2010.[2] He was popular even in white Mirfield.'

He added that, as an experienced polling station chairman, he would never tolerate election day thuggery.

'I believe in law and order, in liaising with the police, in giving back to one's community. It is a Muslim duty to uphold the law.'

I pushed them on Savile Town's extraordinary reputation for producing terrorists, but Afsar and Pandor were having none of it. The 7/7 bomber Mohammad Sidique Khan, they insisted, was from Beeston in Leeds, and had only moved to Dewsbury when he married into a local family, a few months before he blew himself up.

'But what about Talha Asmal, who went to Syria? What about the Munshi brothers?'

'That was tragic, but they were just kids, radicalized over the Internet.'

The Munshis, they said, were from a 'very good family'. Their grandfather Yakub, whom Afsar knew well, was a pillar of Savile Town, the president of the Islamic Research Institute at the Markazi Mosque and a driving force behind the creation of Dewsbury's first sharia court. Naturally, neither he nor the boys' parents had had any idea what they were up to.

'Parents in this country have little control over their young, and none at all over their use of the Internet,' Afsar sighed. 'In schools around here, pupils swear at teachers. In Pakistan when I was growing up, we stood.'

This was, perhaps, the first acknowledgement I'd heard that something is systematically amiss with the Dewsbury Muslim community. It isn't about cultural or religious differences, as the far right believe, but a problem endemic to life in the modern

West, of the older generation losing control of their rebellious young. Afsar and Pandor are the public face of the town's Muslims, the side with which the authorities willingly interact. Yet terrorism, joining ISIS, is an activity almost exclusively for the young, who are the Muslims who matter most to the security services. How much if any influence do they have over them?

I left Cocoa's after dark, warmer and dryer than when I'd gone in but with many questions still unanswered. It wasn't possible to pin all the blame on the Internet. Something else must have made Mohammad Sidique Khan or the Munshi brothers want to murder the kuffar, but these first-generation Asians did not speak for them, the darkest side of al-Britannia, and offered little insight into the cause of their anger and alienation. Here was the paradox: if Islam itself was a loving and peaceful religion, as Afsar and Pandor insisted, then how had a tight-knit community of twenty-six mosques like this one produced so many people prepared to kill in the name of their religion?

I wondered what it must be like to grow up in a town as stigmatized as Dewsbury, and found part of the answer when I returned to Cocoa's a few weeks later for a meeting with Waris Ali. A British Pakistani raised in Ravensthorpe, Waris is famous in Dewsbury for his arrest, in 2007 aged 17, on suspicion of preparing an act of terrorism. He was tried and eventually unanimously acquitted of all charges, but it seemed to me that his experience of the justice system, which included a spell in Feltham Youth Offenders' Institution and another under house arrest before his trial, had changed him and turned him into the impressively passionate but also angry young activist that he had become.

'When you're on a tag and under house arrest you either go crazy or you get focused,' he said. 'I chose to get focused.'

His troubles began at Westborough High School, which he attended in the same year as Britain's youngest convicted terrorist, Hammad Munshi from Savile Town, although Waris said he hadn't known him. Munshi's arrest in 2006 naturally put the school under intense scrutiny by the security services. The whole town, he recalled, was 'crawling' with agents from the newly constituted Counter-Terrorism Unit for the North East, on the hunt for other Munshis. Waris, by his own account, was already a 'very political' Year 11 teenager, infuriated by Western military intervention in Iraq and the thousands of Muslim deaths it had caused, by Abu Ghraib, by Guantanamo. In the paranoid atmosphere following Munshi's arrest it was a risky time to draw attention to this – but that is what Waris did, spectacularly so, with a school art project based on the silhouettes of Guantanamo inmates in their hoods and chains and orange jumpsuits.

His teachers understandably didn't much like that, and then, when Waris 'pushed back with strong rhetoric', the headmaster expelled him, just weeks before he was due to sit his GCSEs. All this was brought up at his trial, where the prosecution tried to portray him as 'some sort of an ideological extremist loon'. His true motives, he retrospectively recognized, were more complex. He had, he said, been going through a 'bad patch'. He suffered from severe acne, for which he was bullied at school. Things were also difficult at home, where he was increasingly looking after his father, a disabled stroke victim. His behaviour, which he now acknowledged as 'stupid', sounded like the consequence of teenage angst and rebellion rather than true radicalization. He reminded me somewhat of Nigel Molesworth, the fictional hero of the 1950s comedy classic *Down with Skool!*

In 2006, nevertheless, his card was marked in the most dangerous way. Westborough High allowed him back to sit his GCSEs, after which he went to Pakistan for a few months before starting at a sixth-form college. Back home in Ravensthorpe, unable to find a temporary job and still looking after his disabled father, he unwisely indulged a pet interest in pyrotechnics, constructing small smoke bombs out of sugar and potassium nitrate and letting them off in the street outside his house.

'I emptied out a firework once. I made no secret of it and there was nothing sinister about it. I learned how to do it by watching YouTube.'

He also downloaded on his computer *The Anarchist Cookbook*, written by an American, William Powell, at the height of the counterculture protests against the Vietnam War in 1971, and still available for free online. In the intervening years it had been read by countless teenage pranksters who treasured it for its recipes for homemade flash-bangs. In the hands of his court prosecutors, however, it became a deadly 'Terrorist Manual'. The smoke bombs, they alleged, were the experimental stage of a plot to blow up the BNP.

This wasn't beyond a possibility in Dewsbury. At the 2005 general election the BNP had won more than 5,000 votes, more than in any other constituency in the country. In 2012, a gang of six genuine terrorists drove from Birmingham to Dewsbury intent on bombing an English Defence League rally using pipe bombs adapted from fireworks – and they might have succeeded had they not been so badly delayed by traffic that their targets had all gone home by the time they arrived.[3]

Waris, though, was found innocent of any such plot. He said it took the jury less than three hours to find him unanimously not guilty – and eight years on, with a degree in politics and international relations under his belt, he had dedicated himself to fighting the many other injustices he perceived in the treatment of British Muslims. He was one of the local representatives of Muslim Engagement and Development (MEND), a new national campaign group against Islamophobia. His many past and present causes included that of Shaker Aamer, the last British resident to be released from Guantanamo, and Munir Farooqi, a 54-year-old from Longsight in Manchester, who in 2011 was convicted of trying to recruit two undercover officers to fight in Afghanistan – a clear-cut case of police entrapment, in Waris's opinion.[4]

He was contemptuous of what he called the counter-terrorism 'industry'. Kirklees Council's budget, he said, had recently been cut by £69 million, with obvious implications for Dewsbury, the most deprived ward in the borough. And yet Kirklees had found the money to take on five extra counter-extremism specialists, whose main job, he said, was 'to carry out the government's agenda to spy on and divide local communities, labelling them "moderates" and "extremists" according to whatever the government deems fit'.

'Dewsbury remains a priority area for the security establishment, but they never seriously *engage* with the community,' he said.

That was a fault of Kirklees Council in general, in his view. Asians remained badly underrepresented at the senior levels of local government. Instead of gripping the issues of race and religion that mattered, the council instead sought simply to avoid confrontation by all means possible. And they were not held to account for this pusillanimous approach by central government, either: Simon Reevell, the Conservative MP for Dewsbury until 2015, had in his opinion been 'useless'.

'That Britain First march? The council refused to condemn it,' he said. 'Instead, on the day of the march, they laid on "activities" for the local Muslim youth to distract them, to get them out of town so that there wouldn't be any trouble.'

He thought the council's approach was at best a holding position, not a strategy – and the cause of social cohesion, he worried, was going backwards as a consequence.

'People won't engage if they think there's no point – and then the project goes awry. It's how you end up with thinking like Russell Brand's [the television celebrity and self-proclaimed revolutionary, who in 2013 encouraged people not to vote]. The government needs to stop targeting Muslims unfairly – it's just creating an atmosphere of fear and prejudice. They need to stop bombing Muslim-majority countries. And they need to start investing in deprived areas, rather than cutting vital services, for the benefit of all.'

Until these things happened, he thought, Dewsbury would likely remain a community troubled and divided, as well as desperately vulnerable to exploitation by the far right. I asked him about Savile Town's rugby pitch, how Danny Lockwood and his mates were forced to pull shards of glass from the turf before matches. It was a story I somehow couldn't put out of my mind.

'What can I say?' He shrugged. 'It's totally messed up. But if you pick out those stories relentlessly and put into the public's mind that that sort of behaviour is commonplace, what do you think will happen?'

Four months later in Birstall, four miles up the road from Dewsbury, the Labour MP for Batley and Spen, Jo Cox, was stabbed and shot to death in the street outside her constituency surgery. She was the first sitting MP to be murdered since Ian Gow, blown up by an IRA car bomb in 1985. The perpetrator was Thomas Mair, a local loner with a history of mental health problems, who shouted 'This is for Britain' and 'Britain First' as he killed her. Cox, a former aid worker noted for her staunch support of the Muslim community, was no doubt an example of what Jayda Fransen referred to in her march-day speech as 'a smelly leftie'. Mufti Pandor told me he was 'stunned'. He had known and liked Jo Cox, and had indeed recently collaborated with her, through his Peace Institute, to set up a cemetery on Lesbos for Muslim refugees drowned while crossing the Aegean.

On Britain First's website, Paul Golding lost no time in denying that Mair had anything to do with them. The group had political ambitions, a reputation to protect. Golding had just stood in the London mayoral elections, in which he received over 100,000 votes. When he lost to Sadiq Khan, the capital's first Muslim mayor, he stole a headline of his own by declaring that London had 'fallen', and ostentatiously turning his back during Khan's victory speech.

Golding called Cox's murder an outrage, but his disavowal of Mair rang very hollow in Dewsbury, where a photograph soon began to circulate online of a small Britain First protest in the town square a week before their main parade, showing a demonstrator with a face strikingly similar to Mair's. Britain First neither confirmed nor denied that it was him.

The killing prompted widespread debate about whether or not it amounted to an act of terrorism. Several MPs announced that they would be upgrading the security arrangements at their own constituency surgeries. Might they also be intimidated into censoring their views on Islam and immigration if these are inimical to the far right? If so, what was the difference, methodologically, between Mair and a terrorist for ISIS? The Oxford dictionary definition of terrorism is 'unlawful violence or intimidation, especially against civilians, in the pursuit of political aims' – and there are some MPs, such as Louise Haigh, the Labour member for Sheffield Heeley, who want Britain First to be proscribed as a terrorist organization on that basis.[5]

West Yorkshire police, however, chose to charge Mair with murder rather than terrorism, and so Mair was not prosecuted under anti-terrorism legislation as he might have been. Rizwaan Sabir, a university professor from Liverpool, was moved to comment on Twitter that there was 'no longer any doubt that "terrorism" is a political and racialized term reserved largely for people of colour'. He perhaps had a point. The following month, when a gunman went on a rampage in Munich, the media reported that the German police were on the hunt for a 'terrorist', but unanimously downgraded the word to 'shooter' when it emerged that the suspect was German-born and not a Muslim. The veteran Middle East correspondent Robert Fisk observed acidly: 'It all comes down to the same thing in the end. If Muslims attack us, they are terrorists. If non-Muslims attack us, they are shooters. If Muslims attack other Muslims, they are attackers. Scissor out this paragraph and keep it beside you when the killers next let loose – and you'll be able to work out who the bad guys are before the cops tell you.'[6]

Terrorist or murderer, the legal status of Thomas Mair made no difference to poor Jo Cox. Mufti Pandor was convinced that Mair had been among the Britain First crowd in Dewsbury on the day I was there. I went back through all my photographs and studied them minutely to see if I had accidentally snapped the killer, but found no match – just the backs of heads and faces too obscured by hats, hoods, flags.

2

Converts to Terrorism

High Wycombe

As HOME TO ONE of the most solidly mono-ethnic Asian Muslim enclaves in the country, poor and crime-ridden in the worst post-industrial northern way, Dewsbury meets every native white preconception of an Islamist extremist hot-spot. I was drawn to High Wycombe precisely because it is so different. Most Britons think of it as a prosperous Home Counties market town, renowned for once making furniture out of beech wood. But it also has a much darker side: Wycombe is actually a more prolific producer of terrorists than Dewsbury.

There is no Asian monopoly on violent extremism here. The town's most notorious sons and daughters include Afri-cans, Afro-Caribbeans, people of mixed race and – especially interestingly – native British converts. Wycombe, indeed, could fairly be called the terrorist convert capital of the country. Its unenviable record demonstrates that Islamist terrorists can come from anywhere, and that the necessary ideology can take root in any culture, including mine – and that demanded a closer look.

The town's record is long and frightening. At least eight local men are said to have volunteered for ISIS or other militant groups. Five Muslims were arrested in connection with a plot to bomb passenger jets in 2006. In 2014, three Wycombe homes were raided over an alleged plot to kill the Queen as she laid a wreath at the Cenotaph on Remembrance Day. The town's quint-essential Englishness could not have been more cruelly traduced. It is only a few miles from the Thames-side village of Cookham, once the home of Kenneth Grahame, who set *The Wind in the Willows* along its idyllic riverbanks and among its woods. In 2006, a wood just outside Wycombe was cordoned off for four months as police unearthed a cache of explosives, deto-nators and automatic weapons.

I was, therefore, surprised to discover that the Pakistani taxi driver who picked me up from Wycombe station wasn't familiar with the acronym ISIS. I assumed at first that he knew the organization by one of its other names – ISIL, IS, Islamic State, Da'esh – and tried my question again, but, no: what the prime minister had recently described as 'one of the biggest threats our world has faced' was barely on his radar.

'I don't know anything about . . . ISA?' he stammered. 'All that mess going on in Syria? It's got nothing to do with me. I mind my own business.'

Stories about ISIS had dominated the media throughout the winter of 2015. The murderous antics of Jihadi John and his London-accented mates, one of whom had once lived and worked in Wycombe, were still big news. Was it really possible that my driver didn't know this? He might have been feigning ignor-ance – a means, perhaps, of avoiding a topic that could be risky – but from his manner I didn't think so.

'What did you make of the attacks in Paris? The Bataclan thea-tre?' I persisted.

It was two months since three suicide bombers, all French nationals of Algerian descent, had killed eighty-nine people at a rock concert there.

'I don't listen to the news,' he said. 'It's too depressing. I just work hard each day, go home, look after the family, you know?'

I looked out at the rush-hour traffic, glistening in the January dark and rain, the mesmeric beat of windscreen wipers the only sound in the car. My driver's cluelessness was a reminder, useful in its way, that lots of people choose to ignore the news, or else peep through their fingers at the horror in Iraq or Syria, the rape and genocide, the crazed suicide bombers, the brainwashed children with executioners' knives. The lesson here was that this man, who spent his working days wrapped against the elements in the warm dry bubble of his car, was no different to anyone else. He was Muslim, but so are a billion other people in the world, and his faith didn't oblige him to have an opinion about what other Muslims were doing – not even terrorist ones from his own town.

I had come here to meet Sally Evans, the mother of Thomas, a white Muslim convert killed while fighting for al-Shabaab, the Somali affiliate of al-Qaida. Sally had taken part in a remarkable Channel 4 TV documentary called *My Son the Jihadi*, which featured footage taken by Thomas himself of the moment he was killed, during an assault on a Kenyan army base in 2015. His camera, recovered by the Kenyan soldiers who shot him, also contained images of Thomas as he prepared for the attack with his comrades in arms. Abdul Hakim al-Britani, as he called himself, looked lean and fit, with the biggest beard of any of them, and a large hunting knife ostentatiously wedged behind the ammunition pouches on his chest. They smiled and hugged each other, pumped up, ready to go. The year before he was thought to have taken part in the massacre of seventy people in the nearby village of Mpeketoni, where he was said to have beheaded a man whose hands were tied behind his back. The Kenyan media dubbed him 'the White Beast'. Sally Evans told Channel 4 that her son was 'burning in hell' for his crimes. And now my taxi was inching me towards the house where Thomas grew up.

I had a lot of questions for Sally Evans. I was hoping among other things to test David Cameron's theory about how and why people become so radicalized that they end up killing in the name of their religion.

'Only if we are clear about this threat and its causes can we tackle it,' Cameron told a security conference in Bratislava in June 2015. 'The cause is ideological. It is an Islamist extremist ideology, one that says the West is bad and democracy is wrong, that women are inferior, that homosexuality is evil. It says religious doctrine trumps the rule of law, and caliphate trumps nation state, and it justifies violence in asserting itself and achieving its aims.'

My first thought, when I read these words, was that radicalization is a lot more complicated than that. I have spent enough time among Muslims to know that there are many roads to joining a terrorist organization, and many factors at play besides Islamist indoctrination. What about poverty, social alienation, anger at perceived racism in white-majority Britain, the lack of opportunity? What about moral outrage at Western foreign policy, the perception that for almost twenty years now the West has been attacking Muslims in their homelands in Afghanistan, Iraq and elsewhere? What about the folly of youth, peer pressure, rebellion against one's parents, the search for adventure or for romance, or for a meaning and purpose in life, the need to belong to something bigger than oneself? Every terrorist's story is different. Thomas's certainly was: as a white trainee electrician brought up in Buckinghamshire, he hardly fitted the jihadist stereotype. Was it really just Islamist ideology that had led him to East Africa? The prime minister's theory on radicalization was beguilingly simple but I suspected it was not reflected in reality – and that, I thought, was likely to lead his government badly astray in its efforts to tackle it.

Sally was a short, quiet woman with a squared-off fringe and big round glasses, who worked as a supermarket cashier. A single divorcee, she lived with her surviving son, Michael, in a small terraced house of startling ordinariness in the village of Wooburn Green just southeast of High Wycombe proper. It was an awkward interview at first. Thomas had only been dead for seven months, and I was sitting in a chair that he must once have occupied. She and Michael had, with some courage, given testimony to a parliamentary select committee on radicalization in early 2015, as well as many interviews to the media following Thomas's death. But the circus had moved on now, leaving her alone with a tumult of emotions to process. Her 'burning in hell' remark had partly been for public consumption.

'Whatever he did, Thomas will always be my son,' she told me, falteringly.

Her sadness was agonizingly mixed with relief that he could do no more harm to anyone.

The encounter became easier when Michael came home from his job – he was a photographer for a skateboard company in Amersham – and in the end I spent two and a half hours with them in their tiny, sparse front room. Michael was a bespectacled 23-year-old who spoke of his late older brother with intelligence and a quiet dignity. He and Sally were obviously very close, a result perhaps of what they had been through. It seemed the only positive consequence of Thomas's awful death if so.

Thomas's radicalization was, as I suspected, the complex product of many local factors and events in his life that no single theory could possibly explain. The 'Islamist extremist ideology' denounced by the prime minister did play a role but it was far from being the whole story. Not even his own brother and mother yet fully understood how it had happened or, in cruel retrospect, how they had missed the danger signs.

Sally described the younger Thomas as an impulsive, energetic, passionate boy. He was sometimes rebellious as a teenager, although not, she thought, unusually so. He and his mates used to ride BMX bikes around the local housing estates after dark and occasionally got chased off by the police for it, but Michael said that this was what all the kids round here did. It was clear, though, that Thomas had eventually fallen in with a bad crowd in Wycombe and that peer pressure had played a significant role in his ultimate radicalization. One of his best friends was Don Stewart-Whyte, who was implicated in a 2006 plot to blow up airliners with explosives hidden in juice drink bottles.

'Thomas brought Don round here once,' Sally recalled. 'I always kept an open house and encouraged both the boys to invite their friends. After he left he wanted to know what I thought of him and I said he seemed very nice. And Thomas went, ha, ha! He's been up on terror charges! It was like he was testing me.'

The trouble for Thomas began at his state secondary school in Beaconsfield, a large and unruly place when he first went there, and ethnically very mixed. Racial tensions were never far below the surface: Thomas used to refer to the black and mixed-race kids, even to their faces, as 'Coolies'. Later, though, as he became interested in Islam, he made friends with some of them.

'He almost went from one extreme to another,' said Michael.

Thomas's circle was often in trouble with the law, usually for petty drug-dealing. But then, in 2009, Thomas was arrested with a group of them on suspicion of burglary. The charges were dropped but he was badly shaken by the experience. He also split from his girlfriend at around this time, which his mother said 'broke him': the final trigger for his descent into extremist Islam.

Thomas, recalled Sally, was already interested in Islam by then; some of his black mates had converted. Now he started attending a gym each night, whose clientele, according to Michael, were rough. They included a number of ex-prisoners from the Young Offender Institution fifteen miles up the road in Aylesbury, almost all of whom had either been born Muslim or were recent converts.

'It was like, if you weren't a Muslim, you either left, or you became a Muslim,' said Michael. 'Thomas fell in with them. He used to say, they're my brothers – my family.'

Thomas, who was soon bench-pressing over 100kg, began to practise Islam for the first time, at a mosque called WISE, the Wycombe Islamic School of Education. To begin with, Sally was pleased by this development: 'It seemed to straighten him out after the burglary business.' The dictum *mens sana in corpore sano*, however, wasn't always true. For Thomas, it seemed more a case of *mens extrema in corpore extremo*. In 2010 he took part in the Road to Hope charity mission, driving an ambulance full of supplies to Palestine, an indication that his faith was becoming more political. On his return to Wycombe, he stopped attending the relatively moderate WISE mosque in favour of the Muslim Education Centre, which in reality was no more than a room behind a shop in Totteridge, the Muslim area of town.

The MEC, according to Sally, promoted a much stricter brand of Islam. The centre, she said, was not at all popular with Wycombe's Muslim mainstream, one of whom had described it to her as 'a really bad place'. In 2007 there were allegations that it was distributing extremist written material and the imam was quietly removed. Precisely what doctrine was promoted there in Thomas's time was still unclear to his mother and brother.

'This is where I get confused between Sunni and Shia and all that,' said Michael. 'It wasn't either of those, it was another one beginning with S . . .'

'Salafi?' I suggested.

'That's it!' said Michael. 'There's a lot of them in Wycombe and they attended the MEC together.'

Adherents of Salafism, a Muslim reform movement that grew out of Arabia in the early eighteenth century, seek to live as much as possible by the supposedly pure traditions of the seventh-century *salaf*, the 'ancestors' or first Muslims, especially those of the companions and first followers of the Prophet known as the

Sahabah. They reject almost everything that came after them, refusing even to adhere to any of the traditional *madhahib*, the four main Sunni schools of jurisprudence. They often nurture their reputation for puritanism, wearing it almost as a badge of honour. By no means are all Salafis anti-Western jihadists, but the doctrine is nevertheless one commonly associated with them. Salafism is also said to be gaining in popularity throughout Britain, not just in Wycombe. It is therefore the Salafi community that has long concerned the security services the most.

In late 2010, Thomas turned his back on Sally and Michael. He refused to enter the sitting room because it had a Christmas tree in it. 'It was proper *Four Lions*,' snorted Michael, referring to the Chris Morris film that everyone involved with radicalization seemed to reference and its absurd, super-Salafi character Mahmood, who is so religious he refuses even to look at his sister-in-law and keeps his own wife locked in a cupboard. The real-life Thomas refused to eat off the same plates as Sally and Michael on the grounds that they were kuffar and therefore unclean; when his mother remonstrated, he called her a racist. Adopting the mores of a Salafist from Arabia, it seemed, was not enough for the white boy from Wooburn Green. In his mind, it was as though he was literally becoming one.

Thomas had been a fan of heavy metal as a young teenager and got into hip-hop and rap as he grew older. Now he stopped listening to music altogether, deeming it unIslamic. He constantly quoted the Koran. He also listened to lectures on Islam online, some of them, Michael did not doubt, of a very hardline variety.

'He really hated that preacher Anjem Choudary,' Michael recalled. 'He thought he was a coward for not acting on his convictions.'

One evening Michael went into Thomas's room and caught him watching *Family Guy* on his laptop. Thomas slammed the lid shut and pretended it hadn't happened.

'I had to smile,' said Michael. 'It was like the older brother I knew was still there.'

Not long after, however, in February 2011, Thomas suddenly told Michael – though not, apparently, his mother – that he was going to Kenya to get married and that they would never see him again. Even then, Sally and Michael did not suspect his real motive for going to East Africa. The notion of jihadism, Sally said, was not discussed so often in the news in those days, and she had never heard of al-Shabaab. Thomas's first attempt to join them was thwarted when he was refused entry by the authorities at Nairobi airport. They had seen jihadi wannabes before and didn't like the look of him. But he soon made another bid for Somalia, this time by flying to Egypt and travelling overland through Sudan. It was the last his family ever saw of him.

It is unusual for white converts to join al-Shabaab and I wondered at Thomas's choice. High Wycombe is not noted for its Somali population and Thomas had no Somali friends. He told his brother that it was Allah's will, but Michael was sure that Thomas's workplace, Elite Electrical Supplies, had more to do with it. A one-time employee called Nero Saraiva, an Angolan convert originally from Walthamstow, was investigated for running guns to Somalia in 2008. He joined ISIS in 2012 and became one of their most senior lieutenants, an accomplice of Jihadi John until he was killed, and one of the men behind the grisly execution video of the American journalist James Foley in 2014.

'Message to America,' Saraiva posted on his Twitter account. 'The Islamic state is making a new movie. Thank u for the actors.'

A photograph of Saraiva taken soon after he arrived in Syria, published in *The Times*, showed him holding a rifle and wearing a T-shirt bearing the logo of Elite Electrical Supplies in Wycombe.

Thomas was not the only white convert jihadi from the area, nor even the best-known one. That accolade belongs to Samantha Lewthwaite, the infamous 'White Widow', who once lived 15 miles away in Aylesbury with her husband, the Jamaican convert Germaine Lindsay who died as one of the 7/7 London suicide bombers. Lewthwaite subsequently joined al-Shabaab and disappeared. There were rumours in Kenya that she was connected to Thomas somehow, and even a report, entirely unsubstantiated, that she had taken part in the village massacre at Mpeketoni.

What was it about this otherwise ordinary town? It was certainly not the place I remembered from the last time I visited, thirty years ago, when my sisters were pupils at Wycombe Abbey school, a grand establishment on the hill leading out towards Marlow. I mentioned to Sally that one of them had been expelled for dangling her legs out of a window at some local boys, which she found hilarious. Wycombe in those days seemed a pleasant if unexciting English country town, but even if it had been that then – which I doubted – it didn't look like one now. My taxi returned to the station through a landscape of new housing estates and light-industrial sprawl, of slipways and clearways and too many mini-roundabouts. Wycombe felt like an extension of Metroland, a dismal, heartless place of form and function. It seemed only a matter of time before development filled in all the remaining space between it and west London and the town's old identity was entirely subsumed by the big city. Wycombe's population already mirrors the ethnic mix of Southall or Ealing. At the last census, one in five of its inhabitants declared themselves Asian, and a third of its schoolchildren didn't speak English as a first language. And yet there are plenty of other towns like Wycombe that have not become terrorist hotspots. There had to be something more.

One thing I learned from Sally and Michael was that it was nothing very unusual for a local English white lad like Thomas to convert to Islam. I spoke later to Paul Goodman, the town's MP from 2001 to 2010, who confirmed that Wycombe in those days had 'an astonishingly high number of converts . . . They were often young people with troubled lives, who then got trapped between two worlds in a space where they could be prone to extremist ideas.'

Thomas certainly ticked the troubled-life box. He had come to the attention of the police for burglary, had broken up with a serious girlfriend, was perhaps traumatized by his parents' divorce, the absence of his father. MI5, in a groundbreaking report on Muslim extremism in 2008 that was leaked to the *Guardian*,[1] identified a tendency to zealotry among new converts, noting that there was a disproportionately high number of them among the hundreds of extremists they studied. As Samantha Lewthwaite demonstrated, white converts can make brutal terrorists. As adherents of a religious culture alien to white trad-ition, they often face rejection by their old peers, yet struggle to find acceptance among their new ones. The transition can be tricky, and hyper-violence is a way of proving themselves and their sincerity to their new brothers and sisters.

Thomas's liking for rap and hip-hop, perhaps first picked up from his 'coolie' black school-friends, offered another clue. There is, I have always thought, a striking similarity between the misogyny entrenched in some forms of conservative Islam and the bitches-n-hoes culture of American gangsta rap artistes like 2Pac or Snoop Dogg or NWA. His radicalization, it seemed to me, had as much to do with the misdirection of testosterone as with the persuasive power of Islamist ideology. Thomas's life before Somalia was about pumped-up music as well as pumped-up muscles, and then he embraced a pumped-up religion.

Islam and rap culture, it turned out, had been cross-fertilizing in Buckinghamshire for years. Not long after my meeting with Sally and Michael I spoke by phone to a Jamaican ex-rapper from London called Andrew Smart, who converted to Islam in 1989 and took the name that he still goes by, Brother Shah Saud. Unlikely as it seemed, he said, Wycombe and Aylesbury in those days were at the centre of a thriving Muslim hip-hop scene, based around acts like Caveman and Silver Bullet. Saud was a frequent visitor there too with his act, the X-Posse.

'People have a lot of time on their hands in these small rural towns. Maybe the Devil makes work for idle hands ... We used to get two thousand people at our gigs. Most converts were hip-hoppers to begin with, into jams, breakdancing. One or two people converted, and others followed – a Pied Piper kind of thing.'

Islam, Brother Saud explained, had long appealed to young British Afro-Caribbeans because the religion is colour-blind, specifically preaching that everyone is equal in the eyes of Allah. Becoming a Muslim therefore offered not just a new identity but a means of opposing the racism prevalent in British society in the 1970s and 1980s. The Islam they adopted was of a political kind from the outset, bordering on the militant. Brother Saud read Louis Farrakhan and Malcolm X, the leading American Muslim activists of the 1960s, and then when he picked up the Koran he was 'instantly converted ... Islam is more accessible than you think. It seems very foreign at first, all that Urdu and Arabic, but once you're past that it's easy to get into. The prophets are the same. It's about reverting to your true nature – bringing people back to the way of Abraham.'

The big boost for black British Islam, he recalled, was the First Gulf War in 1990.

'A lot of people converted then. They opposed what was going on. Bush talked about a new world order, but we just saw a white war over oil. We were good people, sincere and socially aware, who wanted to change things.'

Brother Saud and his friends were energetic proselytizers: 'Doing *da'wah*,' as he called it. They read everything they could lay their hands on – 'It was scary how much Islamic knowledge we had' – and when they weren't gigging, they gave talks in colleges, universities and mosques, at Speakers' Corner or in Leicester Square.

'We'd take buses to places – a big crew of us. There was a talk in Luton once and half the Muslims in our London scene turned up there. It was crazy.'

Of course rap and hip-hop do not necessarily lead to extremism. Indeed, the work of some contemporary Muslim rappers, such as the London-based Krept & Konan or DVS, specifically condemns it. A 2016 track, 'ISIS, Al-Shabaab & Boko Haram (Violating the image of Islam)' by MC Unknown Undercover, is so close to the government's messaging on extremism that it might easily have been written by the Home Office.[2] On the other hand, the existence of a musical sub-genre known as jihadi rap shows that rap's energy also has a dangerous side. The original jihadi rap track, 'Dirty Kuffar' by Sheikh Terra and the Soul Salah Crew, gained cult status after its release in 2004, becoming so well known that it has its own Wikipedia page. It contains worrisome lyrics:

> Peace to Hamas and the Hizbollah
> OBL [bin-Laden] pulled me like a shiny star
> Like the way we destroyed them two towers ha-ha
> The minister Tony Blair, there my dirty Kuffar
> The one Mister Bush, there my dirty Kuffar . . .
> Throw them on the fire

A decade later, a British rap artist called L Jinny – real name Abdel-Majed Abdel-Bary – joined ISIS, and was another suspect in the execution of American journalists James Foley and Steven Sotloff and the British aid worker David Haines.

According to Brother Saud, this polarization of Muslim rap had been foreshadowed in Wycombe and Aylesbury in the 1990s. Some of his convert crew back then, he said, were 'crazies'.

'In the early stages you are malleable. You discover this big new thing in your life and it's very empowering. That can go one of two ways: you can become a good person or the opposite. Like in *Star Wars*, there's a dark side to everything.'

The original Darth Vader of the scene, perhaps, was another Jamaican, Trevor Forrest, better known as Sheikh Abdullah el-Faisal, whose brand of Salafism was so vehemently anti-Western that in 1993 he was ejected as imam of Brixton mosque in south London. He once notoriously told his audience that the *bindi*, the red dot commonly worn on the forehead of Hindu women, was there to make them easier to shoot. He later became the first Muslim cleric to be put on trial in Britain, and was imprisoned and then deported for soliciting the murder of non-Muslims.

'Sheikh Faisal was a trouble-maker,' said Brother Saud. 'I heard him once or twice. I thought he was a maniac.'

He was a popular speaker, nevertheless, particularly among converts, because he was one of the few imams in those days who preached in English. Buses were sometimes organized to take people up to London from Wycombe and Aylesbury to hear him speak.

Shah Saud had heard all about Thomas Evans of Wycombe and spoke about him with pity and sadness.

'I could have helped someone like Thomas,' he said. 'All that energy, that potential: it could have been turned into something good. I remember how it feels when you convert; I understand the romance of fighting for your faith.'

His response to the First Gulf War, he confided, had been to travel to Sudan, the country that would later harbour Osama bin Laden and the nascent al-Qaida.

'I wanted to be in the region in case the fighting in Iraq kicked off into a global war,' he said, 'but after a while there I saw that Islam is a living religion, not just something you get from books. It's about the practice of it, not the theory. I once

stayed with some very poor people who slaughtered probably their only chicken to feed me, yet they were genuinely
happy for me to eat it. I saw the loving side of Islam, and it
calmed me down.'

*

I later met an old acquaintance of Shah Saud's, another London
Jamaican ex-rapper convert, called Ismael Lea South, who once
performed in a 'hip-hop *nasheed*' group called Mecca2Medina.
It made perfect sense to him that Thomas had joined a gym.
At the height of the Iraq War, he remembered hearing some
Muslims shooting the line – 'street talk' he called it – that they
had joined a gym to get fighting fit for the coming jihad in
Britain.

Ismael also remembered Sheikh Faisal and the appeal his
harsh ideology had for the black criminal underclass.

'For gang guys, the Sufi way is too grey,' he said. 'They are
attracted to the *dogma* of Salafism. Its rule system is similar to
what you get in prison.'

In Faisal's orbit, he recalled, the line between religion and
gang criminality was always blurred. The preacher went about
London in the company of a 'very scary' bodyguard known as
Carpet Mohammed. On one occasion, a speaking engagement at
Westminster University, Ismael saw Faisal arrive with not one
but twenty henchmen, all wearing Saudi-style *thobes* and
Timberland boots. And there were other gangs – Ismael called
them 'Yardie Muslims' – who straddled the line between legality
and violent crime, often while rapping about it. SMS, the South
Muslim Soldiers, was one of the earliest manifestations. There
was also PDC, the Brixton-based Peel dem Crew, whose leader
Jaja Soze was imprisoned for dealing crack. On his release,
Soze converted to Islam and turned his gang into a record label,
renaming it Poverty Driven Children, an act of redemption

unfortunately soon undone by a breakaway group known as The Muslim Boys, who were notorious for their habit of forcing people to convert at gunpoint.

Ismael these days is a youth community worker operating on the edges of gangland through his Muslim grassroots organization the Salam Project. With his deep and nuanced understanding of the street Islam that corrupted Thomas Evans, he runs one-on-one mentoring workshops to bring young men like him back from the brink. He has a particular interest in the rehabilitation of ex-offenders, for whom he runs drop-in centres in Manchester and London. His own nephew, he explained, was once a member of a nine-strong gang in Kilburn in north London who were into 'drugs, armed robbery – the usual'. The gang were caught and imprisoned in Feltham, where every one of them converted.

'It's what happens in prison. You join the Muslim gang for protection.'

Prison Islam, Ismael explained, was often quite different from the version of the faith taught in mosques, and would likely have led his nephew down a very dangerous path indeed if he had not intervened.

'They called themselves Salafis but actually they knew nothing about Islam at all. When my nephew was released, he came out telling me that if you converted, it was OK to go on robbing people, so long as you didn't rob Muslims. I said to him, "Hang on . . . that's not Islam!" '

Ismael's intervention seemed precisely the kind of mentoring tactic that might have prevented Thomas Evans from taking the route that he did. And indeed it seemed that the Home Office once thought so too, because in the past they had sometimes funded Ismael's youth work through their counter-extremism programme, called Prevent. Ismael had street cred, a rare commodity among Whitehall civil servants, which enabled him to communicate with young Afro-Caribbeans in a way that they mostly never could. Even his emails were headed, in laid-back Jamaican patois, 'Tingz a gwaan'.

'You have to engage with the youth,' he said, 'and if you want to influence them, you have to do it through people they respect.'

It was dispiriting to discover, therefore, that Ismael these days has nothing to do with the Home Office Prevent programme. After the 7/7 London Transport attacks of 2005, he explained, the Blair government had poured money into youth organizations like his. But the spending was not well organized or properly thought through, and much of it was wasted. Opponents on the right, meanwhile, alleged that government money was in some cases going to community organizations and projects that espoused the very extremist views the programme was designed to eradicate. In 2011, therefore, and with a new government in power, the Home Secretary Theresa May rebooted Prevent. Funding streams to grassroots organizations like Ismael's soon dried up.

Ismael was far from the only British Muslim I met who thought that the Prevent programme had taken a serious wrong turn. The official position after 2011 was to refuse to engage with anything or anyone that smacked of *any* Salafism. To Ismael, however, engaging Muslim youth meant booking speakers like Abdullah Hakim Quick, a Toronto-based imam who had in the past declared that homosexuality should be punished by death.

'Prevent put him on a blacklist for that. But in fact he's an ex-Salafi. He has even apologized for what he once said about gays. He still has a reputation as a hardliner with the youth, though – and that makes him exactly the kind of speaker you need to reach out to them.'

He recalled how, similarly, he had organized a Muslim hip-hop event at SOAS, which ended up being reported because someone there was wearing a 'Boycott Israel' T-shirt. The Home

Office, Ismael thought, was never going to get anywhere if it carried on like that.

'You have to make careful distinctions. What they don't realize is that there are eighty shades of Salafism . . . I know Salafis who condemn ISIS as Kharijites.[3] I even know some who consider Big Macs halal, because it is British meat and the British are "People of the Book". Not all Salafis are the same.'

Prevent Mark II was supposed to be much more narrowly focused on the ideology behind terrorism. Terrorists, according to the new 'conveyor belt' theory, were not born wishing to kill, so had to get their radical ideas from somewhere. As Prime Minister Cameron explained in a speech in 2015:

'It may begin with hearing about the so-called Jewish conspiracy and then develop into hostility to the West and fundamental liberal values, before finally becoming a cultish attachment to death. Put another way, the extremist world view is the gateway, and violence is the ultimate destination.'[4]

Cameron was, I thought, right to call out Muslims on their common attachment to Jewish conspiracy theories. The belief that, for example, all Jews with jobs in the Twin Towers were warned not to go to work on 9/11 remains worryingly widespread. On more than one occasion, otherwise sane Muslims have cornered me to insist that the *Protocols of the Elders of Zion* – a text purporting to reveal a secret Jewish plot to take over the world but revealed as an anti-Semitic fabrication as long ago as 1921 – are true. Such ideas deserve to be scornfully dismissed. But believing in a pernicious myth does not, in my mind, equate to extremism. There is no evidence that it leads, necessarily, to hostility to the West, let alone to a desire to kill or be killed. The logic underpinning the terrorist conveyor belt theory seemed questionable from the outset, if not downright false.

To its adherents like Cameron, however, it followed that the way to beat violent extremism was to take the fight upstream, to the mosques, madrassahs, university Islamic societies, prisons – anywhere that Muslims congregated – and to nip extreme ideas in the bud. Prevent Mark II, in short, was the beginning of the war on *non*-violent extremism, or 'NVE' in Whitehall jargon. It is an approach that signally failed to impede the radicalization of Thomas Evans of Wycombe – and as I was to discover, it is fraught with a great many other problems as well.

3

The Trouble with Prevent

Acton, West London

THERE ARE MOMENTS IN London when it is hard not to adore the capital's crazy diversity and to have renewed faith in the universal human values of kindness and politeness that make it work. An exchange I overheard one morning between two passengers on a bus on the Uxbridge Road was one of them. A stooped, elderly woman in a hijab was lifting her shopping trolley down from the luggage rack. A grey-bearded black man in a woolly hat, sunglasses, and carrying a wooden NHS walking stick, stopped and gave her a hand.

'You,' said the hijabi, surprised and pleased, 'from . . . al-Arabiyah?'

'Al . . .?' said the woolly hat. 'Oh! No, no. From the West Indies. Guyana. Next to Brazil, you know?'

The hijabi, visibly nonplussed, said nothing.

'Very cold there now,' he went on pleasantly. 'Not too much Vitamin D. Where are you from?'

'Iran.'

'Oh, Iran! Very good.' And then, after a pause: 'The Ayatollah.'

Their conversation had nowhere to go after that. They knew next to nothing about each other's countries of origin and barely spoke a common language. Yet when the bus came to her stop she nodded and smiled her thanks, he smiled back, and both went their separate ways with their as well as my spirits lifted – a tiny, everyday encounter where all the fiery public politics of race and religion were joyously trumped by the common bonds of humanity.

I was on my way to Acton to meet my Somali friend Adam Matan, who had offered to take me to Friday prayers at the An-Noor Community Centre, a mosque infamous for its association with extremism. It seemed an excellent opportunity to see how the Prevent programme was doing in west London, itself another noted hotspot for homegrown terror. In 2013 a local Somali man and a regular worshipper at the An-Noor, Mohammed Ahmed Mohamed, was suspected by the Home Office to be heavily involved with al-Shabaab. But there was not enough evidence to hold or prosecute him, and so he was placed under a 'TPIM' control order, the recently introduced Terrorism Prevention and Investigation Measure that was designed to restrict and monitor the movements of suspects in such cases. Mohamed was obliged to report to a police station every day, stay overnight at a specified address and wear a GPS tag on his ankle at all times. He nevertheless gave the police the slip – and he did so from the An-Noor, mingling with the crowds as they disgorged from *jumu'ah*, the main Friday prayers, disguised as a woman in an enveloping black chador. Mohamed had somehow managed to remove his ankle tag, and was never seen again. Was he helped to escape by accomplices inside the mosque? There were plenty who thought so.

The mere mention of the An-Noor made Adam Matan's head droop. I had known him since 2010, when he was fresh out of university and still setting up a Somali youth organization, the Anti-Tribalism Movement, which he now runs from an office overlooking Shepherd's Bush Market. These days he is prominent in west London's large Somali community, for whom he has emerged as an occasional informal spokesman.

'We had such bad press when Mohamed disappeared. There were journalists everywhere, even outside my office. Yet the mosque never even issued a statement. We were so mad.'

The Somali community had other reasons to dislike the An-Noor. One of the mosque's two founding imams was a maverick: Sheikh Khalid Rashad, a Jamaican convert who had once been a follower of the deported Brixton Salafist, Sheikh Faisal. Stories had swirled for years that the mosque was out of control. It had a reputation as a haven for teenage runaways, troubled new converts, young Muslims in trouble with the law or else recently released from jail. The mosque was open 24 hours a day, and anyone was free to doss down for the night in its carpeted prayer hall, no questions asked. There had been instances where Sheikh Rashad had welcomed in 15-year-old Somali girls who had run away from home and married them off in secret to other black converts. Ordinary west London Muslims, the Somalis most of all, were so outraged that some of them organized a protest march. In another incident, a resident Afghan *maulawi* was said to have threatened to kill his sister just for dating a black convert.

Rashad – the brother, divertingly, of Liz Mitchell, the lead singer of the 1970s band Boney M – seemed to like courting controversy, for instance when he booked Uthman Mustafa Kamal, the son of the notorious hook-handed hate preacher Abu Hamza, to preach there for a day; Kamal reportedly offered up a prayer for Islam's 'holy warriors' to 'destroy their enemies'. There were other mosque regulars besides Mohammed Mohamed interested in fighting for Islam, such as the London-born Syrian Ali Almanasafi, who in 2013 was reported to have gone to fight in his homeland for the al-Qaida-affiliated Nusra Front.

The scandals reached a head in 2015 when the mosque's other co-founder imam, a Syrian called Abdul Hadi Arwani, was found dead in his car in Wembley, his body riddled with machine-gun bullets – a contract hit that was later found to have been ordered by Rashad, who was in a dispute with Arwani over the ownership of the mosque. A police search of Rashad's garage uncovered not just bullets but military grade plastic explosives.[1]

In conjunction with the local police, the Anti-Tribalism Movement wrote to the Home Office demanding the mosque be shut down. The An-Noor's reputation, the Somalis thought, was irredeemable. Its teachings had encouraged violent extremism, its imam had led underage girls astray and it continued to damage community relations. The security services knew all about the An-Noor, and indeed had had the place under surveillance since at least 2007, when an agent was reportedly caught photographing sleepers in the prayer hall. Yet the Home Office remained oddly reluctant to act. Matan eventually heard, informally from a local Prevent officer he knew, that MI5 had seven people connected to the An-Noor under surveillance and were worried they might lose track of them if the mosque were shut down.

'He also told me that they had maulawis on the inside who were able to challenge any radical views they heard. They think it's better to keep tabs on extremism out in the open like that, rather than risk driving it underground. But I told him: it just doesn't work like that. And meanwhile, what about our sons, our daughters? Prevent is doing *nothing* for the community locally.'

The An-Noor is a scruffy brick building that looks like it was built in a hurry. The main doors beneath their misspelled sign, 'Annoor Cultural & Community Centr', look more like the loading bay of a light industrial unit than the entrance to a mosque that can hold 1,500 people. I was glad to be in the company of a bona-fide Somali. It being time for jumu'ah, Acton's Church Road, named after a nineteenth-century Baptist church a few doors up, was buzzing with Muslims of every description – Arabs, Asians, Afro-Caribbeans, other Somalis – but no other whites.

'There's big surveillance action around here, see?' said Adam, rolling his eyes at a tall pole nearby with a camera on it, aimed at the very spot where Mohammed Mohamed had vanished in his chador.

The low-ceilinged prayer hall was already packed with

worshippers, coughing and murmuring as they arranged themselves into long lines along the Mecca-oriented carpet, cross-legged, kneeling or prostrated. They were all men – the 'sisters', Adam explained, were out of sight in a gallery up above – and seemed a cross-section of west London's young, ethnic urban poor. Muslims often put on their best clothes for *jumu'ah* – a glittering kufi cap, perhaps, above a pristine white shalwar kameez – but the crowd here seemed not to have bothered. They wore grubby anoraks or cheap leather jackets over mostly ordinary Western clothes. They looked as though they had dropped in from low-paying jobs, if they had jobs, in garages, restaurants, corner shops.

Adam was surprised to see the mosque so busy. He had boycotted the place following the affair of Mohammed Mohamed and his GPS tag, and hadn't been here for two years. We picked our way through the seated crowd to a spot on the carpet with a view unimpeded by pillars just as the main Friday address began. Adam didn't recognize the new Afro-Caribbean imam who had replaced the jailed Sheikh Rashad and the murdered Syrian. His sermon, a homily on the perils of materialism, would not have been out of place in an English country church on a Sunday. What marked it out was that it was being filmed, on a camera conspicuously mounted on a tall tripod a few feet in front of him.

'The mosque's insurance policy,' Adam whispered. 'They are filming themselves so that if anyone accuses them of preaching extremism, they can prove otherwise.'

It seemed to encapsulate everything wrong with contemporary British Islam – the distrust, the paranoia, the constant heavy presence, felt as well as seen, of a fearful, surveillance-obsessed state.

There was little more to see here, and Adam soon led me outside and back to Shepherd's Bush, to a Somali restaurant called Al-Savannah. Over a classic Somali lunch of lamb shank, sea bass and spaghetti, he let fly at the Home Office's Prevent programme. Like Ismael Lea South, he felt deeply frustrated by their refusal to engage with preachers whose views they disapproved of.

'We tried to invite a famous Somali scholar from Nairobi, Sheikh Mohamed Umal. He is well known for speaking out against al-Shabaab. But the Home Office did a background check, found he'd said something homophobic seventeen years ago and wouldn't give him a visa. Yet if we are serious about tackling real extremism, we need people like this. He would have attracted thousands here.'

He recalled how another Somali youth organization, the London Somali Youth Forum, had sought Home Office funding for a proposed symposium on the causes of extremism, which was to have been aired on the international London-based Somali TV channel, UTV. The Home Office were keen at first, but pulled out when they saw the Youth Forum's proposed list of speakers. Only one of the seven sheikhs invited passed the Home Office's vetting procedure. The Home Office objected, too, to the Youth Forum's insistence that the symposium debate British foreign policy, which a preparatory focus group of young Somalis had convinced it was a major cause of radicalization.

'Somali extremists from Britain used to join al-Shabaab, but these days they are choosing to fight for ISIS,' said Adam. 'Radicalization doesn't happen in a vacuum. We have to be able to talk about foreign policy. But the Home Office is too scared to deal with that.'

He took the issue personally. A Somali neighbour, a woman who lived almost next door to him in Holland Park, had recently 'lost her son to Syria'.

His animosity struck me as a real problem for the Home Office, who once saw Adam Matan and the Anti-Tribalism Movement as a key ally in their bid to promote a counter-extremist narrative among British Somalis – for instance through RICU, the department's semi-secret Research and Information Communications Unit. Prime Minister Cameron himself had once visited Adam Matan's office in Shepherd's Bush, in a choreographed public relations exercise designed to demonstrate 'engagement' with the Muslim community.

Adam, however, had since decided to have nothing more to do with Prevent, because it was doing his organization's reputation no good. Too many ordinary Muslims, he explained, regarded Prevent as a government tool for spying on their community and accused organizations like the ATM who co-operated with them of being Home Office stooges. Even senior Muslim figures like Dal Babu, a retired Chief Superintendent of the Metropolitan police, called Prevent 'a toxic brand' for that reason.[2]

'There isn't one Somali group in Britain who wants to engage with them any more,' Adam said. 'They're just too scared.'

The nub of the problem, it seemed to me, was that the government had failed to define properly what it meant by non-violent extremism. The Home Office declared it in 2014 to be 'the vocal or active opposition to fundamental British values, including democracy, the rule of law, individual liberty and mutual respect and tolerance of different faiths and beliefs' – a definition that the government continues to use today, despite its obvious problems. For instance, is it really 'extreme' to vocally oppose the notion of democracy? Even if it is, what proof exists of a causal link to terrorism? And what does 'vocal opposition' mean anyway? Does it mean criticism? Dissent? If so, what does that imply for the freedoms of expression, religion and assembly? Are those not all 'fundamental British values' too?

No politician has ever produced satisfactory answers to these questions, yet the Home Office's definition nevertheless went on to the statute books in 2015, with the passing of a controversial new Counter Terrorism and Security Act. No doubt Prime

Minister Cameron felt compelled by events – or at least by the political requirement to be seen to respond to the terrorist threat. In June 2015, when an Islamist gunman killed thirty British holidaymakers at a beach resort near the Tunisian town of Sousse, Cameron pledged 'a full-spectrum response'.

Yet the fact was that Parliament already had more counterterrorism legislation on its books than any other developed democracy. Fourteen separate Orders and Acts of Parliament, most of them broadening or refining the definition of extremism while ratcheting up the government's power to combat it, had been passed since the year 2000 alone.[3] Did the country really need more?

Many of the new laws have proved controversial. For instance, no civil libertarian has forgotten the case of Walter Wolfgang, 82, a former refugee from Nazi Germany, who was frogmarched from a Labour Party Conference in 2005, under Section 44 of the latest Prevention of Terrorism Act, for shouting 'nonsense' during Foreign Secretary Jack Straw's speech on the Iraq War. But the row that followed was nothing compared to the arguments that soon brewed up over CTSA 2015.

In a preliminary briefing to the National Security Council, using words that the *Independent* described as the 'creepiest thing David Cameron has ever said', the prime minister argued: 'For too long, we have been a passively tolerant society, saying to our citizens: as long as you obey the law, we will leave you alone. It's often meant we have stood neutral between different values. And that's helped foster a narrative of extremism and grievance. This Government will conclusively turn the page on this failed approach.'

What did that portend?

At the heart of the new law was an obligation placed on some half a million public sector employees – doctors, police, health and social workers, university lecturers, teachers – not just to apply 'fundamental British values' in their own work, but to refer to the authorities anyone they came across whom they judged was undermining them, on the grounds that they could be vulnerable to radicalization. 'Prevent Duty', as this obligation was called, effectively outsourced the difficult task of identifying would-be terrorists to the citizenry, who were mostly neither suited to nor qualified for the role.

The misapplication of Prevent Duty was a particular problem in schools. Given that the government's new Prevent teacher-training module lasted all of ninety minutes, it was unsurprising if some teachers got the wrong end of the stick – or else became like Senator Joe McCarthy in the 1950s, finding reds under the bed when there were no reds there.

'Teachers are scared of getting it wrong,' said Alex Kenny of the National Union of Teachers. 'They think Ofsted is going to criticize them if they haven't reported these things.'

The statistics certainly suggested a troubling level of over-reporting. In 2015 nearly 4,000 people were referred to Channel, the government's deradicalization programme: triple the number in 2014. And yet 'supportive interventions' were required in just three hundred cases. Put another way, the referrals in over 90 per cent of cases were unnecessary.[4]

It was the Muslim community who bore the brunt of this, above all the young. In one notorious case, a nursery in Luton tried to refer a four-year-old Asian boy after he produced a drawing of his father making a 'cooker bomb'. It turned out that the teacher had misheard the child's explanation of his drawing, which was actually of his mother chopping a cucumber.[5]

In another incident, the BBC reported that a ten-year-old boy in Blackburn had been referred for accidentally writing that he lived in a 'terrorist house' instead of a 'terraced' one. The Blackburn police later said the BBC had got the story wrong and that Prevent officers had not been called in; rightwingers quickly accused the BBC of leftwing sensationalism. The truth and a sense of proportion were soon lost as the rhetoric swelled and the name-calling intensified, but in a sense that wasn't important: what mattered was the effect the paranoia and negativity developing around the whole counter-extremism narrative was likely to have on British Muslims.

The stories about cucumbers and terraced houses were not hapless one-offs. A 16-year-old in Portsmouth was reported for reading a school library book about terrorism. An eight-year-old in Birmingham was referred for a homework essay that obsessed about violence and guns, even though his parents said his interest came from televised Marvel cartoons. Another eight-year-old, from London, was referred for wearing a T-shirt saying *I want to be like Abu Bakr al-Siddique*, the referrers apparently having confused the First Muslim Caliph, the Prophet's father-in-law known to Muslims as the Truthful, with Abu Bakr al-Baghdadi, the leader of ISIS. The same child was also reported for telling girls in his class that his dad had a 'secret job' selling nail polish. The story was true: his father ran a sideline business selling cosmetics on eBay.[6]

None of this seemed likely to do much for the cause of social cohesion. It was also a potential disaster for the security services trying to root out real terrorists because, as the Council of Europe's commissioner for human rights Nils Muiznieks put it, Prevent 'risked isolating the very communities whose cooperation is most needed to fight violent extremism'. Had the legislative ratchet turned a notch too far?

The Home Office evidently didn't think so – because in 2016, it began to push ahead with plans for yet another counter-extremism bill. The centrepiece of the new law was to be a regime of 'Extremism Disruption Orders', which would allow the government to restrict the movements and activities of any organization or individual it deemed to be extreme. Among the most widely cited critics of this draconian proposal was David Anderson QC, the government's own Independent Reviewer of Terrorism Legislation, who warned in a report:

'If the wrong decisions are taken, the new law risks provoking a backlash in affected communities, hardening perceptions of an illiberal or Islamophobic approach, alienating those whose integration into British society is already fragile, and playing into the hands of those who, by peddling a grievance agenda, seek to drive people further towards extremism and terrorism.'[7]

I went to interview Anderson in his chambers in Middle Temple, where he proceeded to argue, in precise language full of steely charm, that there was enough counter-terrorism law on the statute books already, and that the best way to tackle bad ideas was not to ban them but to counter them with better ones, in line with the 'core democratic freedom' of free speech. He also noted the 'quite astonishing' lack of any formal public consultation by the government as they prepared the new law.

'If you are trying to carry a community with you, consulting them about it is surely elementary – a *basic* prerequisite,' he said.

As a figure so self-evidently from the heart of the Anglo-Saxon establishment – he was the son of an Eton headmaster as well as one of the country's top silks – Anderson's misgivings could not easily be dismissed.

In 2015 the government's Extremism Analysis Unit (EAU) announced that speakers 'on record as expressing views contrary to British values' had addressed students on university campuses at least seventy times in 2014. This prompted the Universities Minister Jo Johnson to write to the National Union of Students to remind them of their duty to challenge extremist views and to protect people from 'the poisonous and pernicious influence of extremist ideas that are used to legitimise terrorism'. A fierce and at times surreal public debate ensued between those who wanted universities to be 'safe spaces' where extremists of all kinds should be 'no-platformed', and those who argued that the free exchange of ideas, however bad, was crucial to academic freedom – a freedom, furthermore, that was enshrined in the Education Act of 2002.[8]

The EAU dug in and named six university speakers whom it regarded as beyond the pale. One of the six, Dr Salman Butt, then sued the government for defamation and breach of civil rights, arguing that the Home Office definition of extremism was unsound. A biochemist from Slough, Butt was the editor of an Islamic news website called Islam21c.com, which described itself as 'articulating Islam in the 21st Century'. As this book went to press, civil libertarians everywhere were awaiting the outcome of a trial regarded as a vital test case, with the Prevent strategy itself in the dock.[9]

How did the government get itself into such a mess?

4

The Hunting of the Snark

Walthamstow, East London

THE FIRST SURPRISE OF the 'Waltham Forest Against Prevent' meeting is how few Muslims are in attendance. The evening, in a community centre in Walthamstow, E17, has been organized by Preventwatch in conjunction with the Waltham Forest Council of Mosques, a body representing 70,000 east London Muslims, which a few weeks ago sensationally announced a 'boycott' of Prevent – the first Council of Mosques in the country to do so. I expect to find a hall full of angry Asian Muslims, therefore. The audience, however, is mostly white, as well as very leftwing. At the entrance I run a gauntlet of pamphleteers, dreadlocked and nose-pierced, from the Socialist Workers Party, Left Unity, the campaign group Stand up to Racism. There is even an organization called Jews for Justice for Palestinians.

I am handed an invitation to a five-day festival of Marxism (*Ideas to Change the World!*) with a special ticket price for the unwaged. The Stop the War Coalition, meanwhile, want me to join a march against nuclear weapons (*STOP TRIDENT – Jobs not Bombs!*).

I wonder what they are all doing here. What does Stop the War have to do with Prevent? But I suppose their presence is in keeping with this part of London's radical left traditions. The old spirit of new Corbynism is strong among these Walthamstow activists, and Prevent has become their new rallying point. It is as though the Battle of Cable Street, the famous 1930s punch-up between East End anti-fascists and Oswald Mosley's Blackshirts, has only just happened.

Waltham Forest's Muslims were in the national news six weeks ago, when a mentally disturbed Somali man, Muhaydin Mire, 29, attempted to cut the throat of a random passenger at Leytonstone tube station, shouting 'This is for Syria!' as he did so. The Council of Mosques' boycott is directed at Waltham Forest Council, who cited the Leytonstone attack as justification for introducing a Prevent-linked programme into local schools called BRIT – Building Resilience through Integration and Trust – which the mosques feel is unfair and racist: 'Another tool being used ... to spy on and denigrate the Muslim community and cause distrust.' Under the BRIT programme, schoolchildren have been asked questions that do indeed seem to be aimed at Muslims, although the council naturally denies it:[1]

I believe that my religion is the only correct one: True/False
God has a purpose for me: True/False
I would mind if a family of a different race or religion moved next door: True/False

I can see why the mosques might be angry. The council seems to have ignored entirely the coda to the incident at Leytonstone tube, in which another passer-by, a non-Muslim identified only as 'John', was filmed shouting at Mire, 'You ain't no Muslim, bruv' – a line that quickly trended on Twitter, and delighted the nation's newspaper columnists who said it encapsulated the true spirit and resilience of multicultural London. John's riposte suggested that Londoners could deal with extremism just fine without the heavy-handed intervention of the state. Even the prime minister said John had 'said it all much better than I could have done'.[2]

The atmosphere in the hall is likely to be heated, therefore – although I actually find it to be supercharged, thanks to Andrew Gilligan, the journalist famed for revealing how the Blair government had 'sexed up' its dossier on Weapons of Mass Destruction ahead of the Iraq War in 2003. Gilligan had trailed the meeting in an article in the previous weekend's *Sunday Telegraph*, in which he described the organizers, a community support group called Preventwatch, as 'Islamist activists linked to the terror-sympathizing group Cage'. Preventwatch's sinister secret agenda, he wrote, was to spread false or exaggerated stories about Prevent in order to inflame public opinion against it.[3] Several of the supposedly ordinary victims of Prevent, according to Gilligan, were in fact Preventwatch 'activists' whose testimony should therefore be dismissed.

I turn to a clean page of my notebook and write: *A Prevent Vent Event*. Speaker after outraged speaker rises to denounce both Gilligan and the government: an official from the NUT, a Midlands university professor called Farooqi, worried parents, the right-on vicar of a local church. Jahangir Mohammed, of the Centre for Muslim Affairs – one of the 'activists' named by Gilligan as a member of Cage, which Mohammed denies – accuses Gilligan of sexing up stories about Muslims. Prevent, he says, is 'McCarthyite'. There is no evidence that religious conservatism leads to terrorism. The conveyor belt theory that underpins the government strategy is therefore flawed. The policy amounts to a reintroduction of an idea as old as the Crusades, that Islam is an inherently violent ideology.

'But terrorism isn't an ideology – it's a methodology! And Prevent is simply a licence for public sector workers to vent their prejudices,' he adds, to pantomime cheers.

The NUT official, Alex Kenny, is scornful of the government's 'Prevent guidance' to teachers, which includes the tip that 'sudden mood swings' in teenagers can be a sign of radicalization.

'I think any parent of a teenager could tell you how useless that piece of advice is,' observes Kenny, who has a 13-year-old daughter.

Schools, he argues, are supposed to be places for debate, but Prevent is slowly shutting down that important role. Some current affairs topics – he gives the *Charlie Hebdo* cartoons and the terrorist murders that followed them as an example – are becoming taboo.

'Teachers are no longer sure what they are allowed to discuss, and mums are warning their kids to be careful what they say. The kids are then internalizing their fear of Prevent. But if you can't discuss something like *Charlie Hebdo* in a school setting, where will that discussion go? I worry, because as we all know there are some very dark places on the Internet.'

A parent on the panel, Ifhat Smith, tells how her 14-year-old son was questioned at his Islington comprehensive because he had used the word 'ecoterrorism' in a class presentation about rainforests – a French class, taught by a teacher for whom English was not her first language. Gilligan has accused Ifhat of exaggerating the ensuing 'interrogation' of her son for her own political ends. He alleges that she is a member of the Muslim Brotherhood, no less.[4] If Ifhat is an Islamist, however, she is a cunningly disguised one. She looks and sounds to me like an ordinary housewife in a hijab.

'I am mocked for wanting Prevent removed from schools, but why shouldn't I be allowed to challenge it?' she says, so quietly that it is hard to hear her. 'I am not and never have been a member of the Muslim Brotherhood. I am against Prevent because it is unjust.'

She describes how her son was questioned by two unknown 'child protection officers', one of them sitting in front of him and one behind, a formation that did indeed sound intimidating. Ecoterrorism, her son explained, meant burying nails in the bark of a tree in order to wreck the teeth of chainsaws.

'Why do you mention chainsaws?' said one of the interviewers. 'Is it because they explode?'

*

I met Ifhat in an Islington coffee shop the following day to hear more details. Ten minutes was enough to convince me that she was no Islamist. She was just an angry mother, standing up for her son.

'My duty as a Muslim mum is to protect my children, including from the government,' she said.

As a former parent-governor at a Muslim-majority primary school in Hackney – where she was the only Muslim on the board – she was more than averagely aware of her civic rights as a parent, and perhaps also more determined than most to uphold them.

'They picked on him because of his skin colour,' she said. 'I have to speak up about this. Otherwise it means Prevent has won.'

Andrew Gilligan dismissed her son's experience as inconsequential, but Ifhat insisted it had changed him from a 'cocky, confident' boy, happy at his school where he was a keen member of the debating club, into someone 'a lot more reserved and quiet'.

Her connection to the Muslim Brotherhood was almost an accident. Five years previously, she explained, she had taken on some unpaid secretarial work for the Muslim Welfare House in Finsbury, a branch office of the Muslim Association of Britain. The MAB, a body best known for its strident opposition to the Iraq War, *is* linked to the Muslim Brotherhood, with a connection through this branch office to Ennahdha, a Tunisian 'Islamist-light' political party that has nevertheless campaigned in the past for sharia punishment for adultery.

'I didn't even know they were connected to Tunisia,' Ifhat said now. 'I thought they were Algerian. I was working from home for them. To be honest, I only took the job because I was suffering from postnatal depression and I thought some work would be a good cure.'

Ifhat, originally from Jhelum in northern Pakistan but brought up in Bristol, is modern, urban and leftwing in her views, and although devout – she calls herself 'Salafist-light' and prays five times a day – she is hardly a traditional British Punjabi. In her private life, indeed, she is an exemplar of the cross-cultural integration that the government desires. Her convert husband is of Jamaican descent, a 'properly black' man whom she met when he was working as a DJ at a WOMAD festival.

'My mum wouldn't talk to me because I'd married outside my culture,' she said. 'But I wanted to be free, to find my own way.'

These details were not reported by Andrew Gilligan. They were probably not details that he *could* have reported, since he had never interviewed Ifhat Smith, nor contacted her in any way before attacking her in print. I wondered if he would have so demonized her if he had. To my mind there was something cheerily and admirably British about Ifhat's awkward-squad refusal to be bullied: not by her mother, not by the government – and certainly not by the *Sunday Telegraph*, which was eventually forced to publish an apology retracting Gilligan's allegations, as well as the editorial it had penned on the back of them. The paper also agreed to pay her 'appropriate compensation'.[5]

A failure to communicate, I was discovering, was one of the worst characteristics of the debate about extremism in general. It was an absurd dialogue of the deaf, an escalating exchange of insults yelled from the battlements like the French and the English in a Monty Python sketch. The media were not the only shouters on the non-Muslim side. The government, too, routinely shot from the hip without checking their target. One of the most embarrassing examples concerned Suliman

Gani, the well-known and entirely mainstream imam of Tooting in south London, whom David Cameron himself accused
of 'supporting IS' ahead of London's bitterly fought mayoral
election in May 2016. Gani's response to this attempt to dis-
credit the Labour candidate, his associate and Tooting MP, Sadiq
Khan, was brilliant in its simplicity: he tweeted a photo of a
poster for a public seminar he had recently given in Mitcham,
entitled 'The Evils of ISIS'. No Downing Street adviser had
thought to ring the imam up and just ask him what his views on
ISIS were.

Gani, for sure, is a conservative, who reportedly fell out with
Sadiq Khan over the latter's support for gay marriage. He is also
a proselytizer. Like all imams, he believes in and prays for the
global establishment of *an* 'Islamic state'. But this is an almost
abstract ambition for some unspecified time in the future; it is
part and parcel of being a Muslim, implicit in the *shahada*, the
profession of faith that forms the first pillar of Islam. No Tooting
Muslim would ever interpret such a belief as extreme, or take it
for one second as evidence of support for ISIS. It turned out that
a Downing Street researcher, tasked with preparing the prime
minister's speaking notes, had failed to grasp any of this, and
had left out the indefinite article in the phrase 'supporter of
an Islamic State', resulting in a catastrophic alteration in its
meaning. The prime minister was later forced to apologize;
the Defence Secretary Michael Fallon, who repeated the prime
minister's assertion in a radio interview, ended up paying
damages.

'The prime minister's desperate dog whistle has now totally
backfired,' Sadiq Khan somewhat colourfully observed.[6]

The episode exposed a worrying level of ignorance at the top
of government about British Muslims that made me wonder
what else they might have got wrong. Tooting, as all British
Muslims know, and as the prime minister or his advisers certainly should have known, is a prosperous place, home to some

of the most successful and Western-oriented international Muslim businessmen in the country. It is in reality almost inconceivable, a laughable accusation, that the chief imam of such a community could be a backer of terrorism.

The names targeted by government are always the same: the controversial 'hate preachers' like Haitham al-Haddad, the political organizations like the Muslim Brotherhood or Hizb ut-Tahrir, the advocacy groups like Cage, sometimes even mainstream umbrella bodies like the Muslim Council of Britain. Are all these people and organizations really as dangerous and influential as the government claims?

The government's flip-flop over the Muslim Brotherhood, in particular, did not inspire much confidence in its judgement. An Islamic Revivalist organization founded in Egypt in 1928, the Brotherhood is one of the largest and most influential political movements in the Muslim world. The methods it advocates are mostly peaceful and democratic. In Egypt in 2012, following the Arab Spring revolution, its candidate Mohamed Morsi contested and won the presidential election. The result was at first welcomed by the British government, but when Morsi was overthrown by the military, who declared that the Brotherhood was a terrorist organization, London began to finesse its earlier position. Britain's Gulf allies, Saudi Arabia and the UAE, also declared the Brotherhood to be terrorists, and complained that Britain was a sheltering hub for them. In April 2014, therefore, Prime Minister Cameron commissioned a review of the Brotherhood's activities in Britain by the former ambassador to Saudi, Sir John Jenkins.

The review's publication was withheld for over a year, with no explanation given for the delay; and when a redacted version finally emerged at the end of 2015, the government response was a fudge. Although there was not enough evidence to ban the organization, the prime minister nevertheless declared that 'membership of, association with, or influence by the Muslim

Brotherhood should be considered as a possible indicator of extremism' on the grounds that 'parts of [the Brotherhood] have a highly ambiguous relationship with violent extremism'.[7] Supporters of the Brotherhood were furious at the aspersion. Were they now to be treated as extremists or not?

The counter-protest was launched at a press conference at Finsbury Park Mosque, an institution controlled by the Muslim Association of Britain (MAB), the Brotherhood-linked organization for which Ifhat Smith had worked. I was curious to see inside this mosque, the onetime fief of the hate preacher Abu Hamza. It was the MAB who had taken control of the mosque in 2005 and evicted Hamza, who famously responded by holding his prayer meetings in the street outside. The government had tacitly supported the MAB back then, but from the prime minister's recent rhetoric – he mentioned the mosque by name in his announcement about the Jenkins Review – it was evident that he believed it was still a den of extremists, or perhaps even the same old wolf in different sheep's clothing. Some members of the public certainly thought so. A few weeks previously, a white man in a hoodie tried unsuccessfully to set fire to the mosque, before being seen speeding away on a moped.

And so it was with mild trepidation that I mounted the steps to the entrance at the appointed time. What I found inside, however, was a blameless community centre. There were posters advertising a weekly youth club, for girls as well as boys, with ping pong, snooker and Playstations on offer. The mosque ran IT courses for non-English speakers and a soup kitchen for local homeless people, including non-Muslim ones. It had won awards for its community work, helping the council to house refugees, organizing neighbourhood street-cleaning and holding regular open days for local, non-Muslim schools. The local MP – one Jeremy Corbyn – had even held surgeries at the mosque. This was no sinister flagship of Islamist entryism, as the government implied, but a conspicuous showcase of Muslim community values, utterly changed since 2005. The government, it appeared, was judging the mosque by a reputation more than ten years out of date.

The press conference was not well attended. There were perhaps thirty journalists there, many of them from Arab websites and news organizations. The mainstream British media that habitually make the most noise about extremists were conspicuously absent. Among the speakers was a charismatic Iraqi called Anas al-Tikriti, the former leader of the MAB and the head of the Cordoba Foundation, a policy think tank dedicated to 'bridging the gap of understanding between the Muslim world and the West', but which David Cameron had repeatedly described as 'a political front for the Muslim Brotherhood'. Al-Tikriti flatly denied being any such thing, although he freely admitted to being an Islamist in its pure political sense, and it was clear where his sympathies lay. The Brotherhood in Egypt, he said, had become the 'victims of a modern tragedy' when the military ousted Mohamed Morsi, killing 6,000 people and throwing 60,000 of his supporters into jail.

Al-Tikriti was a gifted and passionate speaker, with a long record as a hostage negotiator in Iraq. His bald head shone with perspiration as he warmed to his theme.

'There are matters on which we don't agree with the British government: its military policy in Iraq, its position on Palestine, Prevent. But not conforming to their view does not make us extremists. We will call for peaceful protest as an alternative to violence. Political Islam is not the other side of the coin to ISIS. We are democrats, and we are *British* organizations, dedicated to countering extremism. To treat people who say "Prevent is not working" as subversives is incredibly problematic. Why is the government hell-bent on lumping together democrats and non-democrats whose opinions are in opposition? What is the strategy here?'

It was a good question. If the government was to succeed in rooting out extremist ideology, it surely needed willing partners in the Muslim community to work with it; it couldn't hope to do it by diktat, acting on its own. It was, nevertheless, steadily alienating the people it needed: the grassroots social workers like Ismael Lea South, community youth leaders like Adam Matan, the Waltham Forest Council of Mosques and Muslim civil society organizations of every stripe. Even the new Mayor of London stood accused of consorting with extremists.

I wondered if the government properly understood the effect of its actions. It was like watching a big fishing trawler, scooping up everything in its path in an outsized dragnet. Perhaps the prime minister regarded organizations like the Cordoba Foundation as unfortunate by-catch, small fry to be sacrificed for the chance of bigger fish. Whatever the thinking behind it, the technique was doing immeasurable damage to the ecosystem. Scarier still, it seemed as though the ship was on autopilot, with no one on watch to check where it might be headed. Whether through cynicism, or malice, or ignorance or incompetence, the effect was the same. A great injustice was being done to British Muslims, and I felt increasingly indignant on their behalf.

As al-Tikriti pointed out, the Muslim Brotherhood had proved its respect for democracy – one of the fundamental British values identified by the Home Office – when they contested the Egyptian elections of 2012. But it is also a democratic right to disagree with any government policy. To insinuate that a critic like the Cordoba Foundation was extremist when they exercised that right did not just look flagrantly hypocritical, it was an abuse of power. It wasn't good enough simply to assert that the Muslim Brotherhood's relationship with violent extremism was 'ambiguous', or that the Cordoba Foundation was their 'front'. Where was the evidence? The threat these people represented seemed as illusory as the beast in the famous Lewis Carroll poem 'The Hunting of the Snark'.

I spoke later to Dr Abdullah Faliq, the Cordoba Foundation's erudite head of research, at his office at the East London Mosque in the Bangladeshi heartland of Tower Hamlets. Here was another mosque that had been accused in the past of harbouring radicals, and that responded as the Finsbury Park one had done, by opening its doors to the world to show that it had nothing to hide. They took their public relations seriously in Tower Hamlets. The mosque committee had even ordered the construction of a plate-glassed viewing platform above the main prayer hall, so that non-Muslims could observe for themselves the *salat*, the five-times-a-day ritual of prayers and prostration.

Faliq was a former schoolfriend of Ed Husain, the author of *The Islamist*, the bestselling account of Husain's five-year involvement with radical Islam, notably the organization Hizb ut-Tahrir, in Tower Hamlets in the 1990s. Faliq, described by Husain in his book as 'a rather serious, observant young Muslim', rolled his eyes when I mentioned it. Husain went on to co-found Quilliam, the counter-extremism think tank whose views are so close to those of the government that David Cameron once quoted Husain approvingly in a newspaper article. Husain, in Faliq's view, had gone from one extreme to another while he, Faliq, had never joined his friend on the radical path in the 1990s, but had instead stuck steadfastly to the middle way. In his younger days, he said, he had literally fought on the streets of Tower Hamlets with hardliners from Hizb ut-Tahrir or its offshoot, al-Muhajiroun. When they confronted each other inside the mosque, chairs were thrown. And yet Faliq now found himself a member of a think tank officially designated a terrorist organization by the UAE, and which British politicians had implicitly accused of fomenting non-violent extremism.

One of the reasons for the Cordoba Foundation's unsavoury reputation, Faliq explained, was that they had shared a platform at the London Islam Expo conference in 2006 with the Palestinian activist Azzam Tamimi, a Hamas supporter who appeared to approve of suicide bombing. The Cordoba Foundation emphatically did not, but had been judged guilty by association ever since. Nor were they a front for the Muslim Brotherhood, as David Cameron claimed.

'Why would we need to be, when they have their own office in Cricklewood?' he said, disarmingly.

The foundation, he insisted, was just an academic think tank, founded in 2005 on the idea that the clash of civilizations is not inevitable, and dedicated to the principle of interfaith dialogue. It aimed to revive the spirit of Cordoba, the Andalusian city whose heritage was a blend of Muslim and Christian culture, epitomized by La Mezquita, the magnificent, thousand-year-old mosque that was converted into a cathedral following the *Reconquista* in the thirteenth century. The shelves around Faliq's office were spilling over with journals and studies that he had produced. Publishing, he said, was a large part of what the foundation did.

Was it fair to associate such an organization with extremism? It didn't seem much of a security threat to me. The Cordoba Foundation's name had been intoned in grave parliamentary debates about Islamist entryism, yet its staff numbered precisely three, and I had by now met two of them. None of them drew a salary because the foundation was broke. The charitable donations from the Gulf on which they previously depended had dried up under the spotlight of adverse publicity. It didn't help that al-Tikriti's account with HSBC – a bank of which he had been a customer all his life – was abruptly closed down in 2015, on the grounds that he and his foundation 'fell outside the bank's risk appetite'.[8] Lack of funds had forced them to close their office in Ealing; Faliq was working from Tower Hamlets now on a favour from the East London Mosque. The sledgehammer had fallen, and the nut was crushed.

*

In September 2002, on the first anniversary of 9/11, I went to an all-day conference in the London Docklands Arena organized by Hizb ut-Tahrir (HuT), the radical 'Party of Liberation' that had attracted and then repelled Ed Husain, the author of *The Islamist*. By some quirk of my filing system, I still have the programme from that day. It is entitled *Beyond September 11th: The Role of Muslims in the West*. Fourteen years on, as America elected a president who campaigned on a pledge to shut the country to them, it was clear enough that the question had still not been satisfactorily resolved.

My memory of the Docklands conference is sharp. The audience, which was gender-segregated, numbered over 6,000. I watched with amazement as the speakers railed against Western capitalism, denouncing its greed, its racism, its moral corruption. One of them attacked the profligacy of the businessman Sir Philip Green, who had just celebrated his fiftieth birthday by spending £5 million on a toga party in Cyprus.[9] HuT sounded like Marxists, except that the revolution they proposed was a religious one. Islam, as they put it, 'offered the world liberation from the shackles of an ideology that enslaves the masses to feed the few'. They didn't want to integrate, they wanted to live under a caliphate – and the audience chanted its approval with every rhetorical sally, their rumbled '*Allahu akbars*' filling the darkened hall.

I left the conference feeling bewildered and not a little angry at the way HuT denigrated British values while at the same time enjoying Western freedoms, above all the freedom of speech. They wouldn't have got away with *that* in Saudi Arabia, I said to myself. I thought it was dangerous rubbish, and wrote as much at the time.[10] Successive governments appeared to agree and attempted to proscribe HuT for extremism on two occasions, in 2005 and 2009. But they failed each time: HuT never advocated or endorsed violent extremism, and so stayed within the boundaries of the law.

In 2016, however, HuT were under pressure as never before, thanks to the proposed new Extremism Disruption Orders contained in the draft of the latest counter-terrorism law. The EDOs were designed to allow the government to 'restrict the movements and activities' of any organization that it deemed extremist, even if it had not broken the law. It was a licence, in short, to shut down organizations like HuT – and in an interview with the BBC, Prime Minister Cameron had in fact already strongly hinted that HuT would be the first for the chop as soon as the measure became law.[11]

I wondered, though, if HuT justified a piece of legislation that, as the independent watchdog David Anderson QC pointed out, risked undermining some important democratic freedoms. Under the new EDO regime, according to the BBC, the government would have the legal power to ban someone from speaking in public, including on social media or on the news. They would be able to dictate who an individual could and could not associate with, and to ban them from taking positions of authority, such as a school governorship. The libertarian debate was reminiscent of the controversy in the 1980s when Margaret Thatcher sought a law preventing the media from interviewing the IRA, in order to starve them of 'the oxygen of publicity'. EDOs, however, would go further in this draconian direction than Thatcher ever did. HuT was, I thought, a potentially dangerous organization in 2002, but fourteen years had passed since then. Was its peculiar brand of extremism really still the threat to society that Cameron believed? It seemed important to try to find out.

The organization, I discovered, had gone into decline since its 1990s glory days, when it was led by Omar Bakri Muhammad, an infamous north London radical known as the Tottenham Ayatollah, who for many years was the interviewee of choice for reporters filming or writing about British extremism. The big political gatherings of the early 2000s were a thing of the past. HuT hadn't staged any major conference since 2009, when fewer than a thousand people turned up. One study suggests there are as few as a hundred committed activists left in the country.[12] By 2016, Omar Bakri – a genuine extremist who split with HuT in the mid-90s – was doing hard labour in a Lebanese jail for training fighters for the war in Syria, and HuT was run part-time by Abdul Wahid Shaida, who had worked for twenty-five years as a family GP in Pinner in northwest London. The Cameron government's proposal for EDOs sounded like another sledgehammer for a nut.

Dr Shaida picked me up after work at Harrow-on-the-Hill tube station and took me out to dinner at an Afghan restaurant archly named the Maiwand after the 1880 battle in which the Afghans defeated the British. Business was booming in the dining room, which was bright with lights and chrome. We tucked into our kebabs and kabuli pilau a few tables from a large and raucous party of colourfully dressed Somalis, one of whom Shaida recognized, and greeted, as a regular at his doctor's surgery. The party's guest of honour turned out to be Nur Adde, a former prime minister of Somalia. The whole scene was an unintentional advertisement for multicultural, asylum-seeking London, an eloquent illustration of the charm and energy that such strange diversity always seemed to create.

Shaida had dark fierce eyes, an unapologetically thick beard and a trace of the scary, button-holing preacher's style I had observed in his diatribes on YouTube. As the evening wore on, however, I warmed to him. He was London-born, as I was, and almost the same age as me. We had both grown up in Thatcher's Britain, and although our responses to that era had been different our cultural reference points were eerily similar. We talked about Alain de Botton and Salman Rushdie, Frankie Boyle and Roy Chubby Brown, Dire Straits, Peter Gabriel's anti-apartheid anthem 'Biko', and the soundtrack to the *Last Temptation of Christ*. I saw the point, not for the first time, of the online campaign set up after the murder of the MP Jo Cox, #MoreIn-Common. Shaida was thoughtful, well read and good company, none of which I had expected from one of the government's prime exemplars of an 'Islamist extremist'.

He remembered the London Docklands conference well, although he attended it as a marshal, not a speaker in those days. HuT's agenda, he said, hadn't changed since then. It still promoted Islam as an alternative to capitalism, in line with the teachings of its founder, a Palestinian judge of the 1950s called al-Nabhani. I soon understood why the government had found it so difficult to proscribe his movement. He took a hard line on several issues, but was so skilled at hedging his views that it was impossible to pin him down on anything much. For instance, although the establishment of an international caliphate remained one of HuT's core aims – he envisioned it as 'something that brings goodness to people' – he also insisted that it had never been the movement's policy for the UK.

'That was the reason the movement suspended Omar Bakri Muhammad,' he added.

HuT did not support ISIS, which had *not* set up a caliphate, whatever its leader al-Baghdadi claimed.

'Islamic State is not a state, it's a warzone,' he said. 'A caliph needs, at a minimum, stability and security in his territory, as well as the support of local tribal leaders. But ISIS never had that – and even if they did, they would still be classified as usurpers, according to Islamic doctrine.'

What did he think of ISIS's savage treatment of blasphemers?

'I believe insulting the Prophet is a capital offence. But vigilantism doesn't sit well with Islam,' he told me.

Did he approve of the stoning to death of apostates?

'That debate is irrelevant,' he snapped back, 'because sharia does not apply in Britain.'

'What about gays?'

'Morally, I might advise people against if I thought there was a cat's chance in hell that they would listen,' he said gloomily.

'Would you refuse to treat a patient in your surgery if you knew they were gay?'

'Of course not! My default position is to be nice to people, courteous to all. I am a professional and a public servant. It is not my role to judge others.'

Shaida was, I suspected, more innately tolerant than his critics inferred. Respect for the beliefs of others, another of the Home Office's fundamental British values, was very important to him. For all the fire of his public rhetoric, I did not think his private God was an especially cruel one. His reaction to *The Satanic Verses* when he read it was more one of sorrow than of anger.

'I couldn't get my head round why Rushdie would want to hurt people he loved and understood – *his* people. People who attacked the fatwa argued that no one had the right not to be insulted. But if everyone insulted everyone else all the time, society would fall apart.'

Far from despising non-Muslims, he said he greatly admired the poetry of the King James Bible. It turned out that his father, a 'not particularly religious' travel agent, had sent him to a Church of England primary school in the 1970s. He still had friends who were practising Christians.

'Christians have some of the most beautiful ethics and manners,' he said.

It was a paradox that, at bottom, he actually rather liked the society that the government and media accused him of wishing to overthrow.

'HuT does not exist to hate the West. I would love to see Muslims and non-Muslims live together better. In practice, we do get along. Most people say, "They can't all be that bad."'

He recounted how he had appeared on the BBC's *Newsnight* once, where the presenter Jeremy Paxman attacked his views with the withering sarcasm for which he was famous.

'In my surgery the next day, one of my white patients who'd seen it said that they'd felt like slapping Paxman.'

Multiculturalism as a policy, he argued, was an old Labour con, which had never been intended as more than a temporary fix for the ethnic tensions created by mass immigration.

'The message to society was, "Give 'em time to assimilate." But "assimilation" is a terrible concept. It means "being more like us". That is an entirely different goal to peaceful coexistence in a plural society.'

He was filled with righteous indignation at the hypocrisy of the establishment.

'What *is* the problem with segregation,' he wanted to know, 'when NHS wards are segregated? Not to mention the private schools like Eton and Roedean.'

His language reminded me at times of Dave Spart, the loony-left comedy character invented by *Private Eye*.

'Prevent is a form of racial and cultural supremacism,' he said. 'It's the totalitarianism of secularists.'

Where Shaida undoubtedly did fit the government's new definition of an extremist was in his opposition to democracy. He said he refused to vote on principle, partly out of religious belief – because laws come from God, not from man – but also because to do so would be to offer tacit support to capitalism, a system that he had despised since he was a young man.

'I was a political Muslim before I was a spiritual one, because I grew up in Thatcher's Britain,' he said. 'I went backpacking in Pakistan and saw the poverty but also the honesty there. And I saw the homeless numbers in London in the 1980s and how the UK wasn't solving anything. Hizb ut-Tahrir made me think.'

It was touching, almost, the way he clung to ideals forged in another time, a passionate 1980s world of miners' strikes and workers' rights, of agitation for social and racial justice, that I remembered fondly from my own student days. The way he spat the name 'Thatcher' reminded me of Rik Mayall in *The Young Ones*. But that, also, was HuT's problem. Their brand of Islamism was out of date, with declining appeal to the new generation of British Muslims, who faced different challenges and who were looking elsewhere for answers. The new cohort perhaps even included his own teenage son, studying at a local secondary school.

'He's in the school debating club. He's doing really well,' Shaida enthused. 'The latest motion for debate is "Everyone should be made to sit a current affairs exam before being allowed to vote". My son is arguing against.'

'On the grounds that the right to vote is inalienable in a democracy?'

'Hm, well – there's a question,' Shaida grimaced. 'He hasn't asked my advice, but if he does I shall tell him what *I* think about democracy.'

It was seven years since HuT had tried to organize a conference like the one I attended in 2002. Shaida argued that the internet had rendered such mass meetings redundant, and that it was better to spend any funds at his disposal elsewhere. But he still struck me as something of a political dinosaur; and with the threat of the new counter-terrorism bill hanging over him he worried about his extinction, not just as an activist but as a GP.

'I'm a "known extremist",' he said glumly. 'I'm a family doctor, but known extremists won't be allowed access to children under the new Disruption Orders. I could be out of a job soon.'

It was almost midnight by the time he dropped me off at Greenford tube station for the train back to town.

'Look at that house,' he said, nodding at a nearby 1920s pebbledash as I was getting out of his car. 'If the people there lost their jobs, they'd have, what? Three, four months of savings before they defaulted on their mortgage? If they've got any money at all. And it's the same in every house in this street. What real choices do people have in this system? We are all slaves.'

*

Keen to give my hunt for a bona-fide non-violent extremist a final try, I went to meet Asim Qureshi, the research director of

Cage, the Islam-focused human rights advocacy group led by the former Guantanamo Bay detainee Moazzam Begg. Qureshi was the man who, at a press conference in February 2015, called Mohammed Emwazi 'a beautiful young man' and 'extremely kind, gentle and soft-spoken, the most humble young person I knew'. It was a curious description of the world's most wanted terrorist at the time, the throat-cutting ISIS psychopath better known as Jihadi John.

The public reaction came down like an avalanche. Boris Johnson called Cage 'apologists for terrorism'. David Cameron called them simply 'extremists' and urged people to stop working with them. The *Daily Mail* worried how often Cage representatives were invited to speak at universities – thirteen times in the last term alone, they said – and accused the organization of 'poisoning the minds of students'. Theresa May agreed, and said it showed there was 'still more work to be done to challenge those who spread hatred and intolerance'.[13]

I looked forward to meeting Qureshi. Here, surely and at last, was a proper extremist whose warped ideas really did threaten British security and perhaps even justified tougher legislation. But once again it wasn't so simple. In a greasy spoon in Worcester Park in the far southwest of London where he lives, Qureshi disarmed me with his explanation of his incendiary press conference remarks.

'I got emotional,' he admitted. 'I hadn't slept for four days. I failed miserably to control my language.'

His main defence, however, was that the context of his words had also been ignored. Qureshi was not defending 'Jihadi John' but describing Mohammed Emwazi, the man behind the mask whom he had formerly known. His passion was ill-timed and perhaps misplaced, but he was not condoning terrorism or even apologizing for the terrorist so much as trying to explain how he had become one.

Qureshi had known Emwazi, an Iraqi born in Kuwait who

had grown up in west London, since 2009 when, as a 21-year-old graduate from Westminster University, he had first approached Cage asking for help. As the pre-eminent campaign group against the perceived injustices of state counter-terrorism policies, Cage was a natural port of call for someone like Emwazi. His problem was his circle of friends, some of whom had absconded to Somalia to fight for the al-Qaida franchise, al-Shabaab. Emwazi complained that MI5, suspecting that he was interested in doing the same, were watching him so closely that his life was becoming impossible. He was held and questioned almost every time he passed through an airport. MI5 officers also went knocking on the doors of those who knew him, including his London Somali fiancée, whose family were so spooked by the attentions of the authorities that they ordered their daughter to break off the engagement. A second fiancée, in Kuwait, did the same. It was Qureshi's interesting contention – naturally hotly denied by the authorities – that Emwazi had ultimately been pushed into violent extremism not by some backstreet mosque preacher or sinister online ISIS recruiter, but by MI5 itself.

It was the sort of allegation made by conspiracy theorists, or firebrand clowns like Anjem Choudary, but Qureshi was nothing like that. He was a bald, bespectacled, earnest 34-year-old, articulate, sophisticated and bright. He had been privately educated at the Whitgift School, an £18,000-a-year public school in Croydon, and it showed in his middle-class accent, tastes and views. His first love at school, he said, had been history and literature. His favourite author was Dumas, and he described Malcolm X's autobiography as 'the ethnic generation's *Catcher in the Rye*'.

I responded to him as I had to Abdul Wahid Shaida of Hizb ut-Tahrir, with an almost visceral recognition of his innate Britishness.

'My humour, my sarcasm, is British and will remain so,' he said at one point. 'It is who I am.'

I saw that we were products of the same English school system. I could relate to his first encounter with racism at school, which he experienced not just among the 'white rugby lads' but also from some of his teachers, with their 'infantilized view of Islam, never spoken to, always spoken about'. He was the skinny Muslim kid who played squash, an outsider's sport with none of the social cachet of the team games, even though he was good enough at it to play at county level. As it was for so many other young British Muslims – Mohammed Emwazi included – the soundtrack to his coming of age was black American hip-hop by artistes like Wu-Tang Clan, Ice Cube, Tupac: music that he called 'not Brit-hop, and definitely not Bollywood: it was music that spoke to the anxieties of our generation, and gave me an identity outside the mainstream'.

He went on to study international law at London Guildhall before joining Cage in 2004, aged 22, driven by righteous anger at what was happening in Guantanamo, a fire that still burned within him. Cage had since become one of the most controversial but also one of the most formidable critics of Western double standards in the War on Terror, with a long track record of championing public villains such as Anwar al-Awlaki, Abu Qatada and most recently Shaker Aamer, the last British resident to be released from Guantanamo.

Qureshi saw Cage's advocacy work as the continuation of a struggle dating back centuries. He described the Andaman Islands in the Bay of Bengal, where the British incarcerated the leaders of the Indian Mutiny of 1857, as 'the first Guantanamo'. He compared the state-sanctioned persecution of Muslims in modern Britain to the Spanish Inquisition, when 'Morisco' girls – Moorish Muslims forced to convert to Christianity – were raped by bishops. The fiery debate around the legality of the veil in

France, meanwhile, reminded him of Ferdinand and Isabella, the 'Catholic monarchs' who unified Castile and Aragon, and who, after the conquest of Toledo in the 1490s, banned the niqab on the grounds that it was a barrier to integration.

The quality and passion of his intellect helped explain why he was so often invited to take part in debates at universities or on late-night current affairs TV. He was an unapologetic Islamist – 'I see no reason why Islam shouldn't be political if you believe in social justice,' he said – but he was also one propelled forward by convictions that were educated. I didn't know if he was right to say MI5 was partly to blame for Jihadi John's radicalization, but I did think the allegation deserved to be listened to. I knew a little about MI5 harassment, and how clumsy, upsetting and counter-productive the approaches of their officers could be, from my own past interviews with the family of a devout and blameless north London Somali man whom MI5 had tried to recruit. The officer in that case had inveigled his way into the Somali's flat disguised as a postman and threatened him with the removal of his passport if he did not cooperate.[14]

On the other hand, MI5 were only doing their job – and in the end it was not they but Emwazi and his colleagues who cut the throats of ISIS's captives. As an outraged Number 10 spokeswoman observed: '*They* are the ones responsible, and we should not be seeking to put blame on other people, particularly those who are working to keep British citizens safe.' The MI5 chief, Andrew Parker, went further, angrily dismissing Qureshi's claim as 'the sort of thing that our detractors and some people who we need to take an interest in want to say'. [15]

Cage's criticisms are not always constructive and not every broadside hits its mark, but one that emphatically did was Qureshi's attack on the government's Prevent Duty Training Programme. There had been many complaints, particularly from teachers, that the twenty-two risk indicators of potential radicalization they were obliged to look out for were often ambiguous or even contradicted each other. For example, a child who suddenly became withdrawn in the classroom was deemed a 'potential risk indicator' – and yet so was the opposite behaviour, a normally quiet child who suddenly became confident or extrovert. Which one was it? The lack of clarity mattered. In the year to March 2016 some 7,500 people were referred to the authorities under the programme, nearly half of them children.[16] Who had decided what behaviour traits were risk indicators? Where did the new statutory advice come from?

The answer was revealed in a report by Qureshi published in September 2016 entitled *The 'science' of pre-crime: the secret 'radicalization' study underpinning Prevent*. After months of sleuthing in the backwaters of academia – and months too of being stonewalled by the Ministry of Justice – Qureshi discovered that Prevent Duty advice was based on the research of two psychologists, Monica Lloyd and Christopher Dean, who in 2010 had developed an 'assessment tool' called *Extremist Risk Guidance 22+* for use in prisons. Their report, which remains classified, was based on small-scale research and was never intended for use outside the prison environment. Lloyd and Dean, furthermore, had not even meant it to be used to predict the risk of radicalization. Indeed, they were possibly unsure about the validity and reliability of their own findings because, as they said, ERG22+ was still 'a work in progress'.

The underpinning science, in short, was flawed – and it wasn't just Cage who said so. In September 2016, 140 academics, including the philosopher Noam Chomsky, signed an open letter to the *Guardian* expressing their concern. Even the Royal College of Psychiatrists weighed in with a declaration that public policy 'cannot be based on either no evidence or a lack of transparency about evidence', and called on the government immediately to publish its underpinning data so that it could be independently peer-reviewed.[17]

The *Daily Express* accused Cage of touring universities in a bid to recruit 'an army' to fight anti-terror laws,[18] but it wasn't 'Islamist entryism' to disagree with Prevent if even the Royal College of Psychiatrists thought Cage had a point. It was also no wonder that so many people thought the government were embarked on a Muslim extremist witch-hunt. I had conspicuously failed in my own search for a witch, even in London, the source of three-quarters of all terror-related criminal convictions. After meeting Asim Qureshi, the 'non-violent extremism' that the government remains determined to tackle seemed a false construct, a bogey-man, a childish chimera. If it doesn't come from political organizations or activists, where does it come from? Is it from imams, hate-preaching in mosques or madrassahs? Could it be school teachers, pursuing a sinister hidden agenda to Islamize their pupils?

In March 2014, an anonymous letter sent to Birmingham City Council appeared to provide evidence of exactly that: an extraordinary Islamist plot to subvert the state schools of east Birmingham, home to one of the largest and most concentrated Muslim populations in the country. The letter, purporting to be between two Salafist plotters, outlined a five-step method by which any state school could be taken over – a 'Trojan Horse' technique that had been tried and tested in Birmingham and was now ripe for roll-out in other cities with large Muslim populations like Bradford, Manchester and London.

Fundamentalists 'plotting to bring jihad to classrooms' ran the headlines – and public opinion was duly convulsed. The prime minister convened an emergency meeting of his new Extremism Task Force. The Department for Education (DfE) squabbled with the Home Office over whose fault it was and what should be done about it. Doubts about the letter's authenticity quickly surfaced. Some whispered that it had been forged by a disgruntled teacher at another school, for reasons connected to the arcane and internecine world of Birmingham's local authority politics. But as four major investigations into twenty-one Birmingham schools got under way, that no longer mattered.

'Whatever anybody says, the letter was no hoax,' said Birmingham Education Commissioner Sir Mike Tomlinson, because evidence uncovered by the DfE and Ofsted (the Office of Standards in Education) 'mirrored what was said in the letter'.[19]

The affair led ultimately to the replacement of teachers and governors at six schools across east Birmingham. The alleged ringleader of the plot was named in the letter as Tahir Alam, the chair of governors of the Park View Educational Trust which ran three of the schools. He later became the DfE's first 'banned person', formally forbidden to run, manage or work in any British school, on the grounds that he had 'undermined British values'.

From its beginning, however, the Trojan Horse affair disquieted Birmingham education officials who knew Tahir Alam, who always maintained his innocence. His school, a mixed secondary called Park View, had been judged 'outstanding' by Ofsted inspectors many times in the past. What could have changed so suddenly? Some observers thought the allegations were suspiciously convenient for policy makers looking to widen the campaign against non-violent extremism into the nation's schools. Questions were raised about the fairness and thoroughness of the official investigations. The impartiality of Ofsted's chief, Sir Michael Wilshaw, was called into question. The *Guardian* wondered if the row was 'a witch hunt triggered by a hoax'. Even the House of Commons Education Select Committee eventually concluded that the allegations were a storm in a teacup. Not only was there 'no evidence of a sustained plot', the committee also noted that, one incident apart – involving the screening of an inappropriate educational video – 'no evidence of extremism or radicalization was found by any of the inquiries in any of the schools involved'.[20]

So was Tahir Alam a tragic fall guy, a lamb cynically sacri-ficed on the altar of the government's Prevent campaign? How extreme was he, in fact? And what was the impact on the people who mattered most in all this, the parents and thousands of pupils caught up in the scandal? I went to Birmingham to try to find out.

5

Trojan Hoax

Birmingham

IT IS EASY TO get lost in the Muslim marches of east Birmingham, where the plain Victorian terraces stretch on for miles and
one neighbourhood looks very much like the next – particularly
if you are driving through them as I was, after dark, in the rain,
with a satnav on the blink. To my newcomer's slightly panicky
eye, the district's most remarkable feature was simply its extent.
There seemed to be a mosque on every other corner; brown faces
predominated in every direction. I was, I knew, in the heart of a
Muslim community 250,000-strong: one of the greatest urban
concentrations of them in Europe. From Sparkbrook and Spark-
hill in the south, through Small Heath and Saltley up to Alum
Rock and Washwood Heath in the north, the cause of integration
appeared to have surrendered altogether. Of the fourteen state
schools assessed in one government report on Trojan Horse, all
of them within five miles of each other, not one had an ethnic
minority pupil intake of less than 96 per cent. As the think tank
Demos noted, this level of ethnic segregation was higher even
than in St Louis, the Missouri city that had become a byword for
racial violence since 2014.[1]

According to the *Guardian*'s Richard Adams, the education
correspondent who most closely followed the Trojan Horse saga,
the discovery of how big the Birmingham community had
become was a genuine shock to some in Whitehall, which Adams
thought helped explain the force of the government response.

'People in London had no idea about east Birmingham,' he told me. 'They simply weren't aware of the concentrations of Muslims involved.'

In the government's view, communities as deeply segregated as east Birmingham are potential breeding grounds for home-grown extremism. This was why, in July 2015, Prime Minister Cameron chose a local school, Ninestiles Academy, to announce his five-year plan to defeat it.

This mushrooming community has no lodestone, but if it did it would probably be placed in the middle of Small Heath Park, where in the summer of 2016 some 90,000 people came together to celebrate the end of Ramadan, the largest such gathering in Europe. With time to kill early on the morning of my appointment with Tahir Alam, I went for a walk there. It was large and square, a planned Victorian recreation area, bounded on all sides by brick terraced houses with well-kept front gardens and dormer windows for the view. There was a bandstand and a pond with a sign threatening a fine for feeding the ducks. More interesting than either were the other people in the park, who were all housewives in saris and hijabs.

There were dozens and dozens of them, some ambling and chatting in Urdu, some puffing along at a speed-walk, but all of them going in the same, anti-clockwise direction on the tree-lined path around the park's edge. The centre of the park, although criss-crossed with enticing trails through the long grass, was deserted. It was 8.45, evidently the favoured time for a constitutional, with the husband departed for work and the children delivered to school. But I had seldom seen exercise taken with such regimentation or so little imagination. They looked like inmates in a prison yard or, it suddenly occurred to me, like pilgrims in Mecca, circumambulating the Kaaba. I did not envy them. Their exercising hinted at home lives of stifling conformity, restricted by circumstance and the expectations of, no doubt, men. I could not resist a childish impulse to set out around the park in the opposite direction, just to see what would happen. I was scolded for trying to take a photograph, but otherwise nothing did.

Tahir Alam smiled when I described this.

'If you stopped and asked them why they were walking anti-clockwise, they wouldn't even realize they were doing it. It's automatic for Muslims to start off on the right. We eat with the right hand. Arabic and Urdu are written from right to left. The Koran even talks about "the people of the right hand" who will enter Paradise at the Day of Judgement.'

We sat opposite each other in his cluttered study, the front sitting room of a house in Small Heath, which had a Victorian tiled fireplace and flowery wallpaper that could have been from the 1950s. There was also a corner unit crowded with cheap souvenirs, some of which were surprising for a supposed enemy of the state: a moneybox in the shape of a phonebox, a gilt statuette of Big Ben and a model of a red London Routemaster bus.

'Those were there before all this happened, I swear it!' Tahir said, reading my thoughts. 'I love London. I always have.'

He was 47 and had lived in Britain since his father brought him here as a baby from Mirpur, the westernmost district of Pakistani Kashmir where some 70 per cent of British Pakistanis originate.

'My reputation is mud,' he said, 'but the way I think about this country has not changed. I do not accept that we are foreigners here. My premise has always been that Muslims are an integral part of our society. Islam should be normal in the UK, not an alien thing.'

He had been a teacher all his adult life, one of the best-known and most successful educationalists in Birmingham, who had met four education ministers in the course of his career. He was the onetime governor of six different schools, as well as a governor trainer on behalf of the city council. He had been a schools inspector in the past, too. He was a highly paid professional, the kind whose conversation was peppered with quotes from the work of the behavioural psychologist B. F. Skinner or chunks of Section 128 of the 2008 Education and Skills Act.

The hardest thing about his DfE ban, he said, was that he had become unemployable in a profession he loved. He still hoped to appeal, but for now he was in limbo, short of money, stuck at home and left wondering what he was going to do with the rest of his life. He struck me as an intelligent, philosophical man, still struggling to come to terms with the enormity of what had happened to him two years previously, as well as genuinely baffled by the charges.

'Believe me, I am not an extremist,' he said wearily. 'I am a Muslim on the moderate end of the spectrum.'

The press had camped out on his doorstep for weeks when the affair first broke, desperate, an associate of his later told me, to get a 'Captain Hook' shot, the visual shorthand for an extremist ever since Abu Hamza made the look his own. They never succeeded. Tahir Alam, bald and besuited, with glasses and hardly any beard, remained a picture of dull respectability. Nevertheless, it wasn't just the media who had judged him the mastermind of a plot to turn the nation's state schools into madrassahs, but the government as well. Such pressure was bound to take its toll. To me he looked tired, a bit overweight and not a little depressed.

He called himself a moderate Muslim, by which I understood him to mean a traditional, mainstream one. The ethos in his schools was indeed Islamic, and he saw no reason to apologize for it.

'I'm proud to be Muslim and have no problem in promoting it. I think it's inspirational,' he said.

It was his view that the Muslim values of faith, hard work and discipline were the foundation of his schools' success. He said his approach had always been to foster a strong Muslim identity in his pupils because he believed that children who were 'happy in their own skin' grew up to be better, more confident citizens. He was convinced, furthermore, that this was the key to the social integration that the government wanted. The nub of the problem was that the government had come to the opposite conclusion, that fostering a Muslim identity created social division, which led to alienation, which sometimes led to extremism.

'For us, the term "Islamic" is a synonym for excellence, but for non-Muslims it has become pejorative. The government has decided that young Muslims are drawn to violent extremism by ideology. The irony is that we used to cooperate with Prevent. For instance, we referred a kid who had a picture of bin Laden on his Facebook page. Part of our job was to try to bring balance to kids' views. But now they are trying to save children from Islam itself – that's the racket.'

The main reason so many young Muslims have joined ISIS, he argued, is the sense of belonging that the movement offers – a tempting prospect for people who feel rejected by mainstream British society. Ideology, he thought, was a side issue by comparison. As he pointed out, many ISIS recruits know almost nothing about Islam.

'The answer to ISIS is to ensure youngsters receive a higher level of Islamic education so that they can make a more balanced decision. But the government is going in the opposite direction: its solution is to "de-Islamicize".'

He categorically denied ever wanting to 'take over' any state school. As he pointed out, the vast majority of his pupils identified themselves as Muslims when they arrived at his schools, which in that statistical sense were 'taken over' already. All he had done was to try to mould and direct what was already there – and he insisted that he had done so not just within the boundaries of the law, but in line with what, until 2014, he thought had been expected of him by the DfE. He was, in the end, a defender of the old orthodoxy of multiculturalism. His sudden fall from grace was in some respects no more than the effect of a spectacular government U-turn on that policy.

I spent several hours going through the allegations with him, during two long meetings as well as by email and phone, and he had answers for them all. A DfE inspection, for example, had found that boys and girls were segregated into different classes.

'That was never school policy,' he retorted. 'PE classes were segregated, but the other 90 per cent were all mixed.'

'What about the accusation that girls were made to sit at the back and boys at the front?'

'That happened once, on the instruction of one teacher in an Arabic class at another school, Oldknow Academy. It wasn't school policy there, either. The governors were not even aware it had happened. Yet the inspectors repeatedly made it out to be pervasive in Birmingham schools.'

'What about biology? Wasn't that curtailed in favour of "safe" subjects like maths and science?'

'Never,' he replied. 'We followed the national curriculum in every detail.'

'Did you ban music?'

'We had a full-time music teacher.'

'What about the emphasis on Arabic? The inspectors said the corridors were full of posters quoting the Koran.'

'But so what, in a school that is 98 per cent Muslim? And we taught Arabic as a modern language, not classical Arabic. And it was a choice. Even the British Council advocates it as the number three most useful modern language after Mandarin and Spanish. We taught Spanish, French, Arabic and Urdu across four schools.'

'What about banning Christmas?'

'In seventeen years, I never did any such thing. I went to Christmas dinners and ate halal turkey. However, our pupils *are* 98 per cent Muslim, so they simply don't celebrate Christmas as Christians do. I did draw the line at Muslims acting God in nativity plays, but otherwise there were trees and tinsel everywhere.'

And so it went on, with one sensational allegation crumbling after another. There were no 'Salafis' on the board of governors, as alleged.

'There was one niqabi – a Deobandi, maybe. To be honest, I never asked.'

A Tannoy system had been installed in order to call pupils in to prayer from the playground, which certainly sounded inappropriate in a British state school. But it turned out that this was done to safeguard pupils at the behest of their parents, not to indoctrinate them. Until that moment, devout pupils had to walk down a busy road to a local mosque in order to pray. Offering regular prayers on site was a means of protecting children from traffic as well as from preaching that was beyond the school's control.[2]

'We never forced people to come to prayer,' Alam insisted. 'About fifty or sixty would turn up to Friday prayers out of six hundred, and that was fine.'

In 2013, Oldknow Academy arranged a school trip to Mecca and Medina for forty of its pupils, which was deemed inappropriate for a state institution, in part because it was only open to Muslim pupils. But that is true of Mecca itself, and although it might have seemed unfair to the pupils who were not Muslim – of whom there were eight in a school of six hundred – there were no complaints from them about it. Were the other 99 per cent, some of whom were students of Arabic, really to be prevented from visiting the birthplace of the language of the Koran on such slender grounds? Ofsted didn't think so, and even praised a similar trip in 2012 as 'a life-changing experience' for the pupils who went on it. The trip was expensive, as visits to Mecca tend to be, and was condemned as a scandalous waste of taxpayers' money by the press. But the newspapers never mentioned that almost half the cost had been met by the parents.

'It was like a reward for good behaviour and doing well in exams,' said Shabina Bano, whose daughter took part.

It was true that Sheikh Shady Al-Suleiman, a controversial cleric from Melbourne, was invited to address pupils at Park View in 2013. Al-Suleiman was described in one government report as a man 'known to extol extremist views (e.g. stoning of adulterers)'.[3] The Education Secretary, Michael Gove, told Parliament that Al-Suleiman was reported to have said: 'Give victory to Muslims in Afghanistan . . . Give victory to all the Mujahideen all over the world. Oh Allah, prepare us for the jihad.'[4]

That naturally sounded very sinister to the listening MPs. But Alam said that Al-Suleiman had only visited Park View once, and that when he did he spoke not about stonings or the Taliban but the importance of good time management.

Park View came in for particular criticism with the discovery of a closed social media discussion group, set up by a handful of male teachers at the school – though not including Tahir Alam – who called themselves the 'Park View Brotherhood'. Some 3,000 messages were transcribed into 130 pages and analysed by Peter Clarke, the former head of the Metropolitan police's Counter-Terrorism Command, who was investigating on behalf of the Education Secretary, Michael Gove. Clarke found evidence of 'explicit homophobia; highly offensive comments about British service personnel; a stated ambition to increase segregation in the school; disparagement of strands of Islam; scepticism about the truth of reports of the murder of Lee Rigby and the Boston bombings; and a constant undercurrent of anti-Western, anti-American and anti-Israeli sentiment'. Some of this undoubtedly ticked the box of the Home Office's definition of extremism as 'vocal or active opposition to fundamental British values'.

'There were loose comments on WhatsApp,' Alam conceded. 'Some of the views expressed there, like saying that ex-British servicemen shouldn't be allowed to teach, were anti-British. But it was also based on disapproval of British foreign policy. And it

wasn't school policy, it was one, private opinion! It was unpro-
fessional and it merited a warning, perhaps – but surely not an
outright ban from teaching.'

I thought he might be right about that. There was certainly
nothing lenient in the way these Birmingham teachers were
treated – and it did seem harsh to end someone's career on the
basis of a view that was privately held and expressed. But such
lack of compassion was, unfortunately, nothing unusual. The
motive for the crackdown in Birmingham, however spurious,
was national security, and that not only justified but apparently
demanded the toughest of approaches.

Alam's point about British foreign policy was also well made.
I had noticed before that the Muslims' sense that they are part of
a global Islamic community, the *ummah*, often fosters a powerful
empathy for the suffering of their co-religionists abroad – and
also that this is an emotion rarely felt by Westerners of other
religious persuasions. There can be very few Anglicans who feel
an equivalent kinship with, say, persecuted Egyptian Copts.
And of course religious empathy is not felt at all by the West's
irreligious majority. Secular society can feel deep sympathy for
foreigners, but is largely ignorant of the deep visceral connection
formed by a shared faith.

One consequence, perhaps, is that British Muslims' angry
unease at their own government's military actions in Iraq or
Afghanistan – or at its support for those of others, particularly in
Gaza and the West Bank – is commonly misunderstood.
Some non-Muslims dismiss any assertion that the deck is somehow stacked against Muslims as Islamist propaganda. The
propagandists, it is true, know how to play on and amplify
the sense of grievance, but that doesn't mean that it isn't real to
start with. On the contrary, the emotion generated by Muslim
suffering abroad was felt long before al-Qaida or ISIS came on
the scene. It is, in any case, perfectly possible to feel righteous
anger about British foreign policy without being a Muslim. In

2016 I myself felt deeply discomfited by my government's strange moral contortions over the arming of Saudi Arabia, and that country's ill-targeted bombing campaign in Yemen that has killed thousands of civilians – a policy of support that I felt sure was storing up big trouble for the future here at home.

Alam argued that not just he but all the Trojan Horse teachers had been unfairly treated, particularly by Peter Clarke who, he claimed, had not entered a single one of the schools targeted in his report, nor spoken to any of their pupils or parents in the course of his inquiry. (A parent-governor caught up in the affair later told me that Clarke 'never left Birmingham Council's Committee Room Nine'.) Much of Clarke's report, Alam said, was based on 'Jackanory tittle-tattle' that had been extrapolated to fit a preconceived narrative. He wasn't alone in this assessment. Richard Adams also described the report to me as 'very surprising – an elaborately constructed nothing. It was full of accusations like "these schools ban raffles" when only one of them did, once. It was like a stitched-together patchwork quilt, but when you looked underneath there wasn't much there.'

Alam felt it was instructive that the report was not included in the final submission of evidence to the misconduct tribunal that would eventually decide his guilt or innocence.

'Why? Because the DfE barristers knew it wouldn't stand up in court . . . Clarke is a wicked liar who did a dirty job for his political master, and was promoted for his trouble.'[5]

His bitterness was perhaps understandable. In terms of academic achievement, a metric that all conscientious parents care about, Park View had long been a conspicuous success. At one time in the 1990s, only 4 per cent of its pupils' GCSE results were at grade C or higher. By 2013, the figure was 76 per cent. Alam described these as 'leafy suburb results', achieved despite his pupils being amongst the poorest in the country, with 70 per cent of them eligible for free school meals.

'It was the school that every aspirational Muslim parent in

east Birmingham wanted to send their child to. We tried to encourage the kids to think about the future, so that they all had an idea, an aim to pursue in life. We were the *darling* of the DfE. But Clarke ignored all that.'

He was personally proud of the turnaround at Park View, a school that he himself had attended as a pupil in the early 1980s.

'In those days there was a problem with groping,' he recalled. 'Segregation was actually part of the solution to that – putting boys and girls in separate dinner queues, for example. Actually, the girls segregated themselves in that way.'

Once in charge at Park View, Alam made the pupils work hard by, for instance, introducing a revision course over the Easter holidays.

'The staff didn't think it possible, but I *knew* my community – they do have very middle-class aspirations for their children.'

The key to success was discipline. Alam reintroduced ties and blazers and strictly enforced the wearing of them. There was a zero-tolerance policy on swearing and on poor time-keeping. Richard Adams, who saw the school in action, said that the ethos was if anything too intense.

'The emphasis on exam results was very high. Every corridor had posters of the last exam results. I saw a teaching assistant telling off two kids for being last into classroom, even though the bell hadn't gone yet. And I thought . . . Jesus.'

The parents, however, appeared to have no problem with it. Their wishes were being catered to, not ignored. As Alam pointed out, responding to the wishes of the community was one of Ofsted's formal criteria of state school success. Attendance at parent–teacher meetings rose from 25 to 80 per cent.

'The parents felt it was their school. There was one mum, a GP, who wrote in to say that Park View was like an oasis in run-down Alum Rock: "I've seen kids go in and out, and there's not a tie out of place." Her son had been struggling for eighteen months at a school in Harrow. She said that after three weeks at Park View, he was a different child.'

He was, therefore, amazed by the *volte face* performed by the supposedly independent inspectors of Ofsted, who as late as 2012 had rated the school as 'outstanding' in a report that used the word 'exemplary' thirteen times. One inspector told the school head that he had been 'moved' by the school's Islamic assembly and its inspirational themes of kindness and respect. A reporter for the *Times Educational Supplement* told Alam that he had 'never read such an accolade'. The head of Ofsted, Sir Michael Wilshaw himself, told a conference of the National Union of Teachers that 'every school in the country should be like this'. This was a man who publicly argued that Tahir Alam not only had a right to promote an Islamic ethos in his schools, it was actually his obligation. On 9 July 2014, Wilshaw told the House of Commons Education Select Committee: 'It would be the duty of the head teacher and governors of a school where the great majority of children came from the Muslim faith to promote that faith and give them every spiritual support as necessary.'

Ofsted inspectors visited Park View again in 2014, just after the Trojan Horse letter had been made public – and still found nothing amiss. But then, on *another* inspection just eleven days later, they revised their judgement to 'inadequate', the benchmark grade requiring it to be put into 'special measures'. As a former schools inspector himself, Tahir knew how the system worked. Indeed, he knew these inspectors personally. One of them had even examined him once, in London, and granted him his inspector's qualification.

'I could tell from the faces they pulled that they were here to fail the school. They asked loaded questions like, "Why are you wearing a long skirt on such a hot day?" They kept going into the RE class – four times in one day. It was clear they were looking for condemnation of other values. And equally clear that they were operating under political instruction.'

Alam was in no doubt as to the originator: 'The attack came from Gove,' he said.

It was ironic, therefore, that he also admired the former education minister's controversial campaign to reintroduce traditional curricula and teaching standards.

'Gove had passion, and I agree with his education model,' he said. 'The reintroduction of Latin was very good.'

Gove's back-to-basics, *Peter and Jane* approach had been much derided by progressive educationalists, yet Alam thought the wholesome values expressed in those books – on which he himself had been brought up – were actually 'very close to Muslim values'.

So why was the education secretary so determined to clip his wings?

'I'm not a conspiracist, but the neo-cons have got a nice little platform at the centre of government. The whole thing has been centrally arranged,' he said.

I doubted very much that this cabal of plotters existed in reality. The idea that Michael Gove was some kind of evil ringmaster, operating to a secret Islamophobe agenda at the heart of government, seemed preposterous. On the other hand, I had heard the allegation too often on my travels around the country to be able to dismiss it entirely. The fact that it was so widely believed in Muslim Britain made it a problem. My suspicion was that there was a grain of truth in it, a case of no smoke without fire, which was being dangerously fanned by the febrile atmosphere of the times. I thought that the best person to lay such a conspiracy theory to rest, perhaps the only person who could extinguish the fire, was Gove himself. I was going to have to find a way to get to him and ask him.

I was familiar with all the names and organizations behind the purported conspiracy. At the centre of Gove's web, according to Alam, sat the Henry Jackson Society, a right-of-centre think tank that advocates 'muscular liberalism', and whose founding statement of principles Michael Gove had signed in 2005. Alam's implacable local enemy, the Birmingham Labour MP Khalid Mahmood, was a former member of the Society's advisory council and was close to Gove. Peter Clarke, meanwhile, previously worked at the Charity Commission, headed by William Shawcross, a former director of the society. Alam said that Clarke's job at the Commission was to 'hunt down' Muslim charities, which accounted for a quarter of the organizations under investigation by the commission, even though Muslim charities made up just 5 per cent of British charities nationally: a statistical mismatch that Alam characterized as 'harassment as normal'. The neo-con clique was rounded out by reformists like Sara Khan, director of the women's rights organization Inspire, and most of all by the counter-extremism think tank Quilliam.

'These people are seen as lackeys of the government,' Alam insisted. 'There's not one mosque that would let [Quilliam's founding chairman] Maajid Nawaaz speak – not one.'[6]

Quilliam was named after William Quilliam, a Victorian solicitor and the famous 'first' convert in Britain, who founded England's first mosque in Liverpool. Changing his name to Abdullah, Quilliam became Sheikh ul-Islam of the country, on the authority of the last Ottoman Caliph, Sultan Abdul-Majid II. The think tank was founded in 2008 by three former members of Hizb ut-Tahrir, who had seen the error of their radical ways and dedicated themselves to campaigning against Islamism.

I had once heard their CEO, Haras Rafiq, speak at a counter-extremism conference and came away quietly impressed by his knowledge of British Islam and the common sense of his approach. For example, he did not advocate the banning of organizations like Cage or Hizb ut-Tahrir, and actually voiced doubts about the new Disruption Orders under proposal. Like the terrorism legislation reviewer David Anderson QC, he told his audience that the best way to defeat bad ideas was to argue against them, not try to suppress them.

On the other hand, Alam was right to question how much grassroots support Quilliam really has. Their reform-based, secular, London-centric agenda had no traction that I could discern in any of the communities I visited. Maajid Nawaaz, its charismatic founder (and the author of an autobiography called *Radical: My Journey out of Islamist Extremism*), is particularly controversial. In his pointy shoes and natty clothes and with an artfully sculpted beard, he is a passionate and clever debater, but a great many British Muslims suspect that his campaign is more about him and his career than the good of society.

Calling Quilliam 'lackeys' of government was too strong, but as the self-appointed voice of 'moderate' Islam, there is no doubt that their message is very close to what the government wants to hear. Quilliam's work was generously funded by government until 2011 and questions still swirl about its independence. In 2015, David Cameron responded to the accusation that he was not properly 'engaging' with mainstream British Islam by setting up a regular Muslim 'Community Engagement Forum'. This body, however, was widely derided when the first invitation list was published. Far from representing the British Muslim mainstream, the forum was loaded with moderates and reformers like Sara Khan, Lord Ahmad of the minority Ahmadiyya community, the former Bishop of Rochester Michael Nazir-Ali, and – of course – Haras Rafiq of Quilliam. As Ibrahim Khan, a blogger on the grassroots website 5pillars.com observed: 'The objective of actually finding out what Muslims think, and solutions they propose and would accept, is completely defeated.' [7]

A discussion with Alam about homosexuality was, perhaps, the most revealing of the gulf in values between him and the reformists, as well as the most illustrative of the confusion between religious conservatism and extremism.

'Homosexuality is legal, and legality must be respected,' he said carefully. 'The school's policy was always to treat gay kids with respect. It's not the teacher's job to judge them.'

But that did not stop him from regarding it as immoral, a view that he insisted is mainstream in east Birmingham.

'We don't take our morality from the state,' he said at one point. 'Where does this trend end? What is the moral objection to incest, if it is between consensual adults and no minors are involved? What about bestiality?'

According to Prevent, he said, disparaging homosexuality is now considered a potential indicator of extremism. In theory, therefore, teachers are now supposed to report any Muslim pupil speaking ill of homosexuals to the Home Office.

'We used to promote a policy of "Live and let live", but we can no longer do this thanks to Prevent,' he said. 'The metric of improvement at Park View is that they've got posters up now saying, "It's OK to be Muslim and gay." Yet this is a *theological* position, promoted by Quilliam. It means that schools are now directly distorting Islam. These people want assimilation, not integration. We are way beyond Orwell's *1984*.'

He was, I thought, right again. It was horridly ironic, but his belief in Live and let live was actually very close to the Home Office's fundamental British value of 'mutual respect and tolerance of different faiths and beliefs'. State intervention in matters of morality had led the country to sectarian and religious bloodshed in the past. The Home Office appeared to have forgotten its history, for had not Elizabeth I herself come to the throne insisting that she 'would not open windows into men's souls'? She understood, half a millennium ago, that the key to peace in a plural society was outward uniformity within the broad parameters of the law.

It wasn't only Muslim-majority schools that felt uncomfortable with the obligation to promote the Home Office version of Britishness. Earlier in the year I had visited Hymers College, a private secondary school in Hull, a third of whose pupils are from ethnic minorities: the most ethnically diverse such school in the city, according to the principal, David Elstone, who said his student body included 'Iraqis, Iranians, Turks ... lots of recent refugees'.

'We've got to teach the children British values,' said Elstone. 'But what are these, and how are they different from anyone else's values? A friend of mine, the head of a school in Durham, got inspected recently. He passed, but the inspector said, "Your pupils aren't using the right language ... I didn't hear them using the word 'tolerance'." I mean – are the Home Office even going to control the language we teachers use? I heard it on good authority that Theresa May wants the school day to end with us all singing to the flag. I mean, how much division is that going to cause? I thought "live and let live" was the whole point of British values.'

Following Alam's removal, the management of the schools for which he was once responsible was handed to outsiders: a London-based academy chain called Ark, an education trust called Core. The academization of the Park View schools was another source of bitterness for Alam. One of Michael Gove's flagship programmes at the DfE, academization was supposed to help state schools in deprived areas to improve more quickly, by wresting control of schools from local authorities and handing it to the principal and its academy trustees. Part of the accusation hanging over Alam was that he had exploited this programme for his own Islamist ends – despite the fact that it was Birmingham Council and the DfE, impressed by Park View's reputation and extraordinary academic results, that had *invited* him to take over the management of neighbouring schools in the first place.

The wheel had since come full circle. Park View, now renamed Rockwood Academy, was still a 99 per cent Muslim school, yet these days not one of its five trustees was Muslim, a state of affairs replicated in all the other schools affected. The role of parent-governors had also been drastically reduced. Academization, in Alam's view, was insidious, because it ended up distancing the schools from the communities they served, placing them instead firmly under the control of central government and the DfE's own agenda.

'The question is: was that deliberate, or are we all the victims of policymakers sitting in ivory towers? I know what I think.'

Rockwood, the old Park View, had come out of 'special measures' and Ofsted inspectors had recently graded it 'good', a verdict that made Alam hoot with derision: of *course* the system would pat itself on the back in this way.

'It's a shit school now,' he said bitterly. 'All the teachers are supply. The A to C GCSE results are falling, from 76 per cent in 2013, to 65 per cent in 2014, to 54 per cent last year. They've got a Muslim head teacher who says Islam should be kept out. There's no more Islamic education, no more Arabic. It's very belligerent. The 2010 Equalities Act might as well go in the bin.'

He was particularly upset by a new anti-segregation policy, whereby male and female pupils are now zealously directed by their teachers to share classroom desks.

'That's not secularism, that's social engineering!' he spluttered. 'It is bullying: a form of cultural imperialism.'

Peter Clarke reported that in many classes at Park View, students 'sat on different tables with boys and girls segregated'. According to Alam, however, those pupils had segregated themselves: it was not at the behest of any teacher. Like teenagers from any culture, they were hypersensitive to the opposite sex and sometimes preferred the company of their own. To oblige any teenagers to squash up in this way is at best insensitive. But if it was done, as Alam believed, with the intent of expunging the conservative sensibilities of traditional Muslims, I could see why he thought it amounted to bullying. Michael Gove told Parliament in June 2014 that he required academies not just to respect 'British values' but to 'actively promote' them.[8]

Could it be that the schools' new managers had simply replaced Muslim ideology with another?

In an article in 2004, the *Guardian* columnist Andrew Anthony observed that 'the liberal elite can debate equality and diversity, liberty and responsibility, until Abu Hamza turns up on *I'm a Celebrity, Get Me Out of Here*, but it is impossible to legislate for identity'.

Anthony took issue with his fellow columnist Polly Toynbee, who had written earlier that: 'Muslim teaching on women staying one step behind will not do: respect for religion cannot take precedence over respect for British law.'

'Perhaps she's speaking figuratively,' he continued, 'but there is no law that prevents Muslim women from walking one step behind men, which is the formation that I notice increasingly on the streets near where I live. Should there be a secular police, some grotesque parody of the Saudis' Commission for the Promotion of Virtue and the Prevention of Vice, to intervene and ensure that they re-form in double file?' [9]

Twelve years on, it looked as though the secular police had finally arrived in east Birmingham – just as they had arrived on the beaches of the Côte d'Azur in the summer of 2016, where gendarmes ordered one Muslim sunbather to remove her burkini and fined another for not wearing 'an outfit respecting good morals and secularism'. [10]

'I know why they want to make boys and girls sit next to each other,' Alam went on sourly. 'It is about acculturation into nightclubs. It is about hedonism and pleasure. They think, "Let's get some condoms moving here" – you know what I'm saying?'

The word 'condoms' was delivered with such a sneer that it was impossible to miss his meaning.

'At one school they arrange a disco every half term so the kids can do . . . *boogying*,' he added, with a sudden (and startling) lascivious swivel of his hips. 'This school, though, is nearly 100 per cent Muslim, so guess what: hardly anyone goes. So why do they go on holding it? Secularization is about cultural assimilation. And I reject this.'

*

119

Alam was not alone in thinking this way. I spent three days criss-crossing the city, interviewing parents, teachers and pupils from four of the schools affected by the Trojan Horse affair, and found a broad consensus that the government had overreached itself. There were naturally varied opinions of what the schools had been like, and many different versions of who believed what or who once said what to whom. Not all my interviewees were fans of Tahir Alam, whose disciplinarian style was not as universally popular as he made out. The schools, for all their good academic results, were not perfect. In the end, though, they all said the same thing: that Alam and the other dozen alleged Islamist plotters were innocent of any charge of what they understood by 'extremism'.

For a part of the world described by Fox News[11] as a 'no-go zone for non-Muslims', I found east Birmingham remarkably hospitable. I was invited into half a dozen Muslim homes where I drank my hosts' tea and ate their curry. Many of them seemed unshakeably sure of their Brummie identity. They spoke in a flat accent that made me think of oak trees; they exuded stolid calm and cracked dry jokes that I immediately recognized as part of the style of the city. No doubt their confidence derived in part from the immense size of their community, but strength in numbers alone did not explain the sense of belonging that I sometimes detected, a way of presenting themselves as though their residence in the city was a right that they had earned. It turned out that some of them were the grandchildren of unsung heroes of Churchill's war effort. Many of the city's first Asians, if they were not fighting for the British army, had settled here to work in Birmingham's famous munitions factories or on the assembly line at the Spitfire factory at Castle Bromwich, and had suffered many casualties in the Birmingham blitz. Their pedigree was as British as a bulldog's.

And yet the more Birmingham Muslims I spoke to, the more I perceiveed the complexities of their sprawling community and how little of its surface I was scratching. There were subtle distinctions of race and class in play that I knew I would never fully comprehend. The Pakistanis in Sparkbrook, for instance, came from all over the home country, and regarded themselves as cosmopolitan compared to their brethren up the road in Alum Rock – the community served by Park View – which a Spark-brooker from Punjabi Attock told me was even more solidly Mirpuri than Manningham in Bradford. He explained that because Mirpuris were displaced en masse by the building of the Mangla dam in the 1960s – and then invited into Britain by a government in need of cheap labour – the traditional ties of clan and family were preserved like no other immigrant community. And these continue to survive, utterly impervious to the govern-ment's drive for greater integration.

'There's nowhere like it in the UK,' the Punjabi from Spark-brook added. 'You hear Patwari [a Mirpuri dialect] on the street. They're a claustrophobic monoculture compared to us. I'd think twice about living there myself.'

I got my first taste of Alum Rock's monoculture at the home of Amir Ahmed, an IT consultant and father of seven, whose chil-dren had attended Park View as well as its primary school feeder, Nansen. Amir had moved to Birmingham from Reading in 2000 because the religious schooling opportunities were better. It was teatime and his 11-year-old son, Ali, was wearing a spotless white cassock, the uniform required by Hamdh House, a small private faith school of 150 pupils that operated from a converted pub. He was a smiley, outgoing lad who applied perfume to my hand before proudly leading his father in prayer in the cor-ner of the room. He was into park football, but when I asked who he played with, it emerged that not only were there no non-Muslims on his team, but also that he knew no non-Muslims whatsoever.

'Hmm. You've started a thought. That is an issue,' said Amir when I pointed this out.

Another son, Yusuf, eight, was still at Nansen Primary, which Amir said had undergone dramatic change since 2014, not all of it good, despite what Ofsted had said in its latest report.

'There have been a huge number of staff changes. I think there are more non-Muslim teachers than Muslim ones now. They have lost their connection with the community.'

Friday prayers were no longer held there, even though 95 per cent of its nine hundred pupils were Muslim. Arabic was no longer taught as a modern language, although French remained. The school CEO, Adrian Packer, a musician, had introduced lessons in drums, trumpet and guitar, all controversial instruments to conservative Muslims, although Amir was most disquieted by the way 'paedophile safeguarding' was now taught.

'They use outline drawings – quite explicit material – for 11-year-olds,' he said. 'Parents can opt out of sex education, but not if it's taught under the rubric of "science". I know I'd rather teach my children about these matters at home in my own way.'

Amir was a curiously mild-mannered objector but there was no mistaking his bitterness.

'I think [Trojan Horse] was intentional. Government is using bureaucracy to squash our culture. Secular values are being imposed on our teachers as well as our kids, by law. The problem with that is that it *increases* the gap between our cultures, because Muslim values don't just disappear.'

The story of Jahangir Akbar, the 39-year-old former deputy head of Oldknow Academy who was banned from teaching in December 2015, was particularly compelling. He was a Pakistani from Bury Park in Luton, who told me how he had become a teacher in 2000 out of a public-spirited desire to help his community.

'Luton Asians were struggling when I was growing up,' he explained, in a glottal southern accent unchanged by his years in the Midlands. 'The community had turned in on itself. There was a lot of poverty, drug crime, a lack of aspiration – or inspiration. If you don't give youth a good start you've got big problems. It's where support for ISIS comes from, for instance. But I never turned to crime or got angry, thanks to my dad. I was one of nine brothers and he brought us up to be good Muslims. And I thought: why not give some of that back? Middle-class white people can't get into the shoes of working-class Pakistanis. You need people from the community who can do that for you.'

Akbar was not just a teacher, he was also a 'school improvement consultant' who had helped many independent schools judged 'inadequate' or 'satisfactory' by inspectors to raise their standards.

In 2011 he was hired as a consultant to the private Darul Uloom Islamic High School in Small Heath, which was in crisis following an undercover Channel 4 *Dispatches* investigation. The programme, called *Lessons in Hate and Violence*, contained footage of a pupil using highly offensive language about Hindus.

'No one wanted to touch the school after that. The place was in a very bad state, really bad. The press were all over it. But I reintroduced classes in sex education, citizenship, music. I brought in multi-faith religious education: the full whack. I liaised with the community, the police, Ofsted, the governors. I was commuting from Luton, sleeping three and a half hours a night, seven days a week, for months. I turned it around single-handedly. I got it out of special measures within a year. It was brilliant: my biggest project to date.'

This background, Akbar argued, made a nonsense of the later allegations that he had deliberately narrowed the curriculum at Oldknow. He was, he insisted, a modernizer with an unusual and successful record of deradicalizing schools deemed extreme, for which he had been specifically recognized by Ofsted.

'People knew what I was about, what I brought to the table. That's why people in Birmingham simply cannot believe my ban.'

He was as scornful as Tahir Alam of the Clarke report, and

derisive of Nicky Morgan, Michael Gove's successor as Education Minister, who had thanked Peter Clarke for the 'forensic clarity of his findings'. 'Clarke said I introduced a "Koranic memorization programme". But he never even interviewed me. If he had, I would have said, "Come on, mate, it's a bloody state school, not a mosque." There was nothing of the sort!'

The *Daily Mail*, meanwhile, sensationally reported that at Oldknow, 'pupils as young as six were taught to treat Western women as white prostitutes'. Akbar knew exactly where that one had come from: an overenthusiastic teacher who, one morning at a Year 6 assembly, had regaled the children with a well-known parable from the *hadith*, in which Allah forgives a prostitute for giving water to a thirsty dog from her shoe; the story is a Judaic one.

'The head teacher and I took him aside afterwards and said, er, it's probably best not to talk about prostitutes at assembly . . . we laughed it off, really. It was very innocent.'

The version reported in the *Daily Mail* was like the outcome of a game of Chinese Whispers. It was funny, right up until the moment Akbar heard the allegation being used as evidence of extremism by MPs in a debate in Parliament.

Akbar was still furious – 'raging with emotions, and mentally locked,' he said – and a year on, he was still seeking to appeal the DfE's 2015 ruling against him. The tribunal process in his view had been so flawed, in its lack of due process and reliance on hearsay and secondhand evidence, that he thought there might even be grounds for a full judicial review.

'My credibility, my honour, have gone. I can't find work now. Nobody wants to know.'

It wasn't just that a promising career had been cut off in its prime. Akbar seemed genuinely perplexed and hurt that the idealism of his youth had been so traduced and wasted.

'I love my country to the core. I love being British and have not done anything to suggest otherwise. Why do I need to keep explaining that?'

But the Trojan Horse affair had cast such a shadow that every-body associated with it remained tainted. Long before any investigation, he recalled, even Tony Blair had opined that the plotters were driven by the same 'warped' extremism as Boko Haram.[12]

'I mean, Tony Blair lecturing us about ideology. Yeah, right. Move on, mate!'

Many of the parents I spoke to were awestruck by the weight of the government's intervention. Some had had their eyes opened to the power of the state for the first time.

'I was shocked by this encounter with British politics,' said Amir Ahmed. 'Britain has a great history, but the world is get-ting smaller, which makes it more important than ever to uphold freedom. The new system is not promoting British values like tolerance and freedom. Secularism is pushing something else.'

Another parent, Safdar Mir, agreed.

'I've no doubt that the whole story was manufactured by rightwing neo-cons and the media. Islamic education was get-ting above itself. The government didn't like that and wanted an excuse to regain control.'

Other parents felt simply scared. 'Hamid', a former parent-governor whom the DfE was 'minded to ban' – a decision that he was still strenuously appealing – remained so cowed by the experience that he asked me not to use his real name.

'I've got my future to think about,' he said. 'I can't afford to have my name linked to extremism.'

Hamid was a civic-minded delivery driver who had become a parent-governor by replying to a vacancy advertisement in the local paper. His house in Sparkbrook was too small to have any kind of hallway. The sitting room was entered through a narrow front door directly from the pavement. It was a working man's home from the industrial age, complete with mice that scuttled along the wainscoting in the corner of my eye as we talked. In pride of place in his sitting room was a glass cabinet full of trophies awarded for keeping Sparkbrook's streets clean. He had long been a community youth worker, the instigator of a local knife-crime project so successful that in 2003 he had been invited to St James' Palace to meet the Queen. This was a man who knew his neighbourhood so well that he was consulted by and worked with local Prevent officers, which seemed more than ironic.

'There have been a couple of terror arrests in Sparkbrook, and there was one woman who went to Syria, so the press call Sparkbrook a hotbed, but that's ridiculous when you consider the size of the place,' he said. 'There's no support for terrorists here.'

Hamid was still astounded by the accusation that he had used his position at the school to push an Islamist agenda.

'I'm not even a practising Muslim, me,' he said in richest Brummie. 'I don't know anything about Salafism.'

His school had been accused, among other things, of banning the popular annual prom because it encouraged 'free mixing' between the sexes. The reality was that the headmaster, who was not even a Muslim, had decided to organize something different for the pupils that year: a trip to Alton Towers. He had been a parent-governor for just two years before the scandal broke. The full governing body, he said, used to meet for just two hours each term, and everything said in the meetings was recorded in the minutes.

'The words "Islam" and "Muslim" were never even mentioned in the governor meetings. How could we have been plotting anything? We never had the time.'

The charges against him did seem absurd, and would perhaps have been funny were it not for the damage it had caused, above all to his teenaged son, Mo. Hamid shouted for him and he came galumphing down the narrow stairs, glowering at us both. I asked him questions that were becoming standard to me: did the teachers ever try to segregate his classes? Did he ever feel as though religion was being pushed down his throat? But Mo answered in terse monosyllables and so obviously didn't want to talk about it that Hamid soon released him with a nod back up the stairs.

'Mo is still very upset by what happened,' Hamid murmured.

The harm done to the prospects of young Muslims was, to my mind, the worst aspect of the Trojan Horse affair. The story had broken in the middle of the GCSE exam season. TV vans congregated outside the school, with journalists ambushing any pupil they could for interview. Inside, inspectors were everywhere, teachers kept being suspended, and the minds of those who remained were understandably not on their jobs. Mo as well as Hamid blamed all this when his exam results came back and they were all Ds instead of the expected Cs. He had hoped to go on to take A levels but had been forced to opt instead for a BTEC qualification in graphic design. His father had left school with just three GCSEs, one of them in Urdu, and ended up a van driver; he had always hoped for something better for his son. The state's intervention in east Birmingham had cost them both dearly.

Across all the schools affected there were hundreds if not thousands of students who had been knocked back like Mo, yet no education official had ever expressed a word of apology or regret for what happened. That seemed an obtuse way to handle a community as vulnerable to extremist ideas as east Birmingham is supposed to be. Academically, moreover, the schools were in worse shape than they were before the state intervened. How did that serve the government's goal of social integration? Was education not the way out of the ghetto? Like Anas al-Tikriti, the head of the Cordoba Foundation, I asked myself: what was the strategy here?

The longer I spent in Birmingham, the better I was able to understand Tahir Alam's bitterness. Park View's GCSE results, he asserted, sank to their lowest yet in 2016, when just 49 per cent of them were at grade C or above, far below the national average.

'These people have destroyed the education of our children. We built this school up over a decade. Instead of getting awards, this is what they've done to us. It is a grave injustice against our children, our people, our community.'

*

It was another six months, October 2016, before I got the opportunity to put the grievances I had heard to the man held most responsible for them, the former Education Secretary Michael Gove. By then he was no longer the Minister of Justice, the portfolio he had held for the previous two years. That summer he had gambled and lost on a post-Brexit tilt at the prime ministership, and been returned to the back benches as one of the most reviled politicians in the country for his perceived disloyalty to old friends and colleagues. Our meeting was not in some grand ministerial suite but in a self-service café on the indoor piazza of Westminster's Portcullis House. Yet he seemed far from dismayed by this turn of events and was his usual confident, charming, sedulously courteous self. He was, he told me enthusiastically, a foreign correspondent again, thanks to *The Times* who had given him back his column and were about to send him to America to cover the final stage of the presidential election there.

'I've got a choice of pro-Hillary concerts to cover: Jon Bon Jovi or Katy Perry,' he said. 'Which one do you think I should go for?'

He had just published a long essay on the threat of Islamism in the right-of-centre *Standpoint* magazine,[13] which reprised all the old arguments about the 'conveyor belt' from non-violent to violent extremism. He praised both Cameron and Theresa May as 'successive prime ministers who have now "got it" ' – 'it' being the ongoing need to combat Islamism by 'drawing the poison from the well' via the 'upstream intervention' that underpinned his strategy in Birmingham. Michael Gove, in short, had lost none of his Conservative convictions, and still saw himself as a political big-hitter, despite Brexit and all that had happened over the summer. He was down but not out, and I marvelled at the toughness of his professional politician's carapace.

He had, as I expected, no regrets about hiring someone like Peter Clarke, a counter-terrorism chief, to investigate schools – a decision described at the time as 'desperately unfortunate' by Chris Sims, the Chief Constable of West Midlands police, because of the message it was likely to send to the people of Birmingham. There was the worry, too, that when you send in a ratcatcher, you are bound to catch rats. But Gove rejected any notion that rats were what he was hoping Clarke would find. The DfE, he explained, had first been alerted to the threat of radicalism in Birmingham schools as far back as 2010 and had been accused by Labour of not doing enough about it. So when the Trojan Horse allegations resurfaced in 2014, he felt it was his duty, as Education Minister, to investigate properly. He chose Clarke, he said, because he was 'an expert in that area' and also because he was 'a figure of unimpeachable authority and someone who [would] follow the evidence and come to the conclusions without fear or favour'.

He was very confident that this was what Clarke had done. He said he still 'didn't know' who had written the original Trojan Horse letter, or whether or not it was a forgery, but this didn't matter because Clarke's report had shown 'compelling' evidence of 'collusion and a concerted effort by people to Islamize those schools' – a view, furthermore, that had been supported by Sir Michael Wilshaw, the head of Ofsted. He found the idea that Clarke had doctored the facts to fit a preconceived narrative more absurd than insulting.

'Anyone who has looked at the career of Peter Clarke will know that he is not someone who is susceptible to political pressure,' he said. '[That] would imply that I had chosen people to deal with this situation who were either pliant and prepared to do my will . . . or who were prepared to debase their professional reputations in order to make the facts fit a preordained motive. Peter Clarke's professional reputation as a police officer, and also Sir Michael and his inspectors' status as independent figures, point in my mind to the reliability of the conclusion they came to.'

But if Clarke's evidence was so compelling, I asked, how come the DfE's own lawyers chose not to submit it in the NCTL [National College for Teaching and Leadership] tribunal hearings? Gove said he didn't know, because that decision had been taken after he left the DfE.

'But one of the things that I remember from my time there is that government lawyers needed to be challenged rather than having their view accepted a lot of the time.'

'But the DfE's lawyers are £800-a-day silks.'

'In my experience,' chortled the former Justice Minister, 'the more expensive they come, the less reliable they sometimes are.'

This wasn't the only reminder that this was the politician who, during the Brexit referendum campaign, suggested in a TV interview that the British public 'had had enough of experts'. When I asked how it was that the schools castigated by Clarke had previously been praised by Ofsted inspectors as 'outstanding', he said simply that these inspectors had been 'mistaken' – and that even Sir Michael Wilshaw, the Ofsted chief, accepted this.

Gove is, as everyone knows, a conviction politician, as well as a talented and eloquent debater, and there was no dissuading him from his view that the regime at the Trojan Horse schools was not in the best interests of its pupils. He was, he said, an admirer of Islam, 'one of the world's great religions'. The problem was Islamism, 'a specifically twentieth-century ideology' that had no place in any school, not just British state ones.

'I think there were people in Birmingham who were influenced by Islamism.'

He believed, as Peter Clarke reported, that some key institutions – he mentioned the Association of Muslim Schools (AMSUK), of which Tahir Alam was once the vice-chair – had their 'roots in Islamist thinking'. AMSUK was the umbrella body for independent Muslim faith schools, with no remit for state schools, but Gove's point was made: he did not believe there was clear blue water between it and the state sector, in part because the teachers and governors involved in them were often one and the same.

'You know, out of the crooked timber of humanity no straight thing was ever made,' he said, smiling.

The fact that at least 95 per cent of the pupils at all the Birmingham schools investigated by Clarke were Muslim before they arrived there made no impression on him at all.

'These are *British* state schools,' he said. 'What you can't have is a communal enclave within the UK where the institutions of the state are given a particular ideological or religious flavour by stealth.'

His best defence, perhaps, was that if Muslims wished to set up a 'religiously flavoured' school, there were processes by which they could do so by becoming a voluntary-aided faith school or even a free school. He gave as an example the Tauheedul schools in Blackburn.

'There's an argument – I suppose I'd better check it – that as Education Secretary I created more Islamic-ethos school places than any other,' he said.

He was no enemy of Islam, therefore; his conscience on this score was clear. What he was insisting on, in the end, was a clearer separation of church and state.

'There is a very good argument that lots of secularists would put – I mean, I don't think it's necessarily right, because *private* religious observation is fine – but why should a child necessarily be in a school with an ethos that is not explicitly stated as the ethos of the school and not necessarily one to which the child might wish to subscribe?'

The problem, it seemed to me, was that he perceived Islam like other religions, as a faith that could be followed in isolation from one's life as a civic citizen, rather than as a holistic system that governed all aspects of the Muslim identity. It isn't necessarily 'an Islamist project', as Gove asserted, to seek to harness that tradition: it is also a mainstream belief that is surely and naturally bound to come to the fore in a state school with a 95 per cent Muslim catchment area. Tahir Alam didn't want to set up a faith school precisely because he considered Islam to be part of the mainstream, integral not just to the patch of Birmingham that he came from, but to all of British society. But Gove wasn't having it. State schools, to him, were 'institutions that should bring people together'. It was simply inappropriate, in Britain, for a state school to seek to define itself by any single religious identity.

I tried to pin him down on the posters in the corridors of Rockwood Academy that so upset Tahir Alam – the ones that said it was OK to be Muslim and gay. He wasn't insensitive to the provocation. He even compared it to the outrage felt by American Catholics in the 1980s when the National Endowment for the Arts paid for a sculpture by Andres Serrano called 'Piss Christ', a plastic crucifix in a bottle of the artist's urine. But he still wouldn't condemn the posters.

'It may be that there are lots of people who do think it's OK to be gay and Muslim. I mean, a generation ago, people thought it was wrong to be gay and Christian. Now we have gay bishops.'

'But is it a British value?'

'I think tolerance is a British value.'

'But that poster policy is not tolerant of mainstream Islam. The vast majority of Muslims think homosexuality is immoral.'[14]

'As a matter of private conduct or faith, that's fine . . . But this is a *state* school, and it is not appropriate for a state school in essence to incubate or defend homophobic positions.'

'Absolutely not. But that's quite different to saying it's OK to be Muslim and gay. That's going the other way – it's pushing something else, isn't it?'

'I think it's a perfectly legitimate expression of British values.'

I asked him if he called himself a neo-con, but he said no, he was just an old-fashioned Conservative. When I told him that Muslims all over the country had muttered to me about a plot against Islam and that they considered him to be the sinister string-puller at the centre of the cabal, Gove guffawed: a bark like a double pistol shot, so loud that it echoed off the high glass ceiling of Portcullis House and caused other customers at the café to look over in alarm. There was no cabal, he explained when he had regained his composure. Although he was a founding member of the Henry Jackson Society, which he said existed 'to support democratization', he said he had no formal role in it. He had never met Sara Khan of Inspire. He did, however, cheerfully admit to signing off on DfE funding for Quilliam, which he called 'an admirable organization ... fulfilling an appropriate purpose'.

'So is it government policy to reform Islam? Was it the DfE's?'

'No, no, no,' he said, thinly. 'We were not attempting a project of advancing the reformation of an entire religion, no.'

I asked if he stood by what he'd written a decade ago in his book *Celsius 7/7*, a polemic arguing that Western multiculturalist 'appeasement' of Islamism had ended up encouraging more terrorism.

'Yes, almost all of it. I'm sure there are some factual errors, but I think the broad analysis is right.'

At the time of its publication, the *Mail on Sunday* called the book 'lucid, unhysterical, informed'. The historian William Dalrymple, by contrast, described it as 'a confused epic of simplistic incomprehension, riddled with more factual errors and misconceptions than any book I have come across in two decades of reviewing books on this subject'. Either way, *Celsius 7/7* still has political shelf life. In January 2017, when Gove became the first British journalist to interview President Elect Trump in his golden office in New York, he concluded his encounter by offering Trump a copy of his 'book on how to fight terrorism'.

'Good, I'd love that,' said Trump. 'That's fantastic — how to fight terrorism, I can use that.'[15]

There is a popular theory in Birmingham, of which Gove seemed not to have heard, that the Trojan Horse letter was written with his book in mind, perhaps with the intention of spurring the DfE and its minister into action. Chapter eight of *Celsius 7/7* was actually entitled 'Trojan Horse'. Gove wrote:

'The ability to pass a moral judgement, to declare a particular course of action superior, to uphold the values of a particular culture as more worthy of emulation, to declare without shame that what one knows is better than what others would wish to impose, is increasingly rare in the contemporary West.'

The active promotion of British values in east Birmingham's academies, it seemed, had been in preparation for some time.

The implications of the Trojan Horse affair are broad. The Islamist takeover plot, although non-existent, provided the government with a springboard for the introduction of tough new regulations, such as Prevent Duty or the proposed Extremism Disruption Orders. By turning the hunt for Islamist fifth columnists official, it also subtly sanctioned society's deepening discrimination against Muslims in general. Tahir Alam and I discussed an egregious example at our first meeting, a *Daily Mirror* story about the Butlin's holiday camp at Skegness. The holidaymakers there were treated to a spoof wrestling match, in which they were invited to boo a bearded, Islamic flag-waving baddie called Hakim and to cheer on his opponent, 'Tony Spitfire', who appeared in Union Jack shorts to chants of 'Eng-er-land'.[16]

To the Birmingham-born grandchildren of Muslims who had helped build actual Spitfires, it was hard to think of a worse insult, or a grosser inversion of the truth. As Alam said, it was like a return to 'blacking up' – as politically incorrect as *The Black and White Minstrel Show* that was banned from British television in the 1970s. The kicker to the Skegness story was that only one member of the audience felt offended enough to complain.

'It's become acceptable to boo the Muslims. We are the new niggers,' said Alam gloomily. ' "Islamization" is not a pejorative to Muslims. I mean . . . *hello*? The UK has gone backwards. If you'd asked me twenty years ago where the country would be now, I never would have predicted this. And I'm afraid it could take a full-blown civil rights movement to get us back on track.'

Michael Gove wanted state schools to be institutions that bring people together. Many Muslim parents, however, are dissatisfied with the increasingly secular state education on offer and are simply disengaging from the system, opting instead to send their children to private Muslim schools if they can afford to, or else schooling them at home.

'This is the trend everywhere, not just in Birmingham,' Jahangir Akbar told me.

The BBC reported that between September 2013 and June 2015 more than a thousand pupils were withdrawn from fourteen state schools being monitored in London and Birmingham; and that in a third of cases, the authorities have no idea where they have gone, an admission that prompted Sir Michael Wilshaw to worry that the missing children could be at risk from 'extremist ideologies'.[17] The active promotion of British values in schools, in other words, may be leading not to greater social cohesion but to marginalization, alienation and the creation of a new Muslim apartheid – the precise opposite effect of the one intended.

There was no evidence that Muslim children withdrawn from the state system were at greater risk of radicalization, as Wilshaw suggested, but I still wondered where they might be going and what sort of 'religiously flavoured' education they could expect on the outside. Teachers at private Muslim schools tend to be Islamic scholars – imams, in effect – and I knew that the training of those, in Britain, had long been dominated by a particular school of Islam, a movement called Deobandism.

I needed to know more about the Deobandis. Perhaps 45 per cent of the country's estimated 1,750 mosques follow their tradition, far more than any other Muslim denomination.[18] The Deobandis also run the best and the biggest seminaries in Britain: at least twenty-two of them, more than anyone else, with the result that some 80 per cent of the youngest generation of imams, British-born and English-speaking, are Deobandi-trained. Getting to grips with Deobandism was thus critical to understanding the future direction of British Islam itself; and the undisputed centre of the movement was barely 40 miles from Birmingham, in the East Midlands city of Leicester.

6

The Deobandis

Leicester

I FELT THAT THOMAS COOK, the teetotal founder of the epony-
mous travel agency, whose statue I nodded to outside Leicester
railway station, would have approved of my choice of tour guide
in his adoptive city: Sheikh Riyadh ul-Haq, the former imam of
Birmingham Central Mosque, one of the most influential
Deobandi Islamic scholars in the country.

The Deobandis, I had read on the train here, are known not
just for their conservative interpretation of Islam, but for a certain aloofness from non-Muslim society that does not, on the
face of it, lend itself well to the cause of integration. Sheikh
Riyadh, indeed, has been accused in the past of encouraging
his followers to disengage from the world around them. In 2007
The Times published an article entitled 'The homegrown cleric
who loathes the British', which asserted that he was opposed to
forming friendships with kuffar like me because he thought
they exerted an 'evil influence'. *The Times* quoted one of his lectures in which he said: 'We are in a very dangerous position
here. We live amongst the kuffar, we work with them, we associate with them, we mix with them and we begin to pick up their
habits.'[1]

The sheikh, however, picked me up in his car and took me on
a grand tour of Muslim Leicester, from one mosque to another,
to an independent faith school, to his own Al-Kawthar Academy
where he teaches advanced Islamic studies. Originally from the

Indian state of Gujarat, he exuded authority in his white shalwar kameez and skullcap, a billowing black waistcoat and matching bushy beard. He spoke a precise and forceful English in a flat East Midlands accent – 'says' was pronounced as it is spelled, not as 'sez' – just as he did in his many sermons and lectures that I had seen on YouTube. He was quite grand, like a cardinal or a bishop; his students venerated him with kisses to his hands. But I also found him to be humorous and humane, good company, comfortable in his skin, and immensely proud of his community and the city of his upbringing.

Our tour began with a stroll in a park, the centrepiece of which was the ruins of Leicester Abbey, dissolved by Henry VIII in 1538, and the final resting place of Cardinal Wolsey, who died here in 1530 en route to London where he was due to face trial for treason. Riyadh turned out to be a bit of an English history buff, which was also not the mark of a hardcore Muslim isolationist. I wondered if he had brought me here partly in order to make precisely this point. Then again, it is perhaps hard not to be genuinely interested in English history if you live in Leicester, where Richard III was recently disinterred in a council office car park. We stopped by Wolsey's memorial slab, where Riyadh expatiated on the cardinal's rise and fall, a Tudor Ozymandias. We discussed the break with Rome and the role of Thomas Cromwell, as portrayed by Mark Rylance in the televised version of *Wolf Hall*. He saw a parallel between the dissolution of the monasteries and the modern-day treatment of Muslims: 'A community under siege,' he said, whose cultural and financial assets are being similarly stripped away.

This was stretching things a bit. With the exception of some on the far right, no one is suggesting that Britain's mosques should be looted and flattened. Yet it was impossible not to hear the rhythm of history in this place, with Riyadh at my side. The religious life of Leicester was once dominated by this demolished abbey, in which lived forty Augustinian canons, known as the Black Canons because of their dress, a white habit beneath a black cloak. The baton had since passed to the Muslims, and Riyadh even looked like a Black Canon.

There are forty mosques in modern Leicester, serving 70,000 Muslims, a fifth of the city's population. The community's distinguishing feature is how many of them originally came, as Riyadh did, from Gujarat. In fact it is the largest Gujarati community in the world outside Gujarat. And it is still growing: at the 2011 census, when all the other resident ethnic minorities were totted up, Leicester was found to have become the first white-minority city in the country, a milestone passed by only two British towns, Luton and Slough.[2]

I knew the basics of Deobandism from my time in South Asia. The movement began in India in 1867 in reaction to British colonialism, which its founders believed was corrupting Islam and its culture. To counter this they set up a seminary, a *darul uloom*, in the city of Deoband a hundred miles north of Delhi, and began to promote a traditionalist, orthopraxic ideology based on disciplined Islamic scholarship. Through their missionary wing, the Tablighi Jamaat – whose European headquarters, the Markazi Mosque in Dewsbury, I had looked at with Danny Lockwood – Deobandism soon spread around the world.

Deobandi theology is not radically different from that of other Sunni denominations. They follow the Hanafi school of jurisprudence, the one most commonly followed in the world. Sociologists sometimes depict Deobandis as bitter rivals of the Barelwis, the other major Hanafi movement in Britain, who lean more towards Sufi mysticism. Barelwis celebrate the Prophet's birthday, while Deobandis do not. Barelwis sometimes incorporate music and dancing in their worship, which Deobandis frown upon. For the most part, though, the doctrinal differences are small. What is perhaps most striking about the Deobandis is how, as scholarship-based traditionalists, they regard themselves as the guardians and standard-bearers of

Sunni Islam, to the extent that most Deobandis do not even define themselves as such but, often, simply as 'Sunnis'. It is, in the end, the style of Deobandi scholars that marks them out, not the substance of their theology.

The government has nevertheless long looked askance at the Deobandis. It is true that, like many Salafis, many Deobandis incline towards the conservative end of the Muslim spectrum. Wearing the niqab is not uncommon among them; their reputation for self-discipline and unworldly austerity is not unfounded. The security services could hardly forget either that the Taliban, the Afghan Pashtun movement that harboured Osama bin Laden, had grown out of the Deobandi madrassahs in Pakistan in the 1990s. Several other militant organizations in Pakistan, like the notorious TTP (Tehrik-i-Taliban Pakistan), or Sipah-e-Sahaba and its offshoots, have a pronounced Deobandi flavour to them as well. Senior British Deobandis like Riyadh had consistently condemned terrorism in all its forms, but it took more than words to remove the taint of extremism in the minds of Deobandism's critics.

The government's campaign against non-violent extremism began with the easiest targets: Salafist hate preachers like Anjem Choudary, political organizations like the Muslim Brotherhood, activists like the advocacy group Cage or alleged Islamist 'entryists' like the supposed Trojan Horse plotters. In 2016, however, there were signs that the target was moving from these fringes to the mainstream of British Islam, to include Deobandism itself.

One of the main targets of the new campaign was the country's prisons, which the security services have long recognized as a major incubator of Islamic extremism. Richard Reid, the failed airline 'shoe bomber' of 2001, Samantha Lewthwaite's accomplice Jermaine Grant and Cardiff-born Abdul Miah, jailed in 2012 for plotting to blow up the Stock Exchange, were all known to have been radicalized inside. And yet the prison authorities seemed powerless to prevent it. There were more than 12,500 Muslim prisoners in 2016: 15 per cent of the total prison population, a proportion triple the percentage of Muslims nationally. They were almost by definition young, angry and disaffected, a group ripe for exploitation by Islamist ideologues. In December 2015, indeed, the assistant general secretary of the Prison Officers' Association, Glyn Travis, told the *Guardian* that Islamists were deliberately seeking prison sentences in order to reach an audience that was literally captive.[3]

For the last ten years, much of the responsibility for preventing prisoners from choosing the radical Islamic path had fallen on the prison system's 240-odd Muslim chaplains. However, in 2016 a government report by a former prison governor, Ian Acheson, found that they were failing in this important pastoral mission, 'sometimes,' he wrote, 'because they lack the capability, but often because they don't have the will.' The study further revealed that about two-thirds of the Muslim chaplains were graduates of Deobandi seminaries and that chaplains from other persuasions could feel 'marginalized, bullied and intimidated' by them.[4]

Considering how many seminaries in Britain are Deobandi-run, it is hardly surprising if their graduates dominate the prison imamate or that their beliefs are the 'default' theology among them. However, in the hands of tabloid journalists – to whom the report was heavily trailed by the Ministry of Justice – it took on a sinister new significance.

'Majority of prison imams are teaching "anti-western" values,' said the *Daily Mail*. 'Radical brand of Islam contrasts to British values and human rights.'

Even sexist and homophobic literature found in ten prison libraries was blamed on the imams, who according to the *Sun* were not countering extremism at all but 'preaching hate' and 'encouraging lags to murder non-believers'.

A 'Whitehall source' quoted in the *Daily Express* said: 'It is of great concern that the majority of Muslim chaplains propagate a fundamentalist interpretation of Islamic scripture which is contrary to British values and human rights ... Such imams are unlikely to aid the de-radicalization of Islamists in prisons and could potentially even make them more firm in their beliefs.'

Slowly but surely, the blame for prison radicalization was shifting from the systemic or even societal failings of Britain's prisons to the ideology of the chaplains themselves, with the clear implication that they were complicit in what was going on.

Cooler heads, like the Leeds University academic and convert Yahya Birt, pointed out that appointing Muslim scholars to the prison chaplaincy had been a deliberate government policy for a decade because they were the people best placed to counter the warped theological arguments of violent extremists. Moreover, a three-year investigation by Cardiff University's respected Islamic Studies department had found that the Muslim chaplaincy was by and large doing an excellent job.[5]

But that apparently counted for nothing in the new climate of fear. In the eyes of the Ministry of Justice, all Muslims involved in the prison system, even chaplains, were now suspect.

Riyadh was, naturally, very troubled by the anti-Deobandi climate, which was as bad as anything he could remember. He was in particular despair at *The Times*, which had recently renewed an attack on Britain's oldest and most important Deobandi seminary, the darul uloom at Bury just north of Manchester. Many graduates of the 'Muslim Eton', as it is known, had gone on to become prison imams, and Riyadh himself had once been a star student there. *The Times* quoted a website that it claimed 'promoted' the darul uloom's teachings and which denounced integration and warned of the 'repulsive qualities' of Christian and Jewish women. The website also featured a sermon by a graduate of Bury, Maulana Mahmood Chandia, on the evils of the music industry, a means of 'spreading the Satanic web ...

Nearly every university in England has a music department and in others, where the Satanic influence is more, they call it the Royal College of Music.'[6]

Riyadh said it was all an outrageous slur. Even Sir Michael Spurr, the head of the National Offender Management Service, had defended Darul Uloom Bury as an institution that upheld British values. The darul uloom had nothing to do with the website cited by *The Times*, inter-islam.org, which was run not by scholars but by a lone amateur, an IT technician who used to live in Leicester. Some of the material it contained was accurate but some was not, or else was twenty years out of date. The darul uloom, Riyadh insisted, had no political agenda and studiously avoided getting involved in wider community disputes, including doctrinal ones. The school didn't even have its own website. How could it possibly be held responsible for the varied views of the hundreds of people who had studied there over the years?

The Deobandis' difficulties were in part due to a failure of public relations. In line, perhaps, with their raison d'être in the 1860s, the movement's senior clerics tend to be more concerned with the spiritual than the temporal world and feel little obligation to explain themselves or to apologize to anyone. Darul Uloom Bury is, famously, entirely closed to outsiders. Its principal and founder, Sheikh Yusuf Motala, arguably the most senior Muslim cleric in Britain, has never given a press interview. Deobandis as a consequence can seem puritanical, old-fashioned and withdrawn from the world, even to other conservative Muslims.

There had been some steep ups and downs in Riyadh's career, a rough ride that seemed emblematic of the development of British Deobandism generally. He started preaching at Birmingham Central Mosque in 1991 when he was just 20, and soon became the star Friday attraction.

'I drew the crowds because I was young, and because I

lectured in English. I was one of the first *khateeb* in Birmingham to do that. Maybe *the* first,' he recalled.

Imams all over the country began to pay attention to his ability to connect with a new generation of British Muslims. He was passionate and outspoken in a milieu unused to it, a traditionally staid world ruled over by bearded old men. With his impeccable Deobandi lineage and his training in Bury, it wasn't long before he was being called a leader of all British Muslims. In the 1990s, Birmingham Central Mosque was said to be the largest mosque in Europe. In time, the mainstream media suggested that he 'controlled' as many as six hundred mosques. There was speculation, still laughed off by Riyadh, that he was in line to succeed Sheikh Motala at Bury. Some even dubbed him 'the next Muslim Pope'.

His prominence drew flak from all directions. Local politicians, including Muslim ones, fretted at his power and influence. Older imams were jealous. In 2000 he was accused of orchestrating a radical takeover of Birmingham Mosque, although the mosque committee, luckily for Riyadh, didn't believe a word of it and stood by their star performer. The mainstream media, however, proved a more tenacious opponent. *The Times*'s profile of him in 2007 quoted extensively from his past lectures to prove that he was a dangerous reactionary: homophobic, misogynistic, anti-Semitic and an implacable enemy of integration with Western culture. The memory of that attack still rankled. The first he had known of it was when *The Times* emailed him with seventy detailed questions about his past lectures, giving him less than five hours to respond before publication.

'It was impossible. Some of the quotes were taken completely out of context. Others had been spliced together, or attributed to me when I had been quoting someone else. A few of the points they made were valid. I've given thousands of hours of lectures in my time, so of course there are some things I regret saying.

But is it fair to judge a man by words spoken years ago, in a different political climate, a different time?'

He acknowledged that he had made mistakes in his younger days, and had apologized for and retracted his more ill-judged lectures and comments, including by contacting Internet providers and getting them to remove them from circulation. In other words his views, as views do, had changed. And yet the allegations in The Times had never quite gone away, thanks to the Internet. Not every past comment could be expunged; and there were other incidents in his life that had taken on an electronic life of their own. The most unfortunate of these came in 2003, when he was questioned by the police in connection with a drive-by shooting in Small Heath. The word on the street – later repeated by prosecutors on the first day of the trial of the alleged killers – was that Riyadh's wife had had an affair with the mosque secretary, Shokat Lal, by whom she had fallen pregnant. The murder victim, Shaham Ali, 30, was said to have been a friend of Lal's and to have been killed by supporters of Riyadh intent on avenging his honour.

I first heard this murky tale when it was brought up, unsolicited, by a Deobandi contact in Manchester, who said that 'everybody' knew about it; and there were of course many more smutty details online. None of them was true. When I found an appropriate moment to broach the subject with Riyadh, he angrily dismissed it all as 'the worst kind of salacious gossip. It makes me spit.' It was proven at the trial that the mosque secretary was involved not with Riyadh's wife but with another woman. The alleged gunmen were not 'supporters of ul-Haq', as the prosecution first contended. The prosecution's witness evidence was dismissed by the judge as unreliable. In his summing up, furthermore, the judge declared Riyadh to be an entirely innocent party.

The shooting, Riyadh explained, was not about mosque

politics at all, but just another episode in a long-running feud between two east Birmingham drug gangs. This was why, at the time of his death, Shaham Ali was not only armed but wearing a balaclava and body armour. The only connection to Riyadh was that some of the parties involved might have attended one or more of his mosque talks.

'I had no control over who came to listen to me,' Riyadh explained. 'On some evenings I would look down at the front row and see university lecturers sitting next to labourers, or businessmen with PhDs next to ex-cons, ex-gangsters, bouncer types. The Birmingham community in general is not very well educated, frankly. It was a real hotch-potch.'

Some of the hotch-potch, it turned out, contained what he called 'real Birmingham criminals, who had "beef" from the past . . . I caught them fighting outside the mosque twice. They used to stop out of respect for me, but I had no real control over them.'

In his early days at Birmingham, he recalled, he had been 'young and unworldly and non-judgemental. But then I found myself involved in a lot of pastoral care. I dealt with gays who felt conflicted by their religion, with wife-beaters, with honour violence – all sorts. I was always being asked to arbitrate in disputes. I became worldly . . . I had to. I suppose I learned the hard way.'

It was a heavy responsibility for a studious young cleric and he admitted that there were times, inevitably, when he had got it wrong. He surmised that this might have led to resentment among some members of his congregation, who had taken their revenge in 2003 by linking him to the shooting.

Riyadh had since retreated to Leicester, where he still dedicates himself to the teaching of advanced religious studies at the Al-Kawthar Academy in the east of the city. He took me to see the premises, which were low-key for an institution so prestigious and smaller than I expected: a sparsely furnished industrial unit in east Leicester, surrounded by nylon casting factories and roofing and cladding specialists. Al-Kawthar, he explained, is the name of the 108th and shortest *surah* in the Koran and means 'the abundance of good'. I was introduced to two of his student acolytes, Abdul-Hayy and Uthman, both shy, serious men in their late twenties with heavy beards. One day, perhaps, they would become *ulama*, literally 'the learned ones', a part of the scholarly Deobandi elite. Abdul-Hayy kissed Riyadh's hands as he arrived and started to kneel like a disciple until his master impatiently stopped him and asked him to fetch some tea.

They seemed as unworldly as novitiates in a monastery. Their trousers, I noticed, hung short above their ankles, the style supposedly approved by the Prophet because in pre-Islamic Arabia long trousers were associated with the sin of pride. In practice, though, their studies were part-time and their lives were not so cut off from the outside. Abdul-Hayy, for instance, made a living selling shelving for garages, and beneath the austere exterior lay a sharp curiosity about society, as well as flashes of humour.

We talked about beards and of how outward appearances can be taken as an indicator of inner extremism. There had been another case recently of an obvious Muslim being forced off his holiday jet before departure, simply because another passenger didn't like the look of him. Ahmed Ali, 39, a property developer from Derby flying from Manchester to Marrakesh for his honeymoon, told reporters afterwards that it was the twentieth time in four years that he had been questioned in airports.

'I'm so upset about it,' he said. 'What they did was wrong and I think it is purely because I am Muslim and have a beard.'[7]

The Deobandis are more than usually sensitive to this sort of incident. None of them has forgotten how in 2003, Sheikh Motala himself was detained at Heathrow and questioned for almost seven hours, forcing him to cancel his *umrah* pilgrimage to Mecca. It was clear from the security officers' generic questions about jihadism that they had no idea who he was. His treatment caused such outrage among Motala's followers that the Home Office was later forced to apologize.

'That was thirteen years ago, but the airport profiling is worse now than it was then,' said Uthman.

I recounted how I had flown from Edinburgh to Paris earlier in the year and had spotted an Asian Muslim among the passengers who successfully pre-empted any funny looks with a T-shirt that read *I'M THE ONE WITH THE ENORMOUS BEARD*.[8]

I wondered why, at a time of heightened tension around all things Muslim, facial hair for certain young, white non-Muslims – students, hipsters – had become more fashionable than at any time since the 1970s.

'I don't know,' grinned Abdul-Hayy, 'but I think it's very beautiful!'

He had read about a photo shoot, organized in a remote Swedish castle by a group of eccentric beard fanciers, and of how a passing local farmer became so convinced they were a gathering of Islamists that he called in the police. For Muslims too, he acknowledged, beards, veils and other outward signs of a devout soul are just as subject to the whims of fashion, including in conservative Leicester, a city where these days one saw 'more hijabs than in Lahore'.

For adherents of a movement often accused of eschewing the liberal arts, Abdul-Hayy and Uthman seemed well versed in contemporary depictions of British Asian culture. They hated *Citizen Khan*, the BBC sitcom that parodies Pakistani family life in east Birmingham, starring the actor Adil Ray. Abdul-Hayy called it 'out of date and over the top', and ultimately racist because he thought it gave licence to white people to laugh at Muslims. He took particular exception to the daughter character, a stereotype he called a 'slutty hijabi'. On the other hand, he and Uthman were fans of *Goodness Gracious Me*, the BBC sketch show from the 1990s that poked fun at both Indian and English stereotypes. We all remembered the show's best-known sketch, in which four Indians 'go out for an English' after a few lassis, mispronounce the waiter's name and order twenty-four plates of chips.

What really enthused Abdul-Hayy, though, was Chris Morris's 2010 movie *Four Lions*, a 'jihadi satire' about a group of home-grown terrorists from Sheffield. The film, I knew, has a cult following among a great many people, including many Muslims. One critic, after testing the reaction of the audience in Bradford where it premiered, pronounced that it was 'set to be regarded as the most Islamo-friendly jihadi comedy about suicide bombers ever made'.[9] One of the film's funniest lines, comparing a martyr's paradise with the 'rubber dinghy rapids' ride at Alton Towers theme park, has become a well-known Internet meme. The line has been replicated on T-shirts and edited into its own dub-mix track on YouTube. A later photo of three real-life Muslims at Alton Towers, spinning along in their turbans and shalwar kameez, remains a hit on aggregator websites like theladbible.com.[10]

Even so, it was a surprise to find a *Four Lions* fan at Al-Kawthar. 'I absolutely love it,' said Abdul-Hayy. 'It couldn't be more right. That "Barry" character is such a typical convert, more Muslim than the Muslims. My brothers even call me Barry.'

I was pretty sure Abdul-Hayy was a born Muslim, not a convert, but I caught the reference and got the point. Barry al-Britani, in the film, is the gang's only non-Asian, an absurd, angry psychopath who wants to spark a religious war by bombing the local mosque, in order, he says, 'to radicalize the moderates'.

Some time later, in London, I asked Nigel Lindsay, the actor who played Barry al-Britani, where the character had come from. The original idea, he said, was from Chris Morris, who had once met a BNP supporter, 'John', who had bought a copy of the Koran in order better to mess with the minds of the Asians he hated and ended up accidentally converting himself. But then

Lindsay whipped out a smartphone and showed me a 1990 clip of 'Abu Abdullah' preaching Islamist hellfire alongside Abu Hamza outside Finsbury Park mosque. His real name was Atilla Ahmet, a Turkish Cypriot from Bromley. Barry al-Britani leapt into life on the little screen. There was the beard, the shaved head and kufi cap, the same booming Sarf London accent, the same chuntering, aggressive rhetoric: 'Mr Policeman, when are you gonna start telling the people the truth about Islam?'

'I just found him one day on the Internet when I was research-ing the role,' Lindsay recalled. 'I used to watch his videos before each take to get me into character.'

Making a film that ridiculed extremists wasn't without risks. In 2004, the Dutch film-maker Theo van Gogh was murdered for less, for a film called *Submission* about the abuse of Muslim women. The genius of *Four Lions*, though, was that it poked fun at extremism without disrespecting the faith. It also human-ized the bombers without condoning what they did. Built around Chris Morris's insight that terror cells function 'on the basis of inwardly directed group love, rather than outwardly directed hate',[11] the film was so accurate in its psychological observations that, I had found, it is still routinely referenced by counter-terrorism officials in Whitehall. And now, here in Leicester, a Deobandi scholar in shortened trousers was laugh-ing his head off at it.

'*Every* Muslim knows a Barry,' Abdul-Hayy asserted.

It struck me not for the first time that nothing broke down the suspicion and misunderstanding that existed between cultures more effectively than humour. It was somehow exquisite to dis-cover from Nigel Lindsay that he was the son of a man called Lazarus who had changed his name when he emigrated to Britain. Ethno-religious identities were suddenly shifting around faster than in an *Ali G* film. It meant that the Scottish-sounding actor, who modelled his English wannabe-jihadi character on a real-life Turkish Cypriot with an Arab pseudonym, was actually Jewish.

*

Riyadh's guided tour was a fascinating study in the Islamification of a British city, and helped to explain the esteem in which he is held in Leicester. His father, Maulana Muhammad Gora Sahib, came here as one of its first imams, following training in India by one of the heroes of Deobandism, Sayyid Madani. He was from the same Gujarati village as Sheikh Motala, whose first students at Darul Uloom Bury were sent there from Leicester by Maulana Sahib. Riyadh was born the eldest of eleven children and every one of his siblings, including his five sisters, is professionally involved in higher education. The family, in other words, are Deobandi aristocracy. When Maulana Sahib died in 2013, over 10,000 people attended his funeral in the local park.

Riyadh showed me the first mosque, which opened in 1967 in a converted terraced house in Sutherland Street, in the Highfields district east of the city centre. Its congregants were mostly workers in the hosiery and garment industry. The community outgrew Sutherland Street within five years and opened a second mosque, in Berners Street, where Riyadh's father was imam. He pointed wistfully at the third-floor window of a flat next door where, in the mid-1970s and barely six years old, he had first begun to explore the Koran. 'Ah, memories, memories,' he said.

Maulana Sahib helped establish a third mosque in 1977, the Jame mosque, in the former canteen of the Imperial typewriter factory, although there was no trace of the building's past when the imam showed us around. The mosque is the biggest in the city, with a prayer hall easily big enough for 1,500 worshippers, which gleams with chandeliers and marble imported from Dubai. It is a big complex that incorporates a school for 1,300 children and it is still expanding into buildings nearby, including a former police station across the road. We passed along an upstairs corridor of small classrooms, every one of which was crowded with bearded young men squatting at their studies, rocking madrassah-style over their texts.

Leicester has undergone one of the most dramatic demographic transformations in the country since the 1970s. With indigenous whites in a minority for the first time, the city should be a race-relations tinderbox. Yet it is a harmonious place compared to many comparably mixed cities and proud of its record on community cohesion. Leicester Council does not look askance at the mushrooming of mosques in its jurisdiction but celebrates the diversity they signify. The name of the street alongside the Jame mosque, for instance, has been changed to Jame Walk. And there seems to be a lot of interfaith work going on. The Church of England put £100,000 towards the cost of a voluntary-aided faith school, the Madani Schools Federation. The Dean of Leicester Cathedral hosts a regular public forum called *Learning to Live Together*, with discussion topics such as *Understand: The prejudices we do not realise we carry* and *Trust: Can we disagree well?* It was no doubt helpful in 2016 that, for the first time in its 132-year history and against astonishing odds, Leicester City FC finished top of the Premier League, and that three members of the squad atop the home-coming bus as it was mobbed by ecstatic crowds were Muslims.[12]

Leicester, it is true, has produced a handful of recruits for ISIS. Two medical students from Oadby, the British-Sudanese Ageed brothers, absconded to Syria from their university course in Khartoum in 2015. Separately, but at around the same time, an unnamed Leicester woman was stopped at Birmingham Airport while trying to take her three young children there via Istanbul and Munich.[13]

Yet the city has never been labelled a terrorist hotspot as Luton or Bradford or Dewsbury all have been, even though thirty of its forty mosques follow the Deobandi tradition, a brand of Islam that the media and government constantly and explicitly link with extremism. In truth, no Deobandi mosque in Leicester has ever been held responsible for radicalizing anyone – a record that casts further doubt on the official conveyor belt theory of radicalization and perhaps lends credence to the argument that the best way to defeat violent extremism is more, not less, Islamic education.

'We keep out of politics as much as possible,' Imam Imran ibn Adam at the Jame mosque told me. 'Our focus here at the school is all on daily life and ethics, not ideology.'

Relations with Leicestershire police, led by Chief Constable Simon Cole, who also happened to be the national 'police lead' for the Home Office's Prevent programme, were notably cordial. Leicester's imams couldn't have been more specific in their condemnation of ISIS and regularly used their Friday sermons to say so. In the wake of the Paris attacks of November 2015, Dr Ather Hussain of the Association of Sunni Ulama Leicestershire, an umbrella group for a dozen of the largest mosques in the city, told his congregation:

'People have been saying in the press, "Where is this majority of peace-loving Muslims?" You are these people, and you need to speak up. You need to be more vocal and make it very clear that Da'esh are infidels. You do not have to defend them or be held accountable for what they are doing. More than ever before we need to take these terrorists head on, make people in the street realize this is not part of our religion.'

He added: 'I say with great pride, we live in a city – Leicester – where we promote mutual love. There are many cities in this country that are not like this.'[14]

The city's relative tranquillity, Riyadh thought, was partly down to the culture of the dominant Muslim group. He theorized that because Gujarati Muslims were outnumbered ten to one by Hindus in their native state, they were already well versed in the art of co-existing with others when they first came to Britain in the 1950s, an art they had applied with equal success in other countries, such as South Africa and even Barbados. Like others I spoke to, he described Gujaratis as laid-back people with a reputation for cleverness and business nous, who 'punched above their weight through a combination of scholarship and enterprise'. His list of famous Gujaratis was long and surprising: Gandhi, Jinnah, the Tata family, Salman Rushdie. Even Freddie Mercury was born Farrokh Bulsara, to a Parsi family from the Gujarati town of Valsad.

Unlike in some northern mill towns, the Muslim community coped well with the collapse of local industry in the 1970s, by branching out into their own businesses, many of which have thrived. There is money in Asian Leicester – and the opulence of the Jame mosque, refurbished at a cost of £4.5 million, all of it from local donations, is the most conspicuous showcase of their success. The community has been spreading outwards from Highfields for years now into well-to-do suburbs like Evington, a middle-class enclave of big Victorian villas and, since 2000, the site of the smart, copper-domed Umar mosque. Gujarati energy, economic opportunity and the city's strong Islamic ethos have proved a magnet for new arrivals from across the Muslim spectrum. The imam at the Umar mosque said that at Friday prayers these days he barely recognizes a tenth of his congregation, which he thought was the most cosmopolitan in the city. By many measures, therefore, Leicester's Muslim community is a model of success.

And yet it lives under constant suspicion and scrutiny from outside. In an upstairs office of the Jame mosque, Imam Imran ibn Adam recalled how, in 2010, a BBC *Panorama* crew had hidden in the bushes outside to film 11-year-old girls on their way to his mosque's school. In line with school rules the girls were wearing niqabs, which the programme-makers wanted to show as evidence of extremism. By January 2016 it seemed that the head of Ofsted, Sir Michael Wilshaw, agreed with that assessment, when he wrote to all his inspectors instructing them to mark down schools if they judged that the face veil – whether worn by pupils or teachers – was a 'barrier to learning'. His decision, which was expected to affect around 16,000 Muslim girls as well as 1,000 teachers, was supported by Prime Minister Cameron, who had earlier indicated that he would back public authorities who introduced 'proper and sensible' rules to ban face veils.[15]

'They want to go after everyone,' shrugged Mufti Muhammad ibn Adam al-Kawthari, Imam Imran's brother, who ran an online advisory service, daruliftaa.net, that was caught up in the *Panorama* allegations. 'The Salafis were first, now it's the turn of us Deobandis. Next it will be someone else.'

Like Riyadh, he regarded 'Deobandism' as a completely spurious target. He explained that although Deobandism is often described as a 'sect' with a strict set of rules, it is in reality a loose and diverse movement, incorporating liberals as well as conservatives, radicals as well as centrists.

'You can have three Deobandis in a room, as we are now, and you will hear three different opinions. There is no "Deobandi position" on anything,' he insisted. 'I don't identify myself as "Deobandi". None of us do. We are just Sunni.'

It was little wonder, if that was the case, that he thought the government was engaged in a campaign not just against extremism but against Islam itself.

Riyadh and I drove from the mosque to the Madani Schools Federation. Named after the famous Deobandi scholar who had taught Riyadh's father, the Madani is a voluntary-aided faith school, which means that it has government permission to promote an Islamic ethos in its classrooms and is part-funded by the state: one of around twenty such schools in the country and the first purpose-built one. It is an impressive building to look at and has won an architectural award for its glass and steel design centred on an 'Arab-style courtyard'. Academically, the Madani's six hundred pupils – three hundred boys, three hundred girls – are among the highest-achieving in Leicester and there is a long waiting list for places.

Yet even this institution had been subjected to unusual media scrutiny in the past, in its case by a TV crew from Channel 4 News, following a furore in 2014 over its placing of an advertisement for a new science teacher with the condition that 'females need not apply'. Riyadh led me to the office of the school's director, Sheikh Ashraf Mukadam, who I was intrigued to discover was a former chairman of the UK Association of Muslim Schools, the body that Michael Gove told me he believed 'had its roots in Islamist thinking'.

Mukadam sighed when I mentioned the Channel 4 News report and explained that in accordance with Deobandi tradition, both pupils and staff at the Madani are strictly gender-segregated: men teach boys and women teach girls, and where facilities have to be shared, timetables are carefully staggered so that the two never mix. The Madani was accused of flouting the 2010 Equalities Act, but had not, because faith schools in some circumstances are exempt from that law. Even so, he said, Michael Gove didn't like it and asked Leicester City Council to put pressure on the school to withdraw the offending advertisement.

Mukadam, a stickler for traditional Muslim hospitality, had offered us lunch as we arrived in his office, despite it being 11.30 a.m. The meal duly arrived: a microwaved plate of baked beans topped by a meat pie, cheerfully served by an office assistant dressed in the fullest black niqab, right down to a pair of tight, elbow-length gloves. I couldn't take my eyes off these. I was reminded, most inappropriately, of the Belle Epoque cabaret dancer Yvette Guilbert, whom Toulouse-Lautrec used to paint at the Moulin Rouge, which in itself seemed symbolic of the uneasy relationship and many misunderstandings between Mukadam's school and the DfE.

The Trojan Horse business in Birmingham was still resonating in Leicester. It was clear that Mukadam had to exert himself constantly in order to keep the authorities onside.

'Our staff have had all the Prevent training,' he said, with the tiniest roll of his eyes. 'We follow all the protocols, report all suspicious behaviour patterns to the Local Education Authority.'

State funding for independent Muslim faith schools like his is theoretically assured for as long as it is offered to private schools of other faiths – which was no doubt why Mukadam, a shrewd and experienced operator in the sector, made a point of following the Church of England faith school model as closely as possible. Fundamental British values, FBV, were naturally very prominent on the school curriculum, to the satisfaction of Ofsted, who on their most recent inspection had classified the school as 'good'. Yet it was clear that he was still nervous about Ofsted.

'They have a political agenda these days. It is very sad, and very blatant,' he said.

He told a story about a local nursery whose Ofsted rating had been downgraded because the carer in charge had failed properly to define the word 'radicalization'.

'I mean, it was a nursery. For little babies. Are even they considered at risk now?'

Deobandi-style education was under siege elsewhere in Leicester, too. The Darul Uloom Leicester in the city's Belgrave area, a small, fee-paying secondary boarding school for boys, had recently been classified as 'inadequate' at its last Ofsted inspection, despite all previous inspections finding it 'outstanding'.

Ofsted now considered that the boys held 'stereotypical views on gender' that went unchallenged by their teachers. The pupils, they said, had 'no access to television and very limited access to the internet'. All this amounted to 'poor preparation for life in modern British society'.[16]

Mukadam said he accepted that the Department of

Education's criteria could change. What he objected to was that the darul uloom hadn't been granted the customary period of time to rectify the faults found by the inspectors, which included things like fire escapes that are expensive and difficult to install, not just the unsatisfactory promotion of FBV. The darul uloom now faced being 'deregistered' for failing to comply – and that, Mukadam thought, was deliberately punitive.

'The same thing is happening to independent Muslim schools all over the country, to be honest,' he said.

I had asked Riyadh to arrange an interview with the darul uloom's managers, but they were in the process of appealing the Ofsted decision and had been advised by their lawyers not to meet me. Riyadh said that they were scared that the DfE could come after them again, even at some unspecified time in the future, if they dared now to complain to the media. Just as in Birmingham, Mukadam fretted that a state-supported 'cycle of demonization' was at work and that this was playing into the hands of genuine extremists by sowing resentment in young Muslim minds.

Riyadh nodded agreement: 'If there's a radical force at work, it's this negativity from government.'

'We try to keep our pupils away from it,' Mukadam said. 'We teach them to be positive and proud of their nationality, their faith. But it is impossible to shield them from everything.'

Our last stop was a tiny community centre where Riyadh had recently lectured called the Peace Centre, in Thurnby Lodge on the easternmost edge of the city. The imam, another Gujarati Deobandi, called Maulana Mohammed Lockhat, was busy shifting crates of breakfast cereal around when we knocked, unannounced, on his door. The Peace Centre, it turned out, was a busy food bank. The walls on either side were stacked with boxes of baked beans, loaves of bread, catering packs of jam, all ready to be bundled up into food parcels for Leicester's poorest. The parcels made up by his volunteers, Lockhat told me proudly, were worth as much as £20. He had almost three hundred people on his books, some of whom lived on the other side of Leicester and who crossed the whole city to pick their parcels up. The Peace Centre was run as a charity, entirely dependent on donations from the community; the food came from supermarket over-runs, or was donated by nearby bakeries, the local church, or a discount store called Pricebusters.

'These are very good, look,' he said, pointing at a tall stack of Frosties. 'Only just past their BBE date, see?'

He said that anyone who asked, received, with the minimum of paperwork and no questions asked. And the great majority of the askers, he said, were white working-class British.

'We get a lot of widowed pensioners, or people who have been sanctioned by the Jobcentre and are desperate. There's a lot of them like that. We had one old guy in last week who was trying to get by on £1 a week. And it's getting worse, big time.'

'But,' I said, 'what is the Jobcentre doing? Isn't it the state's job to look after these people? What does the council do about it?'

'It's the council who sends them to us,' Lockhat replied.

Despite the obvious saintliness of his charity operation, the Peace Centre is not universally popular with the locals. Thurnby Lodge is a white working-class area where support for the British National Party has been strong in the past. The Muslims who live here are relatively new arrivals – the *maulana* himself only moved here ten years ago from South Africa – and much poorer than the Gujarati grandees of Highfields. In 2012 when they applied to the council to take over the lease of a disused scouting hut, which they wanted to use for children's evening classes, the landlady of the local pub, the Stirrup Cup, complained that they would be bad for business. Then a Facebook campaign was launched accusing them of opening an ISIS training centre. When they expanded into their present premises, a tatty former workingmen's club, someone posted a photo with the big dome of the Evington Umar mosque superimposed on it, 'like a megamosque', Riyadh said. The implication was clear: this so-called Peace Centre was the thin end of a wedge, the start of a stealthy Muslim takeover that had to be stopped.

The BNP co-ordinated demonstrations in the car park outside. The party's leader Nick Griffin, who was an MEP at the time, took a personal interest and once arrived for a demonstration straight off a plane from Brussels.

Maulana Lockhat recalled that there were up to 150 demonstrators, most of them what he called 'local, white-van Leicester', who would turn up after work each evening just in time to disrupt the *maghrib* prayers.

'This went on every night for seven months. The policing bill was £300,000. There was never any violence – I made sure that there was no reaction from us – but there were threats, intimidation. It was not pleasant.'

When Lockhat was followed home one night, the police installed a silent panic alarm in his house. Unfortunately he forgot to deactivate it one evening and the next thing he knew there were twenty armed policemen storming his front garden.

'I don't want to go into detail, but the impact on my young daughters was very heavy,' he said, touching his head.

Calm had since returned to Thurnby Lodge but Lockhat admitted that the community remained watchful for any sign of trouble.

Later, as Riyadh dropped me back at the station and we were talking and saying our goodbyes in the car, we were interrupted by a middle-aged white woman who tapped insistently on his window. Riyadh opened it a crack.

'Please give me some money,' she said, with manic intensity. 'I'm desperate. I'm not a thief or a prostitute and I don't do drugs or anything. And just look at the state of me. I'm only forty-five.'

We looked at her greasy hair and clothes, the broken teeth, the raddled skin: a junkie through and through. Riyadh, wanting to finish a point he was making, calmly and authoritatively asked her to wait; she duly withdrew for a short distance without once taking her eyes off her mark.

'Very tragic,' Riyadh murmured, shaking his head.

She was still hovering when I got out and went off to catch my train, feeling a little guilty at leaving him in that situation and wondering what he was going to do. Give her a lecture on sin? Direct her to a hostel, perhaps? I found out a couple of weeks later when we spoke again, by phone.

'My god, that woman!' he said. 'I didn't have my wallet with me, so I searched all round the car for change. I found enough for her to buy something to eat, maybe even a bus fare too. She took it and started counting it and then you know what she did? As I was driving off, she flung the whole lot at my car.'

Had she mistaken Riyadh for a mean rich man? What amount of money would she not have been insulted by? It was impossible to tell. She was, perhaps, typical of the chaos that lurked beneath the ordered surface of society in all British cities. Riyadh was streetwise enough to be surprised rather than shocked by her reaction, which struck me as very unAsian. You seldom saw Asian drug casualties begging on British streets, for one thing; while on the subcontinent, where begging is a way of life for millions, charity is always received as well as given with good grace, however small the sum. It is a guiltless transaction, an accepted part of a social contract on which the governments of many poor Muslim societies are able to depend entirely for the management of extreme poverty. *Zakat*, the obligation to give away a proportion of one's wealth, is the third and to my mind the most enlightened pillar of Islam. Although there were, clearly, limits to what charity could achieve in situations like that outside Leicester station, I admired the way that so many Muslims do not just talk about charity but routinely practise it, generously, unquestioningly, without fanfare or expectation of any earthly recognition.

The nearest Christian equivalent to zakat was the tithe of

mediaeval times, when the citizenry gave a tenth of their earnings to the clergy, but that practice was more a system of taxation than true charity and is in any case long defunct. The UN has demanded since 1970 that rich countries commit a proportion of their income to the development of the poorest ones, but the spending target, set at just 0.7 per cent of national earnings, is a token compared to the old tithe, and even then very few rich countries (although Britain is among them) have ever managed to meet the obligation. Like Maulana Lockhat's Peace Centre, zakat made me wonder what social good might flow from the serious re-institutionalization of charity in the Western world, locally or abroad.

For me, though, there remained a drawback to the Islamic social system – part of the reason, perhaps, that the tithe is defunct – which was that the obligations it imposes on Muslims seem to require a subjugation of the hallowed Western traditions of liberty, free will and individual choice. Becoming a Muslim is voluntary – the Prophet was clear that there could be 'no compulsion in religion' – but Islam also means 'Submission' and, like many Westerners, I still instinctively distrusted the implications of that. For all the good in Islam, I was wary of the total fealty it demands to its core principles. Because it is based on the literal word of God, Islam comes with a built-in resistance to evolution and reform; it is not good at accommodating social change because the laws and moral values of its patriarchal past, being God-given, cannot be deviated from. And that is problematic for any traditional Muslim living in the West, where laws and values evolve all the time and frequently clash with those of Islam.

In modern Britain, the name alone of the ancient canon of Islamic law is enough to stir controversy. Sharia, meaning 'the way' or 'the path', is synonymous for many non-Muslims with the savage sorts of punishment, known as *hudud*, that are sometimes meted out in Saudi Arabia – or ISIS-controlled Syria – such as the chopping off of limbs for theft or stoning to death for adultery. At the very least it is viewed as a misogy-nistic legal system, another means by which a traditionalist, male-dominated society keeps women in their place. Sharia 'courts' in Britain, moreover, are often seen as another manifestation of the sinister Islamist takeover plot supposedly identified in east Birmingham. Sharia reliably infuriates rightwing campaigners, who portray the courts as a parallel legal system that challenges and subverts the principle of 'one law for all' laid out by Magna Carta in 1215.

I had seen and heard enough by now to suspect that sharia courts – if that was even the correct name for them – were innocent of sedition. But I had never been in one of them: a gap in my knowledge that, after Leicester, I was more determined than ever to fill.

7

The Sisters Are Doing It For Themselves

Oldham

THE MIDDLE-AGED PUNJABI WOMAN on the Skype screen was so hunched and downtrodden she looked as though she had been punched – and as it turned out, she had. Maulana Ejaz, sitting cross-legged on the carpet next to me, sighed wearily. It was the third distressing divorce case we had heard that afternoon. Ejaz thought for a moment, then instructed her to stay on line while the council deliberated and reached forward to press the mute button on his laptop.

'So, James,' he said. 'What do you think?'

His question took me aback. Today was the first time I had observed sharia law in action in Britain and it certainly wasn't my job to pass judgement. Ejaz was the council president. I looked around at his colleagues but there was no guidance to be had there. Maulana Younis, our host here in Oldham, stroked his beard and looked blankly back at me. So did Yusuf, the quiet young mufti from Croydon. The fourth man, a bespectacled older maulana whose name I never caught, went on silently murmuring prayers at the floor, the click of his rosary beads now the only sound in the room.

'I'd say that one was open and shut,' I pronounced, as confidently as I could. 'The police restraining order shows she's not making it up, and the husband has disappeared back to Pakistan. The Crown Court has already granted a decree nisi. So: decree absolute.'

The rosary beads clicked some more. I looked back at the laptop, where the applicant fiddled anxiously with the camera at her end of the line, tunnel-visioned as well as deaf to what was happening here, the decision that could change her life. According to the case papers arranged around the floor, she lived in Nottingham, the long-term wife of a taxi driver who had recently taken a second, younger wife because his first couldn't give him children. Her agreement to this was supposed to buy some respite from the abuse, which it did, for a while, when the husband moved out with his new bride. But one night he came back, forced his way in, broke her nose with his fist. He wasn't supporting her financially, either: she was scraping by on benefits, she said, and odd bits of seamstress work and by selling samosas. Ejaz glanced at Younis, who nodded imperceptibly.

'You are right,' he said eventually. 'This is a very easy decision to make.'

He deactivated the mute button and spoke rapidly in Urdu.

'Jee, Maulana sahib,' she nodded, pulling her hijab tighter. 'Jee, jee.'

Like many British Muslims, she was married both in English law and according to Islamic tradition, having completed the religious ceremony known as *nikah*. A divorce in a case like this was a given under English law, but Islamic divorce procedure is famously different. The power all rests with the husband, who may end a marriage simply by saying *talaq* to his wife three times: I divorce you, I divorce you, I divorce you. A wife, by contrast, may only divorce her husband with his consent – which, for whatever reason, is not always forthcoming. In consequence, a devout Muslim wife can end up trapped forever in a bad marriage, unable to move on with her life or to remarry. Her only way out is to appeal to a religious authority senior enough to dissolve her marriage over the head of the husband. That was the purpose of the Wuzara Ulama Council, whose monthly meeting I was now attending.

While Ejaz spoke into the screen, I asked Maulana Younis quietly why the Nottingham taxi driver had refused to divorce.

'Pure malice,' he said. 'Anger that she didn't give him children, perhaps. Sometimes a sense of family honour comes into play. I'm afraid this is very common in our culture.'

The council's judgement meant that the woman from Nottingham was finally free but she displayed no joy or relief when Ejaz finished speaking. Instead she began to cry. There was a groan of sympathy from the old rosary clicker to our right. The mufti from Croydon looked away and Younis sucked through his teeth.

'I'm sorry, sister,' said Ejaz gently, switching into English, 'but things will be better for you from now on, inshallah.'

The sobbing continued, a tinny sound that still filled the room.

'Come,' Ejaz tried again. 'You have been married for a long time . . .'

'For twenty-eight years!' Younis whispered helpfully.

'For twenty-eight years,' Ejaz continued. 'Surely you have some happy memories from that time? From the early days, perhaps?'

'No,' she said flatly. 'The beatings started from the very beginning when I was sixteen. I never wanted to marry him, it was all arranged by my parents. But now even they say I cannot go on like this.'

Ejaz promised to post her divorce certificate as soon as possible, she hung up and the next case began.

*

Few aspects of Islam are as misunderstood, or as misrepresented, as sharia law in Britain. The allegation that sharia suppresses the rights and freedoms of Muslim women is repeated in the media so often that I had assumed that it must be at least partly true, so it was rather stunning to discover that the exact opposite might be the case. In northern England where his council operated, Ejaz estimated that 60 per cent of Muslim marriages were not registered under English civil law. In those cases, where the state did not recognize a wife's marital status, sharia councils were a would-be divorcee's *only* recourse. The council therefore saw themselves not as oppressors but as providers of an essential service to abused Muslim women; their saviours, even. And from the backlog of applicants on their books, as well as from the sincerity and professionalism with which they worked, it was clear to me that they were justified in doing so. By way of proof, Ejaz later produced a dozen feedback forms from past clients, all of them women escaping abusive marriages, and all of them expressing gratitude for the councillors' help and describing as 'excellent' the service they had received.

And yet the very idea that sharia should operate at all in the West can arouse the fieriest passion in the hearts of non-Muslims. Archbishop Rowan Williams was pilloried in 2008 merely for musing that the adoption of certain aspects of sharia in Britain 'seemed unavoidable'. I knew something of how he must have felt. In Sydney for a book festival in 2011, I was interviewed by *The Australian* about my experiences of sharia in Taliban-controlled Afghanistan, not all of which were negative. I also mentioned Archbishop Williams and what he had said. The reporter, whether out of obtuseness or malice I was unable to tell, wrote this up under the headline 'UK author advocates Sharia law in West'. The following morning a troll called 'Tony' sent me one of the nastiest emails I have ever received:

Any imbecile calling for sharia shite law in the West should be fkn executed. No doubt you will be happy if your children are genitally mutilated. All paedophiles will be grateful to video your conversion. Any UK citizen calling for sharia shite should be hung for treason. Have a shite day you moronic prick!!!!

In the wake of the Paris attacks of 2015, the UKIP leader Nigel Farage claimed there were more than eighty sharia courts already operating in the country. 'Big ghettos', he said, were being run according to sharia law while the authorities 'turned a blind eye' out of 'moral cowardice'.[1] The practice of sharia in Britain was not without its problems, but my afternoon in Oldham convinced me there was no justification for the fears articulated by Farage. For a start, there were no 'big ghettos' run according to sharia. I spent more than a year looking and couldn't find one anywhere. The 'courts' he criticized, furthermore, are not courts at all in the English sense but arbitration panels that have no formal legal power. Maulana Ejaz and the others can offer their jurists' opinion on matters like child custody and alimony, but they cannot enforce anything and nor do they try. Instead, in contested cases, they invariably advise their applicants to seek the help of the civil courts. The council is therefore not operating in parallel to the English legal system but, as they know and fully accept, in conjunction with and subserviently to it. In one case I heard, Ejaz instructed a woman to go away and secure an English law divorce at her local crown court; once this was done, she could revert to them for the Islamic one.

'We always advise this,' he told me afterwards, 'because it means the cleanest possible break for the client.'

Farage's much-repeated assertion that Britain hosts more than eighty sharia courts – or even councils – is also untrue. Maulana Ejaz knew of no more than six. When questioned, Farage revealed that he had taken the figure from a report in the *Daily Telegraph*, who had had it from a 2009 report by the right-of-centre think tank Civitas. Under pressure from the Muslim Council of Britain, Civitas eventually revealed that they had included online forums in their research and that their figure of eighty-five courts was in any case an estimate. The true number, as Civitas admitted, is 'indeterminate'.[2]

There is, of course, no hudud punishment in Britain, nor any

Baroness Warsi observed that Islamophobia had 'passed the dinner table test' in 2011. Britain's Muslims have since grown accustomed to negative headlines like these.

Anti-Muslim street protest has become almost routine in some parts of the country. Pegida UK demonstrate in Birmingham (**left**); Britain First march in Dewsbury, West Yorkshire (**below**).

The killing of MP Jo Cox, like Donald Trump's proposed ban on Muslim visitors to the US, sparked passionate counter-protests (**above**), sometimes from unexpected quarters (Jews and Muslims marching together for Palestine in London, **below**).

"There will always be a group from my nation fighting for the truth, it does [h]arm them if people [avoid?] or abandon them

SHARIAH [W]ILL DOMINATE THE

'Hate preacher' Anjem Choudary (**above right**) was finally jailed in 2016 for inviting support for ISIS. This trio from Cardiff (**right**, in an ISIS recruitment video shot in 2014) are among hundreds of Britons who have answered the jihadi call. **Below right**: Thomas Evans from Wycombe, (**left**) his mother, Sally, and brother, Michael.

An Islamist 'Trojan Horse' plot to take over state schools in east Birmingham turned out to be a hoax, but the heads and governors of six schools were nevertheless sacked, including the alleged ringleader, Tahir Alam (**below**).

The government wants cross-cultural integration (**left**, in Dewsbury), but its counter-extremism 'Prevent' programme has sown division. In Luton, teachers tried to report a four-year-old for describing a 'cooker bomb'; his drawing was actually of his mother chopping a cucumber (**above**).

British Muslims are more politically engaged than ever before. **Above**: Tooting MP Sadiq Khan, elected the first Muslim Mayor of London in 2016. **Left**: Humza Yousaf, the Scottish government's Transport Minister, wears a kilt at his swearing-in ceremony.

Muslim women are increasingly represented, too. **Right**: The mayor and mayoress of Oldham, Ateeque Ur-Rehman and Yasmin Toor. **Below**: Labour's Naz Shah displacing Respect party leader George Galloway as MP for Bradford West in 2015.

A crisis of Muslim masculinity? A cage fighter in Bradford (**above**).

Left: An Asian street gang make their voices heard.

Below: Mad Ash, Bash and Bono Hussain of the Rotherham grooming gang, jailed for up to 35 years each.

British Muslims, though, are resilient. A Luton shopkeeper takes his town's reputation into his own hands (**above**). **Left**: The Wuzara Ulama sharia council in action.

Above: Hundreds of women took to Twitter in protest at the 'traditionally submissive' stereotype. Islam is, if nothing else, adaptable (a backstreet in Oldham, **below**).

Another British religion? Some 88,000 people celebrated Eid at Small Heath Park in Birmingham in 2016: the largest such gathering in Europe (**above**). The state's relationship with Islam, though, remains uneasy. **Below**: A prayer vigil in Rotherham for murder victim Mushin Ahmed ended in rioting and a dozen arrests.

likelihood of it ever being implemented. Islam, Maulana Ejaz reminded me, is clear on the matter of jurisdictional precedence: a good Muslim must follow the law of the land in which he lives. The public image of sharia law is obviously not helped by organizations like Anjem Choudary's Sharia4UK, which, until it was proscribed as a terrorist organization, campaigned to turn Britain into a sharia state. At a press conference in 2009, Choudary explained that in future, proven adulterers as well as homosexuals would be stoned to death – a sentence that he sensationally said might extend to the then Business Secretary Peter Mandelson.[3]

The reality of sharia law is rather less exciting. A collection of legal codes evolved over centuries, modern sharia is most often used to resolve dull civil disputes over things like land ownership or questions about wills and inheritance, as well as divorce. When British Muslims express a desire to live under sharia instead of British law, therefore – as 23 per cent of them apparently did in a poll in 2016 – it is not as seditious as it sounds.[4] Hudud punishment has only ever been a tiny part of the canon. The Wuzara Ulama Council is one of the most respected sharia councils in the country; the greatest surprise to me was that divorce adjudication was *all* they did. Hand-chopping and stoning simply didn't come into it.

I later heard an intriguing defence of hudud from a Salafi traditionalist in Oldham, a secondary school teacher called Samir, who thought of it as a kind of nuclear option, a weapon of deterrence rather than one intended for actual use, except in the most extreme circumstances. The charge of adultery, for example, is punishable under sharia by stoning to death. But the charge has first to be proven, not by one but by four independent witnesses to the act – and as he said, how often does that ever happen in real life?

'There's dogging, I suppose,' Samir said after some thought. 'But to be honest there's not much of that going on in Oldham.'

I wondered about CCTV footage, but Samir said the jurists had thought of that and ruled it inadmissible: an adulterer can only be deemed *in flagrante delicto* if seen by actual people using their actual eyes. Islam, he went on, is more interested in contrition for sin than punishing people for it. The seriousness of the crime is clear from the sanction it theoretically carries, but the 'four witnesses' condition – introduced, as Samir saw it, by the Prophet himself – deliberately makes the punishment almost impossible to issue. To Samir, this was proof of the Prophet's wisdom and ultimate humanity.

*

It took months to find a sharia scholar like Ejaz willing to let me observe a council in action. It was an awkward time for practitioners of sharia and not only because of the invective from Nigel Farage or the far right. In 2016 the government announced an official review of sharia law's compatibility with the British legal system. I had met the review's chairperson, the noted Muslim liberal and Edinburgh University professor Mona Siddiqui, who believes that Western Islam has been 'hijacked' by conservatism, and who was expected to look particularly closely at allegations of gender discrimination.

'The trouble with religious conservatives,' she told me, 'is that they tend to mistake critical thinking for criticism.'

So I could understand why Ejaz was at first reticent. There was a risk of more negative publicity from an unknown journalist like me. He was also anxious about the privacy of his council's clients and I saw his point: who would want a stranger listening in to the most intimate details of their failed private life? But I persisted, and Ejaz finally agreed, on condition that I sign an exhaustive confidentiality agreement.

The council has no permanent home but meets each month in one of the hometowns of its four-man team. Maulana Ejaz is from Dewsbury; the day I attended just happened to be the turn of Maulana Younis, who lives in Oldham. The address I had been given, the Madina Tul Ilm Academy, sounded rather grand – just the sort of place, a UKIP supporter might think, for a gathering of ambitious Islamic scholars bent on subverting the British legal establishment. The reality was so unimposing that my taxi driver overshot it: a tiny, redbrick education centre next to a scruffy industrial park on the edge of Glodwick, the heart of Muslim Oldham.

Glodwick was the district worst affected in the Oldham race riot of 2001, and to judge from the reinforced front door, the grilles on this building's windows and the CCTV cameras that guarded them, the area still has its issues. Maulana Younis said his education centre was focused on outreach work, 'working to get the youth off the street'. The one outside, he confirmed, was a well-known drug-dealing spot.

'The youth get into a lot of trouble, selling drugs, hanging about, driving around in flashy cars with loud music and what have you. This is not good for society.'

I glimpsed what he meant later on: a group of Asian lads a hundred yards from the centre, loitering by a shiny red Mercedes with a personalized number plate. I wondered how successful the maulana was and he admitted it was hard.

'I organize pizza nights sometimes and they do come to those. They will come to prayers on Friday, too. They identify themselves as Muslims. The trouble is that they don't practise Islam.'

Younis, a relatively new addition to Ejaz's sharia team, saw his contribution as an extension of the pastoral work that he had always performed around Glodwick.

'I get quite a few young couples who are living together and want a nikah marriage because they don't want to go on living in sin. I get a lot of grief from the parents for helping them out – the nikah is traditionally controlled by the older generation – but in that situation I say it is better that they get married without their parents' permission if they want to make amends for their sin.'

By the end of the afternoon the councillors and I had heard five divorce cases, including a local one where the husband turned up in person. Both he and his wife accused each other of extra-marital affairs. There seemed scope for mediation between them, perhaps even reconciliation. But Ejaz said that marriage counselling was beyond his remit: his job was simply to apply the letter of Islamic law. Since both spouses in this adultery case wanted a divorce and the questions of alimony and child custody were already settled, it was not for him to try to find out who was at fault or to stand in the couple's way. He showed me his basic reference text, a twelfth-century Hanafi legal manual called *Al-Hidayah* (The Guidance). Ejaz's copy, bound in leather and finely tooled in gilt, was an Urdu translation.

'It lists sixteen circumstances where divorce is justified,' he said, reverently turning its pages. 'If none of these apply, we cannot grant it.'

The other cases, like the Nottingham one, were a lot more troubling. There was a young woman from Bradford who had been forced into a second marriage by a family creditor who had then raped and impregnated her. Another, from Leicester, was heartbroken by the discovery that her new, Pakistan-born husband already had a wife back home and that he had only married again to gain UK residency rights; she had overheard him on the phone to the first wife, promising to bring her over to England (and to divorce wife number two) just as soon as his right to remain was formally confirmed.

The husband in the last case, from London, was another alleged wife-beater. He also drank heavily and attended strip clubs. There were more tears by Skype as his wife told us of the 'disgusting things' he liked to do. She had obtained a video of him consorting with a Polish prostitute in their marital bedroom, filmed by the husband himself while she was away visiting relatives in Canada. The husband had shown it off to a 'friend' who had passed it on to her, not out of conscience but because he thought she might pay for it: as much as £3,000, she said.

By the end of the afternoon I had been at the bedroom key-hole of Asian Britain for four hours, leaving me feeling sullied, depressed and not a little cross.

'Why is it,' I asked, as we were packing up to leave, 'that so many Muslim men behave so appallingly?'

'Now, that is an excellent question,' said Maulana Ejaz with a long look.

'All the marriages we heard about today were arranged ones, weren't they?'

'All,' said Ejaz.

'So isn't that the problem? Parents forcing their daughters into bad marriages, and keeping them there?'

'But I know so many examples of happy arranged marriages,' said Maulana Younis. 'Besides, love matches can end up in breakdown and abuse too.'

'The problem is that so many young Muslims have lost their religion,' said Ejaz stoutly.

It was no doubt true that marital abuse among Muslims would vanish if they followed the teachings of the Prophet, who was unequivocal on the need to treat women with honour, love and respect. But godlessness alone did not quite explain it. There are plenty of atheists, after all, who do not treat their wives like chattels or exploit them so callously for visas or sex.

The Asian attitude towards adultery, Maulana Younis conceded, was confused.

'In India and Pakistan, the tradition has always been that you marry once only. But Islam, as you know, allows up to four wives, which is common practice in Arab countries and many African ones, and even in Afghanistan. So there is this tension there and Pakistani men feel frustrated.'

'You mean they think that if it's OK for other Muslims to have more than one woman, why shouldn't they?'

'Yes. Personally I think it is the natural state for a man to have more than one wife. It is acceptable in white culture for husbands to have lovers outside their marriage, after all.'

'Is it?'

'Isn't it?'

'Maybe in France,' I said.

The maulanas on this council, I thought, were remarkable people. What they dealt with on a monthly basis was enough to sap anyone's faith in humanity. But instead of blocking their eyes and ears to the evil, they gave up their time and energy to try to set it right, and did so cheerfully without expectation of recompense. They operated as a charity and, unlike some other sharia councils, did not charge for their service. I thought what they did amounted to pastoral care of the highest order. But they were also products of a culture that, whatever they or the Koran might say to the contrary, is shot through with ingrained prejudice against women. For instance, there was no escaping the fact that these councillors were all men, even though their clients were almost all women. Why were there no women on the council? Indeed, why were they not all women?

'There would be no objection to that. None at all,' said Younis, 'so long as the scholars can be found.'

Maulana Ejaz thought the nature of his council's work was such that it was 'unlikely to be fulfilled by an all-women council' but agreed that a female scholar on the panel would be helpful. The only reason his council contained no women, he said, was the lack of qualified candidates.

'Indeed, we would encourage more Muslim women to know their Islamic rights and also for some to seek further education in the legal professions so that they can support our women applicants more effectively.'

I had in fact read of one female sharia scholar, Khola Hasan, who sits on a council in Leyton in east London[5], and had heard of another who works at Birmingham Central Mosque. But they are exceptions that prove the rule. For critics of sharia law, including some powerful voices at Westminster, the whiff of gender-discrimination still hangs around councils like this one. In a study presented to Parliament in December 2015, a Dutch academic, Machteld Zee, accused some sharia councils – though not this one – of tending to favour men in their judgements and, even more seriously, of pushing divorce applicants back into abusive marriages.[6] Ejaz, though, regarded that kind of intervention as well beyond the remit of a British sharia council and insisted that it was something he would never do.

In early 2016 Baroness Caroline Cox, an implacable opponent of sharia, was trying for the fifth time to introduce a private members' bill that would outlaw all divorce arbitration on religious grounds.

'The fundamental principles of sharia law are inherently gender-discriminatory in a way that would make the suffragettes turn in their graves,' she told the BBC's *Daily Politics* show.[7]

Ejaz accepted that women were discriminated against in some Muslim communities but insisted that this was a cultural problem, not a religious one.

'Islam actually grants more rights to women, as well as to children, than it does to men,' he said.

Baroness Cox complained specifically that in sharia divorce or inheritance settlements, 'the woman obtains half that of a man in a legacy'. Ejaz acknowledged that this might be true in some circumstances, but explained that Cox had misunderstood that strict conditions applied. Under sharia, he told me, it is the man who must bear all the costs of administration and maintenance, while the woman is free to spend her legacy however she chooses. A woman, furthermore, has separate (and varying) rights of inheritance, according to whether she is a daughter, a mother or a widow – and thus may end up inheriting money from multiple sources at different moments in her life, all of it condition-free. It is certainly a different approach to the standard Western one but the net effect is a distribution of assets much more equitable than it at first looks. In some circumstances the woman can end up better off than the man.

Cox's other complaint, that 'a woman's voice only counts for half that of a man in a court', was another misreading of the intent behind the rule, which is found in a verse – the longest and one of the most technical in the entire Koran[8] – that deals with contract law. In seventh-century Arabia, Ejaz explained, responsibility for financial and business matters generally fell on the man's shoulders. Men therefore tended to be better versed than women in the niceties of the legal process and thus would have the advantage in, say, a dispute between husband and wife. The solution proposed by the Koran in such a case is for two women to attend the court, 'so that if one of the two women errs, the other may remind her'. The Koran does not say that a woman's testimony carries half the weight of a man's, which would indeed be inherently sexist. It seeks, rather, to defend the rights of the female litigant by equalizing the imbalance of legal knowledge inherent in a patriarchal society. Ejaz added that in cases dealing with 'private female matters', men are excluded and only the testimony of women is admitted.

It was clear to me by now that sharia law, at least as it was practised by the Wuzara Council, was far from being the tool of male suppression that it is so often taken for by outsiders. Ejaz's arguments in its favour were both heartfelt and compelling. The real test, though, was what Oldham's Muslim women thought of the council, and as it happened I knew a local Muslim divorcee, Najma Khalid, a Pakistani Pashtun who ran several voluntary women's groups in and around Glodwick.

'Well, it's a man's world, in't it?' she said, in a suitably no-nonsense northern accent. 'In *all* cultures, not just ours. But it's true that all the sharia councils I know of, in London,

Birmingham, Dewsbury, are run by men – and I think maybe that does make it difficult for some Muslim women to come forward.'

She described the Wuzara Council as 'very conservative' but she also acknowledged the vital role that they and councils like them performed. Indeed, she had made use of a sharia council herself when she had divorced in 2008.

She explained that although a nikah conducted in Britain is not recognized as a formal marriage in English civil law, it *is* recognized – automatically so – if the nikah was conducted abroad. In such a case, a Muslim couple seeking formal divorce in Britain is obliged to apply for it twice, through the civil courts as well as under sharia, even though they may only have married under one system. A further complication arises if the nikah conducted abroad is not the husband's only marriage, in which case it is *not* recognized in English civil law, since bigamy in Britain is illegal. Najma said, however, that other marriages routinely go undeclared and that polygamy is widely practised by British Muslims. The consequence is that many Muslim women do not fully understand the status of their own marriages, let alone the divorce rights due to them under either English civil or Islamic law. It often takes the expertise of sharia councils like Maulana Ejaz's to disentangle the knot.

Najma recognized that divorcing men and women might not always be treated equally under sharia – for instance, in the divvying up of a joint estate – but said that this could be remedied if a divorcee wished, at least in this country, by opting to get married according to English civil law as well (if not instead). In her experience, she said, Muslim women are increasingly making a point of formally registering their nikah marriages in English law as a kind of insurance policy in the event of an unfriendly divorce.

Najma's main reservation about the councils was that they are under-regulated, which is no doubt true: Ejaz himself had hinted his disapproval of councils that strayed too far into the role of marital reconciliation. Unlike the Wuzara Council, she added, some sharia scholars charge as much as £500 for their services, a potentially serious obstacle for divorce applicants commonly kept in deliberate penury by their controlling husbands.

'There is a lot of DV [domestic violence] in our community, there's no doubt,' she went on. 'But it's not because of Islam: it's the culture.'

She was referring, although she did not quite say it, to a particular Asian male mindset that views women as intrinsically inferior and wives and daughters as servants or, worse, as slaves – status symbols who merit the harshest punishment should they step out of line, above all when family honour is impugned. The barbaric phenomenon of honour killing has always been commonest among less educated Muslims from rural areas, and Britain has had a preponderance of those ever since it opened its doors to workers from Pakistani Mirpur in the 1960s.

Najma, though, was not trying to point a finger at Mirpuris. There were, she said, many other cultural factors in play, involving race, class, the pressures and temptations of British city life, the lack of economic opportunity.

'I get wives at my groups whose husbands are unemployed and turn to drink and drugs, or husbands with good degrees and qualifications from Pakistan who can only find menial jobs here, who then take out their anger and frustration at home. There are wounded male egos; there are big mental health issues.'

She insisted, furthermore, that domestic violence existed in all cultures, not just the Asian one. She said it was 'statistically proven' that incidents of DV in white households go up after football matches, and that there was no Asian or Muslim monopoly on the abuse of drink and drugs in Britain. Asian Muslims, she meant to say, were in most respects no different to any other group in society.

'I do defend my culture, in the end,' said Najma, 'because I know men are mostly good people, not just bad 'uns.'

I had met Najma on my first visit to Oldham a year previously, when I arrived intending to investigate the town's unhappy reputation for ethnic division. Oldham's race relations had been under the government microscope ever since the race riots of 2001 and I found the town's Muslims unusually nervous of outsiders. It was Najma who saved me with an offer to show me around, just as I was about to give up on persuading any Oldham Muslim to talk.

We rattled around the narrow residential streets of south Oldham in her nine-year-old Honda Jazz. Najma recounted how mobs of whites and Asians rampaged down Harmony Street, stoned and petrol-bombed a pub called the Live and Let Live. Cars, police vans, the offices of the *Oldham Evening Chronicle* and the home of the town's first Asian mayor, Riyaz Ahmed, were torched. Ethnic division evidently remained entrenched throughout the town. At one point we passed a small redbrick terraced house, identical to the houses in all the contiguous streets, except that this one's tiny front garden contained a flagpole from which drooped a full-sized cross of St George. It reminded me of Ulster, or else a colonial trading post in a foreign land. It was the only indication that we had crossed into a part of town called Fitton Hill.

'It's 100 per cent white around here,' said Najma. 'It's where the BNP supporters live.'

The government's report into the riots, the Ritchie review, blamed the violence on years of ethnic segregation. Yet Glodwick today, she said, is if anything more mono-ethnically Asian than it was before the riots. No amount of urban remodelling or government initiatives to promote integration could dissuade the few remaining white families from moving out as soon as they could. The Afro-Caribbeans who once lived here also fled. The paradox is that modern Glodwick, although still very poor, appears to be thriving.

'It's a proud neighbourhood, a strong and self-reliant community,' she insisted. 'The government doesn't like it because it's segregated, but it's the sort of place you can leave the back door open or walk about at night. There's parts of Hathershaw where I wouldn't dare do that.'

She showed me Hathershaw, the next-door ward, which did indeed look marginally rougher.

'There, you see that?' she said, pointing to a back alleyway overflowing with rubbish from overturned wheelie bins. 'You'd never get that in Glodwick.'

Oldham Council had tried to desegregate Hathershaw by parachuting in a handful of poor white families, especially ones from eastern Europe, a social experiment, Najma thought, that had not been a success.

We stopped outside Greenhill Community School where one of her women's groups met. It was called CHAI, standing for Care, Help & Inspire, a play on the common Urdu word for tea. The growing number of women she helped, over sixty of them each week, were mostly Bangladeshi or Pakistani housewives. They were typically poor, uneducated and with little spoken English, sometimes kept deliberately isolated at home by their husbands and living lives of unbroken domestic drudgery – 'virtual house slaves', as she put it.

Najma explained how she tried to teach these women to 'empower' themselves, in the first instance by getting them out of their homes and socializing. The friendships formed at the group, she said, naturally boosted the women's self-confidence while strengthening ties within the community. She spent a lot of time teaching them their civic rights or telling them about public services that they often had no idea existed. She also lobbied the authorities for more services when these were lacking.

'I come across a lot of hidden depression and mental health issues in this community. Oldham is 30 per cent Asian, yet we've only got one female Asian mental health counsellor in the town. Why?'

She organized classes on topics like nutrition because, she explained, Asians are genetically more prone than Europeans to Type 2 diabetes. She arranged lectures, too, by council-funded organizations like KOGS, Keeping Our Girls Safe, which taught mothers how to spot signs that their offspring were being groomed or radicalized.

'We are all safeguarding ourselves,' she observed. 'Not just here in Oldham. It's a national thing now.'

One of the biggest obstacles to empowerment, she knew, was that so many of her women couldn't speak English. For this reason, she was 'always' lobbying for more council-funding for adult English language classes. 'I had a new group the other day. Some were new arrivals from Pakistan, but some had been here for six or seven years already. There were twenty-six of them, yet not one of them could speak English. I was shocked.'

Her view chimed with the government's, up to a point. In January 2016, David Cameron announced plans to spend an extra £20 million on ESOL (English for Speakers of Other Languages) classes for Muslim women. He, too, had identified the lack of English as a key block to the social integration he desired for segregated communities like Oldham's. There were, he said, 38,000 Muslim women in Britain who couldn't speak English at all, as well as another 190,000 who struggled with it. Poor language skills, he added, were one of the reasons why 60 per cent of Pakistani or Bangladeshi women were 'economically inactive'.

Cameron's main motivation, though, was quite different to Najma's: he linked the issue not to social empowerment but specifically to national security.

'If you're not able to speak English, not able to integrate, you may find therefore you have challenges understanding what your identity is, and therefore you could be more susceptible to the extremist message coming from [ISIS],' he told the BBC. One of the main reasons that young men were vulnerable to radicalization, he was reported separately to have remarked, was the 'traditional submissiveness of Muslim women', which prevented them from speaking out against the influence of the radical imams.[9]

The ability to speak English, he was arguing, was not just critical to social cohesion, it was also a way for mothers to stop their sons from becoming terrorists. That meant that ESOL, once the gentlest tool of social integration, was now a plank of national security policy. The seriousness of his intent became clear when he added that, after two and a half years, anyone on a five-year spousal visa would have to take an English language test and could be forced to leave the country if they failed it.[10]

There were, unsurprisingly, loud howls of protest. Civil rights groups asked why the prime minister was singling out Muslim women. Would poor linguists of other faiths and backgrounds face deportation too? And if not, why not? Others accused the government of hypocrisy, pointing out that the Adult Skills Budget used to fund ESOL classes in further education colleges had been drastically cut over the previous five years, and by considerably more than £20 million. As the Labour grandee John Prescott sarcastically tweeted: 'So a Prime Minister who cut lessons for people to learn English wants to deport mothers who can't, er . . . speak English.'[11]

Tim Farron, the Liberal Democrat leader, called the initiative 'dog whistle politics at its best'. Andy Burnham, the shadow Home Secretary, said that linking poor English to extremism in this way unfairly stigmatized a whole community, thereby increasing the risk of radicalism rather than tackling it. The best response, though, came from Muslim women themselves. Scores of them, old as well as young, took to Twitter under the handle #TraditionallySubmissive and posted photographs of themselves in various stereotype-busting poses. They held up placards that read things like: *Black belt in karate. Aspiring scientist. History and Languages Enthusiast*, or *Working in NHS for 22 years. Mother of 3. Grandmother of 10! Community activist. Volunteer. Knows 5 languages AND English.*[12]

Najma's feelings about all this were mixed. On one hand she agreed that if you lived in England it was vital to learn English.

'It's not just about the jobs market. You need English for day-to-day things like going to the doctor or catching a bus. Being able to communicate with the people around you is a part of human happiness.'

On the other hand, she thought it wasn't fair or sensible to force people to learn any language. Gentle government encouragement was fine but the new Cameron approach was too much.

'There's a generation of Asians who are too old to learn English now. And women who live in deprived urban areas are busy running homes, or even busier if they are in work. What if they don't have time for language classes?'

Najma's own mother, she told me, never learned English so was unable to help her with her homework when she was young or to liaise with the teachers at her school. As a Pakistani Pashtun, Najma's upbringing was as traditional as it came. And yet she spoke fluent Yorkshire, held a degree from Manchester Metropolitan University, hadn't worn a veil for twenty years. She was not 'submissive' at all, but modern, emancipated, outspoken, engaging. She had picked herself up after an unhappy divorce and channelled her energies into helping women as vulnerable as she had once been, guiding them in the direction she had taken. She was so confident in her identity as an Asian and as a Muslim that she had sent her daughter to a local Church of England school because it 'offered the best education'. She was about as 'integrationist' as the government could hope for. The difference between her and her parents' generation suggested that, given the time and opportunity, British Muslim women can and do transform themselves and – this was the point – they are doing so without any prompting from Westminster. The sisters, in the words of the Eurythmics singer Annie Lennox, are doing it for themselves.

British public life, if one cares to stop and look, is crowded with examples of self-emancipation. There are politicians like Baroness Sayeeda Warsi or Birmingham's Salma Yaqoob, journalists like the BBC's Mishal Husain, bankers like Farmida Bi. Muslim women compete successfully in the Olympics, in TV cookery competitions, even in professional golf tournaments. Even Oldham had a Muslim female role model, in the shape of Yasmin Toor, the town's first Muslim mayoress. In line with a long local tradition, she shared the role with her husband, Mayor Ateeque Ur-Rehman.

Yasmin invited me to lunch at her home in the well-to-do neighbourhood of Coppice. Her house was three houses knocked through, terraced ones bought long ago when they were still cheap. I was shown into the sitting room – black flock wallpaper, repro chandeliers, vases of silk flowers – by an elderly Kashmiri who spoke no English. I assumed he was the *chowkidar*, but he turned out to be Yasmin's father-in-law on his annual visit from Mirpur. In a diverting reversal of government stereotype, his main role in the house was to teach Ateeque and Yasmin's children Punjabi.

'They don't speak a word of it,' Ateeque explained, 'only English. I'm worried they are going to completely lose touch with their roots.'

The mayor and mayoress were touchingly proud of their civic role and insisted on being photographed in their heavy gold chains of office, which they brought out from a special foam-lined box.

'It's such an honour to wear these,' Yasmin grinned.

They were certainly impressive relics of Oldham's nineteenth-century glory days, when the town produced more cotton than Germany and France combined. Ateeque's livery collar, which was much the larger of the two, contained three and a half kilos of gold. Yasmin counted off the sapphires, rubies and diamonds, of which there were 365, one for every cotton mill there had once been in the town. I found it poignant. It was the cotton industry, after all, that had drawn so many Muslims to Oldham in the first place. But the jobs dried up when the industry collapsed in the 1970s and the mills are mostly gone now, demolished or turned into flats or shopping malls. The town's population has been shrinking for a century, from almost 150,000 in the 1910s to under 100,000 today. It is little wonder that the communities left behind are so divided and stressed.

When the chains were put away again, Yasmin put on a spotty blue and white apron and invited me into her kitchen while she made lunch.

'Now you can see me in my traditional submissive housewife role,' she said archly, as she rolled out chapatis and slapped them expertly between her hands.

She was as scathing as Najma about the Conservative government, which she described as 'totally out of touch'. An Oldham-born Asian woman like her, she was certain, could not have held the position of mayoress a generation ago. Muslim male attitudes, she said, had changed a great deal even within the last twenty years. She remembered how, as a 16-year-old in 1989, she had taken part in a schoolgirls' poetry competition up in Bury, north of Manchester. Most entries, she said, were the 'regular bland love poetry' but not hers. 'You can't see the tears behind the make-up of an arranged wedding', it began.

'I had to read my poem out to the judges, who were all men. My legs were shaking. And when I got to the end, there was this silence – just the tik, tik, tik of my heels as I went back to my seat. The organizer was so gobsmacked he had to call a ten-minute break.'

The response she got afterwards, though, told her that the times were already changing.

'One judge said, "You're a pretty girl. Why write a poem attacking us men?" But another one said, "Well done, it's important to speak up on these issues." So later, I wrote another poem about the negative feedback. But there wouldn't be anyone to attack like that now. Things have changed *a lot* since 1989.'

Her feminism was not the noisy kind. The process of emancipation she described was also no doubt slower than it might have been – so slow, indeed, that it is easy to imagine how it could be missed by outsiders. The signs of progress are subtle and have been drowned out by the headlines. In the years since 1989, after all, Islamic conservatism has boomed. Saudi Wahhabism, or at least a kind of street Islam based on it, has spread everywhere, while the West has been almost constantly at war. And what of the ever-increasing popularity among British Muslim women not just of the hijab but the full-face version of the veil, the Arabian niqab that leaves nothing but the eyes exposed? Is that not a symbol of submissiveness rather than self-assertion – of repression rather than progress and liberation?

At the beginning of my journey around Muslim Britain, I believed that at least some niqabis were, at bottom, the victims of gender discrimination. Eventually, I was sure, I would find one who had been coerced into hiding her face from the world by a husband, a father, a brother. But I was wrong. I conducted at least a dozen interviews with niqabis and every one of them said they wore it out of choice; not one of them said they had been or felt forced.

I remembered Phil Tolson, the retired Dewsbury policeman, and the hostility that he said the niqab engendered in many white locals. I thought I understood that primitive response: the fear of the alien unknown, or resentment of the perceived challenge to indigenous culture. However, the more niqabis I spoke to, the more comfortable I became with it. In fact in one or two instances I found my veiled interlocutors positively alluring, which was not something I had expected in myself. It is, of course, all in the eyes. In the absence of any other visual response clue, a conversation with a niqabi often leads to prolonged eye contact, which in other circumstances is a sign of flirtation, a first step towards intimacy. As John Donne put it in his famous love poem 'The Ecstasy':

> Our eye-beams twisted, and did thread
> Our eyes upon one double string.

Perhaps I was guilty of a primitive response of my own – or else of 'orientalism', the crime so often decried by the left. Nevertheless, I could see why 'veil dances', first popularized by the Dance of the Seven Veils in Oscar Wilde's 1890s play *Salome*, were once so fashionable (and why, indeed, they were considered the forerunner of the theatrical striptease). Seeing no more than a woman's eyes invites the male imagination to fill in the rest, like a blank slate on which a fantasy can be projected. I found talking to a niqabi entirely different to talking to a woman in a burqa, the true full veil, as I had sometimes tried to do in Afghanistan. When the eyes are concealed by a thick mesh of cotton, all clues to the wearer's age, mood or condition are removed and the imagination simply fails.

I was reassured to discover that I was not alone in these reptilian male thoughts. I later met a niqabi in Birmingham, Samaya Ahmed from Alum Rock, who told me she wore it because she liked the 'respect' it conferred, although she didn't wear it all the time, including in front of me when I met her with her parents at her family home.

'It's supposed to be a protection against unwanted attention,' she said. 'Obviously it's pointless if it's attracting abuse. In that kind of environment, I wouldn't wear it.'

The truth was that she wasn't entirely convinced of the niqab's advantages for the same reason that I had identified.

'One thing about it is that it forces you to maintain eye contact when you're talking to someone. But the eyes are the windows of the soul, so that can be more intense, and can be counter-productive.'

One old complaint about niqabis is that it is impossible to communicate with someone you can't see properly, but at no point in any conversation did I think I would understand better if the veil were removed. Britain has been debating this point ever since 2006, when the then Foreign Secretary, Jack Straw, revealed in a column in the *Lancashire Telegraph* that he always asked niqabis coming into his Blackburn constituency surgery to raise their veil.[13]

Straw was not being dogmatic about it, and didn't force anyone to do anything. He just explained that he felt that 'the conversation would be of greater value if the lady took the covering from her face' because 'so many of the judgments we all make about other people come from seeing their faces'. But as he also acknowledged, this was just his opinion; he even added that his concerns 'could be misplaced'. I thought, on balance, that they probably were. The world, after all, has been communicating quite effectively for 140 years without any visual response clues at all, by telephone.

Despite this, I remained curious to know why a British Muslim woman would choose to cover herself up. I kept on asking, and eventually concluded that there was no single reason. No two niqabis' motives were the same, any more than the women behind the mask were the same. Why would they be? The niqab is just a flimsy piece of cloth, in the end, a garment like any other. That it took me so long to realize something so obvious was, by itself, a measure of the prejudice surrounding the veil.

Some, like Zulaikha Farooqi from Longsight in Manchester, wear the niqab out of fierce religious conviction, a means of 'coming closer to Allah'. She refuses to take it off for anyone, a stance, she said, that had cost her a place at her preferred sixth-form college, which had banned the niqab from campus on security grounds. At the other end of the scale, I found women like Ahlam Saed, 25, from White City in west London.

'I'm a make-up kind of girl, and my eyes are my best feature,' she told me, 'so I bought a niqab to draw attention to them. My parents said, if you're not going to take it seriously, don't wear it at all. They tested me, so I kept at it.'

Saed became a fleeting Internet sensation when she posted footage of herself being abused in a shop in Shepherd's Bush. Her assailant, an Afro-Caribbean, began by calling her 'Batman', then asked: 'My kids can't even see your face, who the fuck are you? Are you a man or woman?'

'I only wanted to get a packet of Starburst,' Saed told the *Evening Standard*. 'My parents don't want me to wear [the niqab] because they fear for my safety. But why should I take it off because of other people's opinions? It's my choice.'

Her abuser, who was later arrested, also ranted about Britain being 'a Christian country in a Christian, Western world'. Yet it wasn't religious conviction that first led her to don the niqab, but vanity.[14]

For others, the niqab is as much a political statement as a religious one: something much closer to what Jack Straw once described as 'a visible statement of separation and of difference'. I first spotted Sahar al-Faifi, a Saudi-born activist from Cardiff, on a notably bad-tempered edition of *The Big Questions*, a BBC current affairs programme, debating the topic 'Do we need a British Islam'? Sahar took exception even to the premise of the debate, which duly descended into a shouting match between defenders of traditional Islam like Sahar and those who would reform it, led by Adam Deen of Quilliam. Her eyes flashed and as the volume rose, the curtain covering her mouth danced like the bass cone of a loudspeaker. Traditional she may be, but no one watching *The Big Questions* that night could ever call her submissive. She is no housewife either, but a molecular geneticist and NHS cancer specialist, who in her free time enjoys extreme sports like canoeing, abseiling and skydiving.

She was generally impatient with the British media obsession with the niqab – 'Don't we have more important things to talk about?' she once wrote in the *Independent* – but I found her gentler than her TV persona when I met her in Cardiff.

'It's a struggle wearing a niqab. I'm a target,' she told me frankly. 'I get abused once a month on average. My mother used to wear it around town but she stopped out of fear. I have to tell my family where I'm going when I go out.'

'So why do you persist?'

'It deepens my faith. It's my own manifestation of worshipping God. And I find it forces people to see you how you are. I prefer to be judged on what I think and say, not on how I look.'

I texted her later with a question that I worried might sound facetious: how did one skydive in a niqab?

'I take it off,' she replied. 'You see, I am not really fanatical about it. I wear it as much as I can, as I believe I will be rewarded for it, but at the same time I do not consider it a barrier at all. Same thing when there is a need to check my identity. I happily take it off, then wear it after.'

Sahar was impressive in her determination to demystify the veil but as a campaigner for Muslim women's rights I thought she was also unnecessarily constrained by it. Telling people not to judge a book by its cover, however successfully, can only get you so far. The political controversy around the niqab, the prejudices associated with it, condemn her to forever having to explain her appearance, and I could sense and sympathize with her frustration at that. However articulate and right she was, she remained a kind of one-trick pony.

A better advocate for modern Muslim womanhood, I found, was Siema Iqbal, a Manchester GP to whom I was introduced by Najma in Oldham. Siema was the national woman's lead for MEND (Muslim Engagement and Development), a new, community-funded campaign group that I had heard a lot about. Their mission to persuade British Muslims to become fuller citizens by exercising their civic rights is much the same as Najma's, except that they operate not at the grassroots but on a national scale. Since their inception in 2014 they had set up twenty-five working groups in cities around the country, with new ones being established all the time. They specialize in seminars that teach Muslims how to register to vote or how to lobby government, and distribute natty printed 'toolkits' explaining how to respond to Islamophobia in the press. Successive London governments have complained that because British Muslims are so disunited, there is no efficient way of engaging with them or of dealing with their concerns. Mona Siddiqui told me that in Whitehall circles, it is now a cliché to preface one's speech with the observation that there is 'no such thing as the Muslim community'. MEND is one answer to that charge.

I met Siema and her orthopaedic consultant husband at their home in middle-class Cheadle, a cul-de-sac house with a Range Rover with a personalized number plate parked outside. Their sitting room was white and airy with a huge flat-screen TV on the wall above a designer gas fire of matching size. It was all very different to the grunge of Glodwick. The fire was switched to full power when I visited, perhaps because Siema had a cold: one of the hazards of her job, she said.

It was the fighting in Gaza in July 2014 that first politicized her. Thousands of people, including hundreds of women and children, were killed that summer in the Israeli Defence Force's ground operation against Hamas militants.

'I used to be your average Cheshire housewife, more interested in shopping at Selfridges than politics. But I saw what was happening in Gaza on TV and it made me really angry.'

Not content with shouting at her television, she went demonstrating in the city centre, starting with a street boycott of Kedem in King Street, a smart shop for Israeli-made beauty products.

Manchester is home to the largest Jewish community in Britain outside London. The pro- and anti-Israel demonstrations went on for weeks, with riot police deployed to keep the two sides apart. Then Siema began to receive abusive tweets and emails from pro-Zionist trolls. She had been identified at one of the demonstrations and singled out as the target of a concerted psychological campaign that lasted for six months.

The tweets turned into nuisance calls to her NHS practice, then into more threatening ones to her private number. One anonymous caller berated her as 'a Nazi doctor'. The General Medical Council, the Medical Defence Union and the police became involved. She didn't feel safe going out, even on the school run. She worried she could lose her job. The campaign against her finally stopped when it was traced back to the North West Friends of Israel, an organization led by a staff member at the Manchester-based *Jewish Telegraph*.

Siema was shocked by the experience as well as profoundly changed. The playing field for Muslims, she saw for the first time, was not level.

'The Jewish community around Prestwich have their own paramedics and ambulance service, but no one tells them to integrate,' she said sourly.

The end of apartheid in the 1980s, she pointed out, began with public boycotts of South African goods and services. Yet the Cameron government had declared it illegal for councils to boycott pro-Israeli businesses, and ordinary Muslims who spoke out against Israeli policy risked being labelled extremists. The accusers sometimes even included other Muslims, such as Commander Mak Chishty, Britain's most senior Muslim policeman, who announced that refusing to shop at Marks & Spencer could be a sign of radicalization.

'Mak Chishty is an idiot,' observed Siema.

Since 2014 she had become a prolific contributor to the

Guardian, the *Huffington Post*, the activist website 5Pillars.com. She had pointed her guns at targeted stops at airports, at Theresa May's Fundamental British Values, at Muslim-bashing in the *Sun* and the hate crime it provoked, and, most of all, at Prevent.

'Schools aren't safe places any more. My eight-year-old came home the other day asking what ISIS was. He thought it was "a place in Iraq". I left it. I didn't want him going back to school saying, "Mum was talking about ISIS." '

For the first time, she told me, she felt genuinely fearful of the future.

'When I was growing up my parents used to say I should think of an alternative place to live because this country will turn on you. I used to tell them they were talking rubbish. But now we talk about it all the time.'

What made Siema effective as a campaigner was that she spoke and wrote not just as a modern Muslim woman, but as a family GP and 'mum'. She was feisty, funny, didn't wear a veil, spoke with no accent other than Mancunian. She was as British and as 'integrated' as they come. The government often dismisses Muslim activists as religious conservatives with a hidden Islamist agenda, but it was impossible to do that to Siema. She too obviously belonged to one of those 'ordinary hard-working families' that ministers like to talk about at party conferences. One of her articles buttonholed the prime minister himself: 'I need you to listen to someone like me', it began. 'I need to have confidence that the person shaping my children's future has an understanding of the impact of legislation imposed by you and your government.'[15]

Her opinion of domestic abuse, honour violence, forced marriage and female genital mutilation was the same as any other educated Westerner's: she thought it all appalling. Being a doctor, she also had strong views on cousin marriage and the increased risk of birth defects that this custom carried.

'I've advised against it a couple of times in my surgery.

Sometimes a patient shrugs and says, "It's in God's hands," to which I say, "Yeah, but God gave you a brain" . . . That line really annoys me.'

There was, she said, a need for more or better education on genetic health.

'It seems to be a big thing among Mirpuris. Blackburn is particularly bad. But *educated* Mirpuris do not marry their cousins.'

She was no religious conservative but defended those who were.

'The government has confused extremism with conservatism. Yet the Paris bombers were out clubbing the night before they attacked.'

She understood the liberal elite's moral outrage at the penalties decreed by sharia law but thought the debate around it was shrill and overdone, on both sides.

'Growing up, if one of my friends announced they weren't going to mosque any more, they might get a slap off their mum . . . It doesn't make them "apostates". And they don't have to be public about it. Why don't they just call themselves "moderate Muslims" and shut up?'

It was the same with homosexuals, none of whom, when she last looked, had been pushed off any high buildings in Britain as they had been in Raqqa.

'My hairdresser's gay. His customers are all Muslim women, but none of us has any problem with it.'

MEND was not exclusively a women's organization but it knew how to channel the energy behind the British Muslim feminism that Siema articulated. I later went to a MEND fundraising dinner at a plush banqueting hall in Miles Platting in northeast Manchester, a much regenerated industrial slum that once featured on *Coronation Street*. The speakers for the night, side by side on the podium, were three stars of British Muslim womanhood: Lauren Booth, the convert sister of Cherie Blair, in her trademark tight red hijab; Naz Shah, the up-and-coming Labour

MP for Bradford West; and Baroness Warsi, the most senior female Muslim politician in the country.

All three spoke about their success in a world of men, the glass ceilings they had to break through to get to the top. Naz Shah dedicated her speech to Sayeeda Warsi, whom she called her 'inspirer' and 'sister'.

'She refused to be bought out by the system,' she said. 'Like her, I carry my resignation in my pocket.'

The all-Muslim audience, which included a large number of women glittering in their best saris and hijabs, lapped it up, especially when Lauren Booth compared the panel to the Spice Girls – although unlike those 1990s pop-stars, the 'girl-power' they stood for was more than a slick marketing ploy. Naz Shah's rise from the back-streets of Bradford was the real deal. Her celebrated story brought to mind what I'd heard at the sharia council in Oldham. It perhaps also showed why women's support groups like Najma Khalid's were so necessary and important. I read the details online, even as Naz Shah was speaking.

Her parents came to Bradford from Mirpur in the 1970s; Naz was born in 1973. But her father didn't want more daughters and forced his wife Zoora into several abortions. He also regularly and violently beat her, even when she was pregnant, which led to the loss of another child. Eventually he took up with the neighbour's 16-year-old daughter, and Zoora and her three small children were thrown out on the street. She was rescued, so she thought, by Mohammed Azam, a local notable, who helped her get a mortgage. But Azam expected sexual favours in return for his help and turned violent when she refused. She turned to the community elders for help but, to their shame, they also refused. Azam was briefly imprisoned for heroin-dealing but there was no respite for Zoora, who now found herself repeatedly answering the door to men demanding sex, sent along by Azam from inside jail.

'I was the bed mattress for all the men in the community,' she later recalled.

On Azam's release she realized that his attentions were turning to Naz, who was then 12. It was the moment that turned this battered, passive, tormented woman into a vengeful tigress. In 1993 she was imprisoned for fourteen years for murdering Azam with arsenic.

With her mother gone, Naz became the primary carer of her teenaged siblings. Aged 15, she was also forced into a marriage while away in Pakistan, where by her own account she was raped by her new husband. Her truncated youth led to a career back in Britain as a carer for the disabled and then as the head of a mental health charity, before she went into politics and defeated George Galloway and his Respect party in 2015. It was a film script of a life, in which she had fought misogyny, racism and hardship every step of the way.[16]

Like Siema Iqbal and so many other British Muslims, Shah was deeply troubled by events in Gaza in 2014. Her job, too, was briefly put in doubt when she was later accused of anti-semitism. Her crime, committed before she became an MP – but for which she was nevertheless suspended from the Labour party – was to have re-posted on Facebook a jokey diagram entitled 'Solution for the Israel-Palestine conflict: Relocate Israel to the United States'. Her punishment seemed harsh to some observers, including even to the diagram's main online propagator, who turned out to be the well-known American political scientist Norman G. Finkelstein.[17] Shah apologized and was reinstated at Parliament, but the episode again demonstrated how risky it could be for a Muslim in the public eye to step even fractionally out of line on the Israeli issue. As the Jewish journalist Ben Judah noted, she was no more than a product of her time and place. Thanks in part to the fiery rhetoric of the Respect leader George Galloway, Palestine was a huge issue among Muslims before and during the 2015 general election. Israel-bashing, according to Judah, was 'normal politics in Bradford'.[18]

Of course there was also a dark side of female empowerment, perhaps even darker than Zoora Shah's poisoning of Mohammed Azam. One of the most memorable photographs of 2015 was of three bespectacled school friends from Bethnal Green in east London, two of them not yet 16, passing through passport control together at Gatwick airport on their way to Raqqa. Despite the blurriness of the CCTV image, there was no mistaking their youthful inexperience, nor the girlish care with which they had dressed for the occasion, all stylish jackets, sweaters and artfully draped woolly scarves. It was a shock. In the popular imagination until this moment, joining ISIS was the preserve of crazed young men, not innocents like these. The truth was that by 2015, some 550 other Western women and girls had trodden the path taken by Amira Abase, Shamima Begum and Khadiza Sultana, while the proportion of women arrested on terror charges in Britain had risen from 10 to 23 per cent in a year.[19] The old certainties about gender and violent extremism were turned on their head. Girl power, it seemed, had turned jihadist.

Counter-terrorist experts as well as the press pored over the case. Much was made of the fact that Amira's father, from Ethiopia, had attended an Anjem Choudary rally in 2012, where he was photographed chanting 'Allahu akbar' as the American flag burned in the background. Examination of her social media accounts, however, revealed a teenaged girl of terrifying normality. She loved to shop for clothing brands like Victoria's Secret and Vans shoes and was an ardent Chelsea supporter. She agonized over which A levels to take, expressed a hatred of statistics classes, huffed at the vicissitudes of London Transport and wondered if nose-piercing was haram.[20] She reposted some heartrending photographs of starving children in Syria, but it was hardly unusual to be upset by the suffering there and did not by itself point to sympathy for ISIS. There was, in short, little in her background to suggest she shared any of her father's hard-line views.

The experts were baffled. But in the unlikely surroundings of the Edinburgh Fringe Festival in 2015, I heard someone who was not: Shazia Mirza, billed as Britain's only female Muslim stand-up comedian.

'I know why those girls went,' she deadpanned her audience in her flat Birmingham accent. 'They wanted to get laid.'

Her interesting contention was that the young ISIS fighters so often paraded on Western television were 'hot . . . they're macho, they're hairy, they've got guns', as she put it. ISIS had let it be known that they needed broodstock for the brave new state they were building, and the schoolgirls from Bethnal Green had answered the call.

'They think they've gone on a Club 18–30 holiday to Ibiza . . . They're not religious, they're horny. They're looking for a halal version of Brad Pitt.'

It was an alluringly simple explanation, as well as a plausible one. In 2015 Sahima Begum, the distraught younger sister of the absconded Shamima, told a Home Office select committee: 'There was nothing that indicated that she was radicalized in any way. She used to watch *Keeping Up With the Kardashians*.'

Shazia's show was called *The Kardashians Made Me Do It*.

I met Shazia a year later at Shoreditch House, a media-world members' club in the heart of hipster London. The club seemed a parody of itself, with a swimming pool on the roof and a res-taurant selling poached hake with lovage for £18. The bar zone, she observed acidly, contained so many people tapping on lap-tops that it resembled a student library. And yet she seemed perfectly at home in this peculiar place. With her long, languor-ous face and heavily lidded eyes, she seemed a sophisticated, citified kind of Pakistani, quite different to the working-class

Asians I had been spending time with in the ex-mill towns of the north. She had been brought up in the 'very white' Birmingham suburb of Harborne, by parents who were very definitely not rural Mirpuri but from Lahore and Rawalpindi.

'I know Pakistanis who think of Mirpuris as self-ghettoizing, cousin-shagging Neanderthals,' she noted.

Bethnal Green was just down the road, and yet a world away.

Her observations on the schoolgirls were not idly made. As an Asian Muslim brought up in the traditional way in 1990s Birmingham – her father, she said, knew 'all eight thousand hadiths' – she felt a kind of kinship with them.

'I used to be one of those girls,' she said.

This made her particularly perceptive on the matter of teenaged sexual frustration. Her father used to drive her to school every day, taking her right to the school gates to avoid any possibility of socializing beyond them. She used to enjoy swimming but her mother stopped her when she was 13 because the costumes were unseemly. She hung posters of Tom Selleck and Don Johnson on her bedroom wall but there was no chance of even talking to a real boy, let alone kissing one. Shazia also had experience other than her own to go on. In her twenties she had taught science at a Tower Hamlets state school, close to and very like Bethnal Green Academy, where her pupils included the London-African rapper Dizzee Rascal. The Muslim girls she taught, she recalled, 'never talked about Islam or foreign policy or anything. All they ever talked about was boys.'

Since the Edinburgh Fringe she had taken her show on an extended, year-long national tour that had sold out almost everywhere. Her material was close to the bone and upset some, mostly white people who misunderstood it. The audience response in towns like Banbury and Tunbridge Wells had been 'a bit cold'; a turn on the ITV panel show *Loose Women* elicited a handful of complaints from viewers calling her 'disgusting' and 'an idiot' for making light of terrorists. To Shazia, the most telling aspect of that episode was the way it was reported in the tabloids.

'The *Star*, the *Mail*, the *Express* all took a few negative tweets and blew them up into a furore that didn't exist. They just made it up. They did the same thing to Sadiq Khan in his London mayor campaign. It is *clearly* Islamophobic.'

Ultimately, though, and for all its edgy humour, her show was rooted in empathy – and the response it had received among ordinary Muslims, the measure that counted the most, proved that she had got the tone just right. Her reception in towns and cities like Aylesbury, Bradford and her native Birmingham was rapturous. She had been on the stand-up comedy circuit for sixteen years – since 9/11, in fact, when she gained notoriety for her introductory line, 'I'm Shazia Mirza. At least, that's what it says on my pilot's licence' – but never, she said, had she played to so many Muslims. Her audience in Bradford mostly comprised Asian women, who gave her a standing ovation.

'I get letters all the time from young Asian girls saying, "You just said what we talk about all the time." I think that's because, in comedy, no one has really spoken for them before.'

I wondered if she had ever received threats from anyone for poking fun at ISIS, but there had been none.

'It's weird, actually. I half expected it but there's been nothing. I had more confrontation over the jokes I made in my last show about my mother's moustache. I'm baffled – but I think it must mean that you can't argue with the truth. Everything I say in my show is true.'

Shazia clearly didn't lack courage. In February 2016, three months after the ISIS Paris attacks, Shazia performed in a venue directly opposite the Bataclan theatre. It was another sell-out. Just as poignantly, she was also invited to perform for the girls – interestingly, only the girls – at the Quintin Kynaston Community Academy in north London, the alma mater of the late Mohammed Emwazi, the ISIS killer known as Jihadi John.

'There were two hundred girls, all in headscarves ... they thought it was hilarious. There was a good Q&A about ISIS afterwards and they all agreed with what I was saying. I hope it helped.'

It was brave and imaginative of the staff to book her. They, but few if any of their pupils, were aware that Jihadi John's sister was still at the school, using a different, assumed name.

Laughter, Shazia agreed, was not just an antidote to people's fear of terrorists, but an excellent way of pricking the pomposity of ISIS's death-cult ideology. At a recent US Senate subcommittee hearing, she said, Bono of U2, apparently in all seriousness, had proposed deploying famous comics to Syria as an alternative to airstrikes. The singer was much derided for the proposal, but Shazia thought maybe he had a point.[21] Humour, she observed, has the power to draw people together, Muslim and non-Muslim alike.

'We are all laughing at the same thing – and we are laughing at ISIS, not at Islam.'

Was she, I asked, religious herself?

'Yes – I'd say so,' she replied after some thought.

From Sharia to Shazia: laughter was the most empowering quality of all.

8

Men Behaving Badly

Bradford

IT WAS OBVIOUS THE bout was going to be short from the
moment the fighters stepped into the cage. The Asian one, Hassan Mahmood, didn't skip so much as bounce around its edges,
like potassium in water in a school laboratory experiment. He
climbed and even straddled the top of the high mesh fencing,
from where he flexed the square slab of his chest and roared,
like King Kong on the Empire State. His supporters, standing
teetering on chairs ranged too close behind me, bayed back their
approval. It was the highlight of their big Saturday night out in
Bradford and they were almost as pumped up as their champion. His opponent, a wiry professional flyweight from Stockport
called Reece Street, seemed no pushover with his jug ears and
Charles Atlas stomach muscles, yet he shuffled his feet and
looked at the floor when Mahmood came circling with his hard
man's stare, their faces inches apart.

It was hot as well as deafening in the Bradford Hotel's win-
dowless conference hall, which by this late stage in the evening
smelled strongly of beer and marijuana as well as sweat. The
police had been called, twice, to break up fights in the 700-strong
audience. On the second occasion they had passed a message
via the compère in the cage, a beefy Asian ex-boxer (and
ex-policeman), that the evening would be cancelled and the conference hall forcibly shut if the audience didn't sit down and
behave. The marshals had been losing their grip all night and

now, as the penultimate fight got under way, they lost it completely. I ducked aside as the mob surged from behind through the ringside seats, overturning chairs and kicking over beer glasses, clambering the cage where their champion was already pummelling the flyweight from Stockport.

'Fuck him up, Haz!' they shouted. 'Fucking destroy him!'

They wore sharp shirts and sharper haircuts, carefully parted moptops over short back and sides, sometimes with natty patterns etched out with a razor. It was my first encounter with suburban Asian rudeboy culture and it didn't feel comfortable. One or two of them hung back and filmed the melee on their phones, whooping at the anarchy they had unleashed on the desperate marshals. Some of them seemed very young.

Adil, an ex-gym fighter himself and my companion for the evening, tapped my shoulder and leant towards my ear.

'This is when we use the phrase "Fucky Paki",' he yelled, rolling his eyes.

It was not, I reflected, a phrase that I could ever use. Adil, as a Pakistani Pashtun, was more entitled. I had asked him some weeks before to show me the 'real' Asian Bradford and this was what he came up with. It was good of him to bring me because, as he said, he didn't like fight nights as much as he once did. For most of the evening he sat scowling with his arms obdurately crossed, an incongruous woolly hat crammed down over his head.

'They're not from Bradford, that lot,' he added. 'They're from Dewsbury. Bloody inbreds.'

Hearing this was like a jigsaw piece falling into place. I had heard so much about the lawlessness of Dewsbury youth – the drugs, the petty and not so petty crime, the disdain for the police and the authority of their own elders – but had never seen any evidence of it until now. Dewsbury was barely ten miles away. It was fascinating to hear a Bradford Asian dismiss them as country bumpkins.

Adil said that cage fighting is increasingly popular among Asians, not just in northern cities like Bradford but in London, too. The sport has some conspicuous heroes for them, notably the Bolton-born boxer Amir Khan, a former Olympic medallist in the lightweight division, who in 2016 was busy setting up the world's first Mixed Martial Arts league. But it isn't an exclusively Asian sport. Only about half of the fighters at the Bradford Hilton were Asian, a proportion reflected in their audience. The fact is that cage fighting is on the increase in all communities, which made me think that it might be symptomatic of a wider social malaise. Youth violence is on the rise everywhere; it has nothing to do with Asians or Islam per se.

The sport presents itself as a controlled outlet for violence, a social safety valve. Amir Khan once took part in a Channel 4 documentary called *Amir Khan's Angry Young Men*, whom he steered away from trouble on the streets through the discipline of the ring. But the fact that the need for such a safety valve is growing points to a crisis of masculinity, including and perhaps especially among young Asian men, which traditional Islam seems unable to resolve. It was this issue that I was hoping to explore in Bradford, famed as one of the most densely Asian Muslim cities in the country.

There were various styles of cage fighting on show at the Hilton, from classic boxing to K-1, a mixed martial arts discipline that combines several skills including kick-boxing and wrestling, although to my untrained eye it looked a lot more martial than art. The fighters, most of whom were affiliated to back-street gyms with names like Caged Steel and Rock Solid, seemed more like glorified street-brawlers. The cage itself, I realized as the night went on, was mostly just a stage prop. It was a Victorian freak-show trick: stand back or you might get hurt, it said. It separated the civilized from the uncivilized, a symbol of control over the violence that also sanctioned our prurient animal interest in it. The fighters at least wore light-weight boxing gloves but there were few rules that I could discern. It seemed perfectly acceptable to go on smashing your opponent after he was down, with elbows as well as fists. The paramedics on duty were in and out of the ring as often as the competitors. Many of the night's fights ended in brutal knock-outs, in one case after just 14 seconds. The dazed and bleeding losers were dragged away like expended gladiators, some of them leaving such a trail of fluids behind them that the cage floor had to be mopped.

Reece Street didn't last long. Haz Mahmood flipped him into a hold that was going to break his spine if he didn't submit. Their bodies were locked together on the ground, a strange ser-pentine heap of sweat-slicked arms and legs. Street's fists briefly flailed for a target but then it was over and Mahmood was off around the ring again, a victory lap this time, pumping both fists, riding the fence like a motorcycle stunt rider on the Wall of Death.

'You see?' crowed one of his fans to a mate, 'didn't I tell you? I *told* you!'

The fights were not deliberately arranged on racial lines but they tended to fall that way. Was cage fighting a *Hunger Games*-style outlet for the racial tensions Bradford was famous for? The symbolism was none too subtle if so. The cage was the frustrating trap of society; beat up the white man, as Haz Mahmood had just done, and you could literally escape it. There was some clunking religious symbolism on display, too, espe-cially in a Yorkshire title fight between Khatib Rehman and Brad Carter, a local white bouncer nicknamed 'War Machine', whose back was tattooed from neck to waist with a crucifix bearing the legend: *If today I should die, then may I die well.* Another Asian, Addy Khan, ostentatiously fell to his knees to pray before his fight. Adil, who took his Islam seriously, was unimpressed. Fighting for sport, he observed, is actually haram according to some interpretations of Islamic law. He didn't spell it out, but I suspected this was one reason why he no longer followed the sport.

The atmosphere in the conference centre, certainly, was about as far as one could get from that of a mosque. This hall was filled not with the sound of prayer but the thump of trance music by the Pakistani-American artiste Nadia Ali. ('Not to be confused with the porn star of the same name,' Adil said.) I had recently interviewed a senior imam in Leeds, Qari Asim MBE, who told me that only 20 to 30 per cent of the young Muslims in his area regularly attended mosque. Some of the remaining 70 per cent, he frankly acknowledged, probably never attended at all, even while continuing to identify themselves as Muslims. A Saturday night cage fight, perhaps, was where they ended up instead, lured away like Pinocchio to Pleasure Island.

Thanks to his brother who worked for Solid Impact, the fight-night promoters, Adil had secured us ringside seats right by the prize table, which glittered with belts and gold and silver cups. But what we mostly looked at between the fights, along with all the Dewsbury boys behind us, were the ring girls as they sashayed back and forth, with their hands on their hips and million-dollar smiles on their made-up lips. They weren't quite the only women in the crowd although they might as well have been. They were working-class white girls in stiletto heels and fishnet stockings beneath the shortest possible hotpants, with a Hotmail address for their modelling agency imprinted across their bottoms in shocking pink.

The Dewsbury lads were so fixated that I felt almost sorry for them. They came from a culture where boys and girls are forbidden to mix. It seemed crazy to tease such a dog with such a bone. Was the atmosphere in here not charged enough already? What confusing message did the ring girls send in the context of this evening, a festival of male combat in a cage? What, in fact, did the Dewsbury boys imagine would be the victor's real reward – the gold and silver trophies on the table or the pretty white ones standing next to it? There was, I could see, a kind of pornography about this spectacle of semi-naked, super-fit bodies violently writhing on a floor. But cage fighting is also about domination through the infliction of pain and humiliation; it propagates the fantasy that might is right. It is no kind of substitute for normal healthy relations between the sexes. At the beginning of the evening, one of the ring girls had handed me a business card promoting the event's main sponsor: *Tariq Khan LL.B (Hons), Solicitor*, it read. *Criminal Defence Specialists. 24 Hour Police Station Attendance. Serious Crime and Fraud.* I remembered Najma Khalid in Oldham telling me that domestic violence always spiked after football matches. These solicitors clearly knew a good business opportunity when they saw one. Taken from the hand of a ring girl, the business card seemed like a kind of warning: *Keep your testosterone in check*, it seemed to say. *You can look all you want but you'd better not touch.*

It was almost midnight when the last fight ended and the crowd, many of them drunk, carried us back through the hotel lobby towards the street. The air remained thick with aggression. Two po-faced policemen stood in the middle of the reception area, as still as rocks in a turbulent stream. There was a commotion over by the lifts where a shouting middle-aged blonde woman, over-tanned and heavily bejewelled – the companion of one of the white fighters, for sure – was being hauled backwards towards the lifts by her friends, her face contorted with rage at an insult someone had just thrown her. The policemen looked on but didn't move. A minute later a lurching white drunk whispered to Adil, slowly and deliberately, that he was a batty boy.

'*What* did you just call me?' said Adil, wheeling.

'A *batty* boy,' repeated the drunk, prodding his chest, with glazed eyes and a crooked smile on a razor's edge between bonhomie and anarchic violence. It was the crudest possible invitation to a fight and I hastily pulled Adil away.

We drove to a late-night diner called Shimla's where we met up with his brother Kamran and three friends who had also been at the cage fight. The tables were packed with a clientele that was all Asian, all male.

'The women can eat upstairs in a separate room,' said Adil when I asked, 'but they tend to eat earlier and they're mostly all at home now.'

I squeezed into a booth next to Ibby, Asif and Shuayb. It was like a scene from *Grease*, but without any girls to wink at. Kamran, in a leather jacket, was the John Travolta character. He was moodier and quieter than at our last meeting at the family home over in west Bradford. Solid Impact's fight night had not gone according to plan. There was some doubt as to whether the hotel would ever have them back again, thanks to the attentions of the police during the evening. All the talk at Shimla's was about the aggro in the crowd, who'd done what to whom.

'It was Copa, and Rooney from Speedball, you know? Fighting over a scrat goree,' said Ibby.

Speedball, Adil translated, was another Bradford boxing gym; a goree was a white chick and scrat meant hot. Ibby had the whole thing on video on his phone, filmed and forwarded on by a friend. He passed it round the table so that everyone could take a look, although there wasn't much to see: just a shaky shot of backs and a forest of upstretched arms holding smart phones.

There was general disgust at the behaviour of the posse from Dewsbury.

'Did you see those idiots drinking?' said Adil, his outrage unabated. 'They were drinking openly! And it will all be on YouTube later. To be honest, I'm surprised.'

Kamran, who unlike his brother identified himself as a Salafi, shook his head grimly and said nothing. It was hard to make out what bothered him more: the upset to his big event or the breakdown in public mores. But Muslims drinking in public like that, the others all agreed, used to be unheard of.

'Were they Gujarati?' I asked, thinking of Savile Town and its notorious mono-ethnicity.

'Definitely not Gujis,' said Ibby firmly, 'just Pakis like us.'

'To be honest, it's happening more and more,' said Adil thoughtfully.

That, perhaps, was the real story here – the imams and elders losing control of the younger generation as never before.

The group's mood improved once we'd eaten an enormous curry feast. The talk turned to gentler subjects, like Pakistani recipes. Someone recommended cooking chicken with honey and fried eggs. Someone else swore by his mother's 'pye', a traditional sauce made from lamb's feet, laboriously washed and stewed in a pressure cooker. After dinner we drove through a rough part of town to a shisha bar called Junoon. Adil pointed out a jagged hole in a wall where a cashpoint machine had recently been levered out. Gang crime, it seemed, was quite an issue in Bradford. Only the other day, he said, a gangster was shot at the wheel of his car outside a pizza shop near his house, yet the neighbours barely remarked on it.

Junoon was on the top floor of a converted mill. With its anonymous security door and narrow staircase, it felt like entering a Bradford version of a Chicago speakeasy. The decor inside, though, was faux-Egyptian. There were more booths, these ones filled with plush leather sofas and special holes cut into the tables for the shisha pipe smoking tubes. It was novel, although I found myself wondering slightly what the point of it all was. It was a very Muslim version of a British nightclub, with no dancing, no girls, no drugs and no booze. It was hard to make oneself heard above the Asian electro-pop on the sound system and the bar served nothing stronger than milkshake. Tobacco, in a bewildering variety of fruit and spice combinations or brands with names like Starbuzz and Fumari, was the only fun on offer – and the local authorities had tried to spoil even that two years previously when the police raided, found the owners to be in breach of the enclosed public spaces smoking ban and fined them £2,500. Adil said that shisha spots like this one were all the rage but I couldn't imagine the Dewsbury lads wanting to come here. It was a Saturday night but I was not surprised that Junoon was half empty.

*

None of the cities I visited for the first time in 2016 was more amazing to me than Bradford. I knew it by reputation as 'Bradistan', the most uncompromisingly Muslim city in Britain, and I wasn't disappointed in that respect. It was a sunny Friday morning when I arrived and the streets were teeming with families in hijab and shalwar kameez on their way to prayers. At the last official count, Bradford contained an astonishing 125 mosques, serving a Muslim population of at least 130,000, a quarter of the city total. One in five Bradfordians is a Pakistani, the highest proportion anywhere in England. It seemed a city in another country.

And yet nowhere is more evocative of northern England's glorious and not so glorious industrial past. It was hillier than I expected, and there was an austere beauty in the way the terraces marched around the contours, like cornrows braided on a girl's head. Some of the streets were like postcards from another time.

In this digital age, the neighbours still shared a communal telephone mast, the lines radiating outwards like streamers from a maypole. The crumbling back-to-backs they still inhabited were discoloured by soot from factory chimneys that had gone cold years before. Adil's hometown tour included an introduction to his father, who had worked for twenty-seven years in one of those factories, a famous city landmark called Lister's Mill, the world's largest silk factory until it closed in the early 1990s. The old man, a specialist velvet weaver, had met Margaret Thatcher, Prince Charles and the Queen on three separate tours of the shop floor.

There was nostalgia everywhere Adil and I went, even in a chippy called Mother Hubbard's, an institution famed for its scallop butties, where a framed, yellowed newspaper cutting recalled its opening by the cast of *Coronation Street* in 1972. In Victoria Square we stopped by a poppy-strewn war memorial commemorating the Bradford Pals battalion, 1,770 of whom died in a single hour on the Somme. The bronze-cast figures on the cenotaph's flanks, a soldier and sailor perpetually frozen in a bayonet charge, were unequivocally white Anglo-Saxons: there was no mention here of the 400,000 Muslim soldiers who fought alongside them in World War One.

There is, of course, another side to Bradford. In 2001 the city suffered rioting almost as serious as Oldham's. Just as it had there, a subsequent government inquiry identified poverty, alienation and years of deep social segregation as its major causes. Adil said things were better these days, in part because after the riots, 'all the bad guys got locked up'. But he also observed that the local *Telegraph & Argus* still made very gloomy reading with its apparently endless reports of drug crime, violence and murder.

He took me to Laisterdyke in east Bradford, the district from where, in 2015, twelve members of the extended Dawood family, three sisters and their nine children, absconded to ISIS. It was as poor and depressed as anywhere I have seen in Britain. The tiny houses were either derelict or crumbling towards that state. Rubbish blew about the streets like tumbleweed. We passed a corner store called Bargain Food, a third-world shack of a shop selling unappetizing vegetables from beneath a canopy of corrugated iron. Across the road was a drug-dealer's den, its windows reinforced by grilles, its walls defaced by graffiti. There were notably few cars about, moving or parked. The folk around here mostly couldn't afford them.

We stopped by a small recreational area called Attock Park, where I found a plaque explaining that it had been named after a stabbing victim. Some Asian children were playing cricket on an all-weather football pitch surrounded by a high metal fence that, I fancied, looked a lot like a cage-fight ring. A niqabi passed by, and I surreptitiously photographed her with the cage, and the plaque, behind her. I looked up Attock Park in the *Telegraph & Argus* later on. In the previous six months, I discovered, the pitch's floodlights had been vandalized, again; a fight over a swing between three traditionally dressed Asian girls, two of them aged seven, had resulted in an assault requiring hospital surgery; and a 21-year-old Gambian man, Beyake Keita Ann, had been clubbed to death with a baseball bat following a row over a game of football.

Callous violence no doubt exists in all societies, in every part of Britain. But there is one form of it that the wider public particularly associate with Asian Muslim men, especially in northern England. Two weeks before I visited Adil, a group of twelve Asian men from Keighley, an attractive ex-textiles town in Brontë country ten miles northwest of Bradford, had been jailed for 130 years for trafficking vulnerable white schoolgirls for sex. One of the victims, who had been multiply raped by the gang, was 13.

'None of these defendants had any concern for the victim,' said the sentencing judge at Bradford Crown Court. 'They saw her as a pathetic figure who had no worth and who served no purpose other than to be an object that they could sexually misuse and cast aside. They showed her no shred of decency or humanity when as a vulnerable child she so needed care and understanding.'[1]

The Keighley case was just the latest in a series to reach the courts, over two dozen of them around the country in the previous ten years. Bradford's Muslims were still abuzz with the news, forced into yet another round of soul-searching and recrimination.

The scale of Asian child-grooming was one of its most disconcerting features, ensuring that it remained the rawest nerve of British race relations. The Alexis Jay report of 2014 on Rotherham, the most notorious case, estimated that 1,400 young girls had been sexually abused in that town alone. The figures were hotly contested by some Muslims, including ones as senior as Rotherham's Lord Nazir Ahmed.

'There were never that many girls being abused,' he told me. 'There were eighty-seven incidents reported in one very bad year. Baroness Jay was told that the grooming had been going on for sixteen years, so she multiplied 87 by 16 and came up with 1,400.'

Nevertheless, the figure caught both the media's attention and the public's imagination, and led some non-Muslims to conclude that the sexual abuse of minors is culturally endemic to Islam. That argument naturally plays particularly well with white supremacists. Britain First, for example, referred to the Rotherham statistic at their march in Dewsbury to justify calling all Muslims 'Paedo Scum'.

In his speech, their leader Paul Golding also reached for another far right trope: the allegation that Islam itself sanctions paedophilia, because the Prophet had married his favourite wife Aisha when she was just six (and shared a bed with her when she was nine). Adil dismissed this Aisha story as a pernicious myth, and later sent me a scholarly article explaining where it came from: an unreliable hadith narrated by a single eighth-century scholar in his seventies, Hisham ibn Urwah, whose memory was known to have been faulty, and who may in any case have been misquoted. Aisha, I read, was not *tisa* (nine) when her marriage was consummated, but *tisa ashara* (19); the ashara bit had somehow fallen off the end of the sentence in the course of the hadith's transcription. It seemed extraordinary that so much should turn on the exegesis of a single ancient Arabic symbol.

Perhaps campaigners against Muslim immigrants were always going to find the Asian grooming phenomenon useful as ammunition. Less expected, but just as troubling, was the extent to which the 'culturally endemic' argument appeared to be believed by senior figures of authority. In October 2016 the former head of the government's troubled inquiry into child sex abuse, Dame Lowell Goddard, was alleged to have said that the reason Britain had so many paedophiles was 'because it has so many Asian men'. She was also said to have voiced shock at the size of the country's ethnic minority population and to have complained of having to travel 50 miles from London to see a white face.[2]

The grooming phenomenon is often blamed on the old New Labour policy of multiculturalism, including in Rotherham. The local authorities there, Alexis Jay found, had known about the problem for years, but had turned a blind eye out of misplaced respect for a different culture, or else for fear of being labelled racist if they called that culture to account. This was much the same complaint that I had heard from indigenous whites in Dewsbury. In Rotherham, the problem was disastrously compounded by police attitudes to the girls themselves – an assumption, as one Rotherham resident told me, that if young white girls were in the company of older Asian men at night, it was because they were 'slags' and therefore 'asking for it' and complicit in their own abuse. In one notorious incident in Rotherham, Bannaras Hussain, 36 – the second of the three brothers at the centre of the grooming ring, known locally as Mad Ash, Bash and Bono – was caught abusing an underage girl in a police station car park.

'She's just sucking my cock, mate,' he told the police officer – who then drove off.

There can be no question that such blatant official failings have given succour to far-right organizations, whose narrative of 'taking back control' found many willing listeners among the outraged citizenry of towns like Rotherham. Britain First, EDL, National Action or regional organizations like the North West Infidels marched or demonstrated in Rotherham's town centre an astonishing fourteen times between August 2014 and September 2015, and every time they picked anew at the scab of the scandal's wound.

Contrary to the public's impression, Rotherham's Muslim community is small – smaller, even, than the national average. Unlike in towns like Dewsbury, therefore, the common complaint that they were 'taking over' did not apply. As in every other grooming scandal, the gangs who had caused such harm were tiny in number and in no way representative of the community as a whole. The disaster was fixable; Muslims and non-Muslims alike were desperate to rebuild the trust lost between them. But the far right would not let them and race relations in consequence were perhaps worse there than in any town I visited in 2016.

The nadir came in August 2015 when Mushin Ahmed, 81, a popular local figure known as 'Texas', was kicked and stamped to death as he headed to early morning prayers at his mosque. Sheffield Crown Court later heard that one of the two killers, Dale Jones – who had spent the previous day and night consuming cocaine, diazepam, Southern Comfort and Sambuca – was in a 'raging fury' by the time he encountered Texas, whom he accused of being a 'groomer' as he killed him. Jones assumed his victim was Pakistani, as most of the real Rotherham groomers were, although Texas was in fact a Yemeni. He was moreover married to an Irish Catholic and had only recently 'reverted' to Islam; his children and grandchildren had been brought up in both persuasions. It was the grimmest of ironies that his murderers had targeted one of the town's conspicuous examples of both religious moderation and social integration.[3]

The following month, Rotherham's Muslims demonstrated against racism in the town centre, where they also held a prayer vigil for Texas. But even that was marred by yet another Britain First march, which included a group of veteran football hooligans who styled themselves 'Yorkshire's Finest' and who had a long history of provoking racist violence. The two sides came to blows when South Yorkshire police channelled the Muslim demonstrators past the William Fry, a pub well known for the extreme rightwing views of its clientele. It was, however, twelve Rotherham Muslims who were arrested and tried for violent disorder. They were acquitted in October 2016, following a major public protest campaign. One of the defendants, Abrar Javid, a 38-year-old NHS project manager, later suggested to the press that the police decision to send the Muslims past the William Fry was no accident, and that he and the others were victims of 'political policing'. He told reporters:

'I believe that because the police had failed in terms of child sexual exploitation, they were trying to make examples of a community – in whatever shape or form – and say: "Look, we're doing our job now. We're actually putting a few Asians away." '[4]

Years have passed since Rotherham's grooming scandals were first exposed, yet the consequences reverberate as strongly as ever. A 'Peace Day' seminar I attended in the town, organized by the anti-extremism campaign group Hope not Hate, gave as good an indication as any of the scale of the challenge the town faces. There were maybe fifty people at the seminar, a ragbag of councillors, vicars, local journalists and LGBT spokespersons, but noticeably few Asian Muslims. It was, as one delegate muttered to me, a room full of 'the usual suspects', a diverse group of white liberals who meant well but were essentially just talking to themselves.

'Rotherham has got nasty now,' said Angham Ahmed, a Yemeni who runs a group called Rotherham Ethnic Minority Alliance. 'There have been five or six race attacks since Texas was killed. The grooming scandal has been a brutal education for the whole country.'

All the town's 8,000 Muslims, she said, have been branded guilty by association. And yet they had no more idea of what was going on than anyone else.

'My friend's brother actually shared a house with one of the five Asians convicted of grooming in 2010 but even he had *no* idea,' Angham said.[5]

No doubt Asian child sex abuse could and should have been stopped sooner than it was and the fallout for the communities affected could have been handled much better. But why did it happen in the first place? Before coming to Bradford I had asked Elizabeth McDonnell, the adoptive mother of Lara, one of the girls caught up in the Oxford grooming case of 2013, in which a seven-strong, mostly Pakistani gang were found to have groomed and sexually exploited some three hundred girls over a period of nine years. McDonnell, a high-flying charity worker in her sixties, subsequently wrote a book, *You Can't Have My Daughter*, which told in wince-making detail how Lara was plied with drugs in filthy crack dens, raped and tortured, and trafficked to cities all over the country, including to Bradford: the victim of what the judge called 'a series of sexual crimes of the utmost depravity'. The book also documents the appalling failure of the Oxford authorities to help McDonnell protect Lara from the gang, partly through a misplaced fear of appearing racist, as in Rotherham.

McDonnell had thought hard about what had turned the gang members into such monsters. The victims were almost all white girls; the perpetrators, as well as the customers, were all black and brown men. Was there, I asked, an element of racial empowerment at work? Did the men get satisfaction from symbolically turning the tables on the white society that lorded it over them by raping their daughters? Were they perhaps subconsciously seeking revenge for colonialism, the oppression of their ancestors? For slavery, even?

'That's a big, *Guardian*-type question that nice middle-class social workers steer a mile from,' she replied. 'But the fact remains that one girl, who was groomed from eleven, was branded with a hot iron by one gang-member so that people would know she belonged to him.'

McDonnell thought the sense of moral impunity with which the gang acted was partly down to the way they had been brought up.

'What I saw in my neighbourhood was these unbelievably spoilt and undisciplined young men and boys, turned into little gods by their mothers . . . the phenomenon of mothers driving their eight-year-old 250 metres to school, while the daughters walked.'

Two associates of the gang, who were never charged, lived at the top of the road where McDonnell lived, and used to 'swagger past making obscene comments . . . there was always this sense of projected anger towards the local white community'.

She knew a primary school teacher who had taught the Dogar brothers, two of her daughter's tormentors, in east Oxford.

'She said they were difficult, unruly boys, but when she tried to discipline them, the mother came in and made a formal complaint – and the school refused to back her out of political correctness.'

The school's sensitivity was, in retrospect, tragically misguided. Mothers are capable of spoiling their sons in all cultures but I knew from my reporting experience abroad how common it is in traditional patriarchal societies, where men rule the roost and women are born as second-class citizens. The phenomenon is even more prevalent in societies like Iraq or Somalia that have been atomized by war, where the father figure who might normally rein in a wayward son is frequently absent, if he isn't dead. For that reason, it is common for children who come to Britain as refugees to be brought up by single mothers. And it is, perhaps, understandable if some mothers, lonely, unable to speak English, afraid of or mystified by the customs of an alien land, should cling fast to the reassuring ways of home, including an unswerving adherence to the principle of patriarchy. When taken to an extreme, it is almost inevitable that some Muslim boys will grow into men who believe that they are entitled to behave as they please and that they can get away with anything.

McDonnell didn't think that Islam, as such, had anything to do with the creation of groomers. The men who had tormented her daughter were about as godless as they came, far beyond the reach or influence of the mosques. Nevertheless, they were often identified as Muslims by the wider public, who didn't always make much distinction between that term and 'Asian'. The community's reputation was in jeopardy, either way. What, if anything, could the mosques do about it?

Adil took me to Friday prayers at the Jamiyat Tabligh-ul-Islam, a big Barelwi mosque in Manningham, chosen for me because the *khutbah*, the main sermon, would be in English.

'It's usually in Urdu and that's half the problem,' Adil remarked. 'About 80 per cent of the young here in Bradford can't understand a word of Urdu, so why would they even come?'

The sermon was delivered by an ascetic-looking young mufti called Wajid Iqbal, whose unexceptional theme was the avoidance of the sins of the world. Adil and I cornered him after the service and I asked him about the Keighley case.

'I have talked about the evil of grooming many times in my sermons,' he said. 'Drugs are always involved in these cases: it always starts from there. The Keighley gang got teenage girls to work for them as drug couriers before trafficking them for sex.'

Grooming, he argued, was a criminal enterprise like any

other – a symptom, like drug crime, of social decay. This was something he knew all about: the Bradford suburb of Girlington had been 'lawless' when he was growing up there in the 1990s.

'Women couldn't go to the shops. There were muggings and a massive drugs and car theft issue. There were chop-shops all over. I knew a junkie called Hamíd who could black-box any car in under three minutes. Yet it started as harmless fun. He used to practise on his neighbour's car.'

He acknowledged the seriousness of grooming as a crime, the awful damage it inflicted on its victims. But he also insisted, as many Muslims do, that there was nothing specifically Muslim or even Asian about it, and that it occurred within all communities; it was just that the media distorted this picture by only reporting on grooming when Asians were involved.

He was right up to a point. For example, a review for South Yorkshire police, the force responsible for Rotherham, found that just 19 per cent of those investigated in its area for child sexual exploitation in 2014 and 2015 were Asian, compared to 65 per cent who were white north Europeans.[6] In 2012, similarly, police in Greater Manchester revealed that only 5 per cent of the men on its sex offenders' register were Asian, and that the rest were white.

A great many white non-Muslims have nevertheless bought into the far-right narrative that preying on young girls and women is an exclusively Muslim habit. In February 2016 in Birmingham I attended a demonstration by Pegida UK, an offshoot of the anti-Muslim German movement founded in Dresden in 2014. (Pegida stands for *Patriotische Europäer gegen die Islamisierung des Abendlandes*: Patriotic Europeans Against the Islamization of the West). The British branch was set up by Tommy Robinson, the Lutonian founder of the EDL, who hoped to mobilize the respectable middle classes, as the movement had very successfully done in Germany. The crowd he drew in Birmingham was not huge, partly no doubt because of the atrocious weather on the day, but it was certainly very different to the thuggish crew I had seen demonstrating in Dewsbury. It included mothers with their families, retired soldiers, dog walkers, a man with a furled umbrella and a bowler hat. All of them wanted a halt to Muslim immigration – and the assumption that Islam silently endorses the abuse of white women was one of their main motivations.

We will not stay silent while our women are raped, read their placards. *'Rape Culture' is being IMPORTED.* Robinson deliberately tapped into the old Churchill vs Hitler narrative, Britain's finest hour. One poster explicitly equated Islamism with Nazism. *We defeated fascism. Now we import it*, read another. Most chilling of all, perhaps, was the poster that read *Donald Trump is right*, although they might not have used that one eight months later when allegations emerged that Trump, too, had molested young girls and women in the past.

Why did white people think only brown ones were guilty? One answer is that white groomers tend to operate singly, often online, and are therefore much less visible than Asian ones, who tend to groom girls in organized gangs on the street. Pakistanis unquestionably dominate this version of the crime, which also grabs most of the headlines.[7] One popular sociological explanation is 'the night-time economy' in which a disproportionate number of Asians work – as taxi drivers, for example, or in late-night fast-food restaurants. The girls groomed by Asians are generally from troubled backgrounds, often living in care homes or with foster parents. They are already vulnerable to abuse and are statistically more likely to be out on the streets at night. The opportunity for the wrong kind of interaction comes ready-made.

The solution Mufti Iqbal preached to his community was more self-discipline.

'The first lesson is to stay away from women and children,' he said, 'because the best cure is abstinence.'

I wondered about that. Abstinence might be the answer for a

man married to God, but for the rest of us, wasn't it just a recipe for sexual frustration? Back outside the mosque, Adil broadly agreed: he thought the sermon we had heard was a high-flown waste of time.

'The *khutab* are all the same. There's never anything in them for or about the community. That's what these mosques should be doing. Is it any wonder that kids go off and do stupid stuff?'

Not all of Bradford's imams were as out of touch as Adil intimated. One celebrated preacher, Alyas Karmani, was so outspoken on the matter of Muslim sexual frustration that the BBC had dubbed him 'the Muslim sex doctor'.

'You have a red-blooded young man, 19 years old, his testosterone surging,' he told me. 'His culture, his whole upbringing, forbids sex before marriage. Yet his parents are telling him to wait eight years before getting married. That's just stupid.'

Muslim society in Bradford, he thought, was unhealthily stuck in what he called 'a 1950s morality bubble', increasingly at odds with modernity. The tension was exacerbated by what he described as the 'sexualization' of Western society, which increased a Muslim's sense of isolation, as well as fostering resentment that they were not as free as young Westerners. Bradford's moral orthodoxy, very interestingly, was also quite out of step with the culture back home in Pakistan. He had just returned from a visit to Lahore, the red-light district of which employs 30,000 working girls.

'They are much more open and progressive there, with a culture of buying sex that goes back to Mughal times. How come? As an imam here, I encourage Muslims to marry young. I tell them to use a condom. They say, are we allowed? And I say, shut up, just go away and have great sex!'

It was not a message likely to win many friends among Bradford's Muslim conservatives but Alyas was refreshingly unafraid to speak his mind.

'I get it in the neck from the community for my sex-doctor stuff, but I say, look: it *is* OK to masturbate . . . Some parents are so uptight, I tell them that maybe they should too, just to help them relax.'

He was in no doubt that the traditional Muslim alternative to licensed sexual activity – enforced abstinence – was potentially much more dangerous. At best it fostered what he called 'the double life syndrome':

'A lot of young Muslims have this nice lovely mosque life and behave like dutiful sons and daughters at home, but then they get up to the craziest shit outside. I had this myself in my youth.'

That sounded something like an explanation for the behaviour of the Dewsbury lads at the Saturday night cage fight.

At worst he believed, as the stand-up comedian Shazia Mirza did, that sexual frustration could lead to violent extremism, the first step on the road to Raqqa.

'It's not about ideals – 90 per cent of them never subscribe to the ideals,' as he once told the *Observer*. 'It's other factors that are a draw. This is the new rock and roll; jihad is sexy. The kid who was not very good-looking now looks good holding a gun. He can get a bride now, he's powerful. The ISIS gun is as much a penis extension as the stockbroker with his Ferrari.'[8]

The Friday khutbah was only one means by which he communicated with Bradford's young, and certainly not the most important to him. Like Adil, he thought the mosques in Bradford generally were 'inept'.

'Eighty per cent of them don't talk to their congregations in a language they can understand. Only about one in ten of them run a youth club. It's better in London but up north it's a real problem. It's such an important vehicle for change.'

Alyas was a Londoner originally, and the co-director of a well-known youth-mentoring project in Brixton in south London called STREET (Strategy To Reach, Empower and Educate Teenagers). His experience there had convinced him that mentoring young men was far more useful and effective than lecturing from a *minbar*.

'The south Asian parenting model has been a terrible failure. I work with young men and I very often find that I am the first older man that they have ever held a mature discussion with. It's no wonder if they have no moral compass. My task is to find a way to put one in.'

These young men, he went on, often had what he called 'the one square mile mentality . . . a complete disconnection from reality' in the way they viewed the world. He thought this was another partial explanation for the appeal of ISIS. Young English Muslims saw the propaganda videos and naively interpreted them as a 'real-life *Call of Duty II*'.

'ISIS, dysfunctional as they are, do also provide something meaningful to believe in. And they spend not one hour but a hundred hours coaxing recruits to join them. It is a kind of mentoring.'

Like Elizabeth McDonnell, he viewed the child sex-grooming phenomenon as an extreme effect of parental failure. At the same time, like Mufti Iqbal, he thought that it had also been unfairly politicized.

'There's nothing unique about Muslims. They become paedophiles for the same reason as any other group – and they *don't* only target white girls,' he insisted. 'The Nazis vilified Jews as sexual predators, defilers of the Aryan race. Think of the Goebbels propaganda film, *The Eternal Jew*. The same narrative is being peddled against Muslims now.'

Adil agreed wholeheartedly with this. In the past, he said, grooming was seen as someone else's problem because the victims were perceived as all being non-Muslims.

'It's not reported, but Asian gangs groom Asian girls too where they can. I've heard stories . . . It's going to come out.'

In fact, even the Jay report referred to research conducted by the UK Muslim Women's Network in 2013, which knew of at least eighteen cases where Asian Muslim girls had been exploited in just the same horrible way as the white girls of Rotherham.

Alyas's youth work with black 'postcode gangs' around Brixton had taught him that sexual violence happens everywhere. Organized grooming was just the method favoured by British Asians; it was, he added, a uniquely British Asian practice.

'Gang rape happens nightly in south London. But no one is going to say that black boys are innate rapists. Why not? Because if you did, London would be on fire tomorrow.'

He agreed with Iqbal that grooming is a criminal enterprise closely linked to the drugs business.

'It's a reflection of demographics. In Bradford and Rotherham, the drugs are supplied by Pakistanis. In Liverpool sink estates, it's a white business. There are Bengali groomers in Tower Hamlets, Turkish ones in north London. It's all connected to drugs.'

That, however, helped explain but did not excuse the grooming phenomenon. The politics and fierce arguments around grooming and the way it is presented (and distorted) were, to him, an unhelpful distraction.

'My concern here is simply that children are being raped. This is my message: this is *all* my community. And the Muslim community is not doing enough about it.'

Alyas, at bottom, was a social policy maker as much as he was an imam. He was a radical in his youth, a follower of the infamous Salafist 'godfather' of Western jihad, Abu Muntasir. But then he began to specialize in youth work, studied psychology and spent twenty years in the public sector, holding positions like the head of Race Equality for the Welsh Assembly. He was consulted by probation services in Yorkshire and London for his knowledge of how to resettle Muslim offenders, and was even now working on a PhD entitled *The Crises of Masculinity and Urban Male Violence*. He had also flirted with politics, and as a member of George Galloway's Respect party he became a Bradford City Councillor in the so-called 'Bradford Spring' of 2012.

Bradford, he explained, was the youngest city in Britain, and one of the youngest in the EU.

'Half the population will be under 20 by 2020. It's got bundles of potential. And yet we are massively failing our young here, with the third worst education authority in the country. Why?'

The blame lay with a supine local government, which had been dominated for years by a cosy coterie of Mirpuri politicians in cahoots with the Labour party. Respect, in its early days, appealed to progressive third-generation Muslims – what he called 'a significant cohort for change' – who were fed up with traditional biradari clan politics and its self-serving ways and wanted a different system based on merit, not patronage. Galvanized by Galloway's fiery rhetoric, it became a high-energy youth movement that promised to at last start making use of Bradford's wasted human capital. But the Bradford Spring failed when Galloway revealed himself to be more interested in his career as an MP in London. Galloway lost his seat to Labour's Naz Shah in 2015, the Respect party imploded, and the old biradari culture, according to Karmani, took over again. He had quit the party, and although he now sat on the council as an independent, he said he would not be seeking re-election, having concluded that he could 'do more on the outside than from within'.

As a reformed Salafist radical, and as a Muslim from the street who has demonstrably experienced the frustrations of a British Muslim upbringing, Alyas had a credibility that a cleric like Mufti Iqbal never would. Bradford's Muslim youth listened to him – and I felt sure that his thesis about sexual frustration, as well as his sex doctor's prescription for it, was right. The one-on-one mentoring of troubled Muslim youths seemed key not just to the well-being of British society but to its security as well. And yet, quite extraordinarily, the Home Office refused to work with him.

My introduction to Alyas came from a friendly former

Prevent officer who had tried to hire him to address a youth group in Wandsworth in south London. He had recently quit his job in protest when his boss refused him permission on the grounds that Alyas was a 'Salafist' and therefore 'too Islamic'.

'This is advice from the Quilliam Foundation,' Alyas said bluntly. 'It's frustrating and toxic. The term "Salafi" is meaningless. I'm an elected councillor and one of the most outspoken imams on sexual politics and forced marriage. Many of my own community see me as a sell-out. If I am not allowed to talk to young people because I'm an extremist, who's left?'

Alyas was, of course, not the only Bradford Muslim dedicated to speaking up for Asian youth, and nor were his methods the sole ones, as I discovered when I spoke to Aki Nawaz, the drummer and lyricist of Fun-Da-Mental, a band formed in the 1990s that was once wonderfully described by the music press as a 'multi-ethnic hip-hop-ethno-techno-world fusion music group'. Aki defined himself rather more comprehensibly as a 'punk', raised on much the same music that I was in the early 1980s by bands like the Sex Pistols and The Clash. He was, in that sense, a remarkable example of cultural integration. Fun-Da-Mental are sometimes called 'the Asian Public Enemy', a reference to the influential New York hip-hop group of the same era. Aki previously played drums for a forerunner of the band The Cult.

'I'm still a punk,' he told me. 'Anyone who speaks out against the system is a punk.'

His music, he said, had always been about trying to 'normalize' the Islamic presence in Britain, while expressing and explaining the anger and frustrations of Muslim youth, including those frustrations that might lead towards violent fundamentalism. His lyrics are often controversial, notably on a track called 'Cookbook DIY' from the 2006 album *All is War (The Benefits of G-Had)*, which appears to give the recipe for a homemade bomb. He sang on the same album about Osama bin Laden and the spirit of resistance he personified, and compared him to Che

Guevara. The album remains publicly restricted; it is unavailable on Spotify, for example. Aki maintained that *All is War* was misunderstood.

'Roy Hattersley said I should be arrested and MI5 turned up at my house while I was gardening,' he recalled. 'It was an edgy time for me. I couldn't walk the streets for a few weeks. I didn't go on the tube in London for six months.'

Western foreign policy was a subject he knew quite a lot about. Fun-Da-Mental had performed in Bosnia to an audience that included war-traumatized children. ('Music heals,' he observed.) He had travelled to Afghanistan and Gaza, and written angry songs about what he saw there. His work dealt with the nuanced reality of being Muslim and British, a status full of confusing and fluid contradictions, much more complicated than the stereotype. Another of his tracks, 'White Tongues', was 'all to do with people like George Galloway . . . when *he* criticizes Western foreign policy, everyone claps, but if a Muslim says it, they say, "Arrest them." '

His work naturally found favour with a section of young Bradford men who had never heard anything like it before.

'Kids used to come up and say we were wicked, thanks for sticking up for us.'

The portrait he drew, the mirror he held up to the community he came from, had a compelling warts-and-all authenticity about it.

'Muslim society has never been completely mosque-going . . . I know people who pimp and do drugs and mad stuff and still go to mosque. We are all messed up. I know kids I grew up with in Bradford, some of them amazing, some of them full of shit, just the same as my punk mates in London. Just the same as everyone. There are no rules about it, no clear lines of demarcation.'

His conversation was occasionally as gnomic and sage-like as his lyrics.

'We're just another football league,' he said at one point. 'Not premier league maybe, but we're still the same as you. It doesn't need a superior intellectual analysis to break things down and see that we're all fucked.'

Like Alyas, he had a street appeal that the outreach officials of Prevent could only dream of. He, too, had fallen foul of Muslim conservatives, and stood up to them. The music-averse Deobandis, in particular, objected when he overdubbed some lines from the Koran on one of his early albums.

'People rang up threatening to burn our office down. But we didn't run away. We went into a Muslim radio talk show with a Koran and said, tell us where it says music is haram?'

Bollywood movies in the mid 1980s, he added, were full of Koranic recitation, yet no one complained.

'The truth is that the Koran is full of music. It is incredibly poetic. And what is the adhan if it is not music? The tuning is amazing . . . it's pure musical notation.'[9]

The Home Office, he said, understood that music like his spoke to some young Muslims in a way that the mosques never could and wanted to exploit that power.

'They've been trying it through the hip-hop scene recently – picking up Muslim artistes as a kind of backdrop to speaking out,' he said. 'But I did that ten years ago with *All is War*, and all I got was people talking about arresting me.'

I asked him how he felt his overall mission, to 'normalize' the British Muslim Asian experience, was going.

'It's going terribly,' he said bluntly. 'I've failed.'

I had to agree that, twenty-five years after Aki Nawaz's career began, it was still not considered 'normal' to be a Muslim in Britain, in the way that, say, British Judaism feels normal. Racist snobbery maybe played a role in that, since Judaism is commonly treated as a white, culturally European religion. Yet neither Hinduism nor Sikhism hangs around the necks of their adherents as Islam does. Islam seems to challenge the Anglo-Saxon sense of identity in a way that other religions do not. Perhaps Christianity is more important to the Anglo-Saxon sense of self than our god-less society realizes, and we are all still subconsciously fighting the Crusades. Talking to Aki Nawaz made me think of Prince Charles, the future supreme governor of the Church of England, who once suggested changing the old Tudor title, *Fidei defensor* (Defender of the Faith) to 'Defender of the Faiths' or even to 'Defender of Faith'. Like Archbishop Rowan Williams who once spoke up for sharia, he was attacked and derided for his gentle inclusive ambition. The ideas of both men, it seemed to me, were mistaken only in that they were ahead of their time.

Meanwhile, in the present, Nawaz felt that the stakes were higher than ever for British Muslims. He said that John F. Kennedy's observation that 'if we make peaceful revolution impossible, we make violent revolution inevitable' – a statement that appears in graffiti form in the video that accompanied the release of his track 'Cookbook DIY' – remained as true today as it was fifty years ago. And yet he hadn't entirely given up, and indeed felt encouraged by Jeremy Corbyn's rise to the top of the Labour party.

'Maybe he can help us get to that level of normalization,' he mused. 'They say he's unelectable, but what is wrong with being too nice? What do you want: Hitler? Trump? What *is* this obses-sion we seem to have with icons of strength?'

The political fervour of his punk heyday still burned within him.

9

#NotinmyName

Luton

THE MOST I KNEW of Luton before 2016 was its airport. Like every Briton of my generation, I remember those famous Campari advertisements of the 1970s and thought of the town as at best a transit point or else as a place to escape from. By casting Luton as the dreary antithesis of Paradise, Lorraine Chase had done the town's public relations no favours at all.

In the intervening years it has garnered a more evil reputation as one of the country's most prolific producers of extremists. Anjem Choudary's al-Muhajiroun was based here before it was banned. Luton was also the birthplace of Tommy Robinson, who set up the English Defence League in 2009 in response to al-Muhajiroun demonstrators when they burned poppies in the town centre in protest at a parade of troops come home from Iraq.

Non-violent extremism, moreover, has a habit of turning violent in Luton. The 7/7 bombers who met here before setting off to attack London Transport in 2005 were not one-offs. Two other terrorist cells had been uncovered in Luton the previous year. A Luton man blew himself up in Stockholm in 2010. In 2013, police arrested four local men, all of whom had received terrorist training in Pakistan, in connection with a plot to blow up a local Territorial Army Centre using a remote-controlled toy car. In 2015, Luton father-of-two Abu Rahin Aziz fled to Syria and became an ISIS bomb-maker; in 2016, Junead Khan was convicted of plotting to murder an American airman at RAF Lakenheath. The list is so long, it makes Luton sound like a bomb factory. From private conversations with senior politicians and intelligence officials, I knew that Luton's Muslims worried them more than those of any other town or city, Bradford and Birmingham included – and that alone called for investigation.

But Luton also drew me for another reason. Its proximity to the capital makes it a gateway of opportunity for all Muslims, not just aspiring suicide bombers. It is also a noted entry point to Britain for new migrants. Luton came up in my conversations with Muslims almost everywhere I went in the country. Its Muslim population is young and energetic and ethnically very mixed, and when its leaders speak out, which they often do with verve and confidence, it is as though they speak for all British Muslims. I recognized long before I went there that it was a crucial piece of the jigsaw and that if I did not get to grips with this town, my portrait of al-Britannia would be incomplete.

I spent days there, but came away with no conclusive explanation for its tendency to extremism. It had characteristics with which I had become all too familiar – the warp-speed demographic change, the urban poverty, the dreary lack of economic opportunity for the young – yet there was nothing about it that I saw or heard that might explain its particular history of terrorism.

'Luton's problem is parenting,' said the Asian cab driver who took me into town on my first visit. 'The kids all want to get rich quick. All the drug-dealers around here are Muslim. But that's got nothing to do with Islam.'

He made his own three boys go to mosque twice a week.

'You have to, to keep them on the right path.'

He reminded me of Jahangir Akbar, the Luton-born Trojan Horse teacher whose career began here with an impassioned mission to help the next generation through Islam. Luton's drug-dealers thrive on the proximity of London, the country's biggest market for them. I suspected that the difference between rich and poor, the perceived glitz and glamour of the big city and drab old Luton, was more keenly felt here than in some northern Muslim towns precisely because the capital is so near. The town, my cab driver confided, sometimes felt a 'rubbish' place to live.

The town is, nevertheless, special. Bury Park, the suburb around which Luton's 52,000 Muslims cluster, is one of those places repeatedly described as a 'no-go zone' for non-Muslims by rightwing American think tanks,[1] but of course it is far from being that. What I found was a community more spirited, resilient, intelligent and proactive in its determination to counter extremism than any other I had come across in Britain. The years of obloquy, furthermore, have turned its leaders into experts not just at fielding questions about extremism, but also at presenting themselves in a benign alternative light.

The most obvious example was Dawood Masood, the 20-year-old son of the imam of Luton Central Mosque, who responded to ISIS's murder of aid worker Alan Henning in 2014 by launching an online campaign called #NotinmyName. This quickly went viral, with 9 million hits in a single day – and Dawood, in his geeky glasses, a parka and pill-box hat, briefly became the public face not just of Luton's Muslim youth, but of Britain's. He was named Bedfordshire's Young Person of the Year in 2015, received a Child of Courage community award, and was invited to meet the Queen. I went to meet him at the al-Hira Islamic education centre that he manages for his father, where he answered my questions with the polish of a seasoned professional. In the last eighteen months, he told me, he had given no fewer than 150 media interviews.

'Luton is everyone's favourite whipping boy. We get referenced every time something happens – Alan Henning, the Brussels and Paris attacks – and it isn't fair,' he said.

It surely isn't. No mosque in Luton, including and perhaps particularly the main Salafist one, has ever supported violent extremism. As long ago as 2002, when a posse of al-Muhajiroun attempted to preach in the town, some local Salafists drove them off in a much-celebrated fist-fight. They wanted nothing to do with a group who had recently described the 9/11 attackers as 'the magnificent 19'. The Luton Salafist imam, Abdul Qadir Baksh, has been promoting the message ever since that Salafism is not the same thing as extremism.

'These ignorant misfits who have an acute lack of knowledge of the true teachings of Islam have ruined the image of Islam and the Muslims,' he said in 2013. 'We the majority who preach peace, tolerance and good manners have been silent at our own peril.'[2]

I was interested by Baksh. His outspokenness made him a potentially powerful ally of the counter-extremist campaign. As the *Independent* journalist Memphis Barker wrote: 'What is more likely to persuade a 16-year-old already agog at ISIS propaganda – a Westminster voice preaching British values? Or a local one that says, yes, an Islamic Caliphate is a desirable thing, but ISIS's is not legitimate, nor is the violence it uses.' Barker argued that instead of vilifying Salafists, the government would be wise to speak to them, and 'even, perhaps, quietly promote their peaceful views – however offputting the whole package – as an alternative to ISIS'.[3]

But Baksh had been vilified. A small primary school annexed to his Islamic centre, the Olive Tree, was linked to the Trojan Horse affair when Ofsted inspectors found two books in the staff room, one of them called *The Ideal Muslim,* which condoned among other things the beating of 10-year-olds who didn't pray properly. I later heard from an Olive Tree teacher who insisted that the book was for 'the information of the staff only', that there was 'a big difference between providing information about a topic and promoting it', and that the pupils were never beaten.

The children's parents also came to the Olive Tree's defence. Yet the school was still declared 'inadequate', and the mud of course stuck in the press, which reported that the books found in the staff room 'promoted stoning'.[4]

I approached Baksh for an interview but found him reluctant to talk. Or rather, he told me that he would talk to me, but only if I paid him for the privilege.

'I apologize if I sound rude but my time is valuable, and the number of people that come for interviews and information is actually disturbing,' he emailed.

No British Muslim interviewee had ever asked me for money before. His rebuff spoke volumes about the community's impatience with their usual media portrayal and the constant demands to apologize and explain. I was not disheartened. On the contrary, I gave a silent cheer for his testiness, or at least for the stubborn pride and self-confidence (and entrepreneurialism) that underpinned it – qualities lacking in other divided towns I had visited but which are surely essential if they are ever to heal themselves.

Another example of local self-confidence was a drop-in centre called Discover Islam, in a former bank in the main shopping precinct. Set up in 2011 and still entirely funded by public donation, it operated as a kind of safety valve for Islamophobia. There was no other centre like it in the country. Non-Muslims were invited not just to come in and learn about the religion that has become so prevalent in their town, but also to vent their frustrations at it.

'The news drives people in,' said Sufian Sadiq, its chairman. 'Some come in shouting and swearing. I think that's brilliant. It takes them off the net forums. We give them a cup of tea, and they end up saying things like, "All Muslims are scum – apart from you, of course." '

Discover Islam ironically owed its existence to the town's most notorious Muslim-baiter, the EDL founder Tommy Robinson.

'He's a Lutonian like me,' said Sadiq (who once studied psychology at Luton Sixth Form College alongside another famous scion, Nadiya Hussain from *Bake Off*). 'He wasn't always so angry, and he's civil when you meet him in person . . . He challenged us. He said, "If you don't support al-Muhajiroun, why don't you come out and tell us what the truth is?" He said he didn't want to go to a mosque or to Bury Park to talk about it because it made people like him feel "uncomfortable". We thought that was a fair point.'

Following a survey of 2,000 local Muslims, the original idea for a library-style information point was rejected in favour of something more welcoming: tea, sandwiches and comfortable furniture arranged by a sunny window. It was also decided to make the centre culturally 'neutral', for instance by avoiding any Arabic calligraphy on the shopfront and anything overtly (or covertly) Koranic inside. Sadiq and his committee also kept firmly out of local politics, and a low profile generally, including talking to journalists. Whatever else it was, Discover Islam definitely wasn't public relations window dressing.

'We would lose focus if we allowed ourselves to be current-affairs-driven,' said Sadiq. 'I get a hundred media requests a year. You're only the second one I've agreed to.'

The centre was full of racks of second-hand school clothes when I visited, giving it something of the atmosphere of a charity shop. It also organized a 'curry kitchen' for the homeless, doling out up to 150 meals to the town's shelters every Friday.

'We are like the Salvation Army and Age Concern! But we are *not* in the business of religious propaganda. We go about our business quietly.'

The project, he thought, was working. Both EDL and al-Muhajiroun had 'lost traction' since 2011. In another mark of success, Sadiq had been approached by Muslim leaders in Birmingham and London who wanted to replicate the Discover Islam formula, although he had declined to help them.

'It isn't something you can just parachute in. It has to be grassroots-driven.'

My guide for one Luton day was Samia, a young journalist student I had met at a conference in London, who epitomized the new generation's impatience with conservative tradition and hunger for change. Not every young Muslim woman would have agreed so readily to show a lone white male around Bury Park. At one point, as we strolled together along Dunstable Road, the area's busy main shopping drag, she was tutted at in Urdu by an older woman in a hijab. Samia, her hair uncovered and her shoulders draped in a bright red coat with a collar of fur, answered back.

'She was basically calling me a tart,' Samia smirked afterwards. 'I told her it was none of her business. No one tells me how I should behave.'

She took me to meet Mohammed Nadeem, an entrepreneur once described by BBC's *Inside Out* as 'Luton's answer to Alan Sugar'. His shiny new restaurant at the top of Dunstable Road, the Nadeem Plaza, is a local landmark, popular for the all-day halal breakfasts it serves for £3.49. With its four floors, roof garden and round glass street front, it dominates the surrounding area like the prow of an oncoming ship. There was a Land Cruiser parked by his office (Numberplate: N17DEM), the right car for the man himself, with his bald head, a wrestler's physique and a flashy gold watch to match. The corridor outside was decorated with a photograph of Bury Park a hundred years ago and an expansive display of framed community investment awards. A pinboard cluttered with cheeky inspirational aphorisms also seemed to typify the area's brash, raspberry-blowing spirit. *Kill them with success, Bury them with a smile!* I read. *If people are talking about you behind your back, then just fart.*

Nadeem headed a group called the Bury Park Business Corporation. On the front edge of his oversized desk was a small wall of business cards for local enterprises: a letting agency, a private GP practice, a wedding car-hire firm called A1 Phantoms Ltd. Like the mosques, Luton's many Asian small businessmen had long been at war with the radicals, who by impugning the reputation of the town were also damaging trade. al-Muhajiroun's poppy-burning stunt in 2009, he recalled, was a turning point for many of them.

'The police defended them on the grounds of free speech. We were cheesed off with that.'

Nadeem presented me with a fat file of cuttings from the *Luton News* detailing the campaign that he organized in response. *On the Brink*, I read. *Angry Shopkeepers hit out at al-Muhajiroun radicals who are accosting people in Bury Park.*

'It's our town,' he said. 'I get emotional when people talk bad of it. These people bring shame to our community. Bury Park is not a no-go zone.'

Posters went up in almost every shop in Dunstable Road, warning that anyone associated with al-Muhajiroun would not be served.

'We are Brits. Those soldiers they insulted were our soldiers, too. I hate those guys. I've had threats. But when they go about the place telling people that voting is haram, even while they are claiming benefits? I mean, come on.'

He insisted that Luton was a 'warm, loving place', but it was also one that could show teeth when necessary, to fill the void left by officialdom. He worked closely with the police, whose community relations work had 'improved' since 2009, although it was still not what it should be, thanks in part to funding cuts.

'You can wait eight hours for a robbery response around here. The Crime Commissioner came to us asking for money for more beat bobbies, which is ridiculous.'

He added that Luton's MPs were 'useless', although in contrast to the radicals he opposed, he was a staunch defender of democracy. It was, he believed, a civic duty to vote. At the last election, he had deliberately put up posters in his restaurant promoting both Labour *and* Conservative, although he drew the line at UKIP. He was particularly contemptuous of a UKIP candidate in Bristol, John Langley, who was revealed in 2015 to have a second life as a porn film actor called Johnny Rockard.

Nadeem was just as scathing about Luton's Muslim councillors and the continuing baleful influence of biradari politics.

'They can't speak a flipping word of English. I went to the inauguration of our new Muslim mayor the other day. A Bangladeshi, Tahir Khan. He could barely read his own speech. I was so embarrassed. We're trying to break into this by promoting younger councillors who can speak properly for us. We've got two or three youngsters here who went to Oxbridge.'

He clearly had clout in Luton, as much and maybe more than the town's two dozen mosques. The small shops and businesses of Bury Park felt like the engine of this community, not the imams; and the business corporation Nadeem had set up was surely leading it in a direction of which any British government could approve.

We talked about Syria and the town's terrorist problem. Shutting down radicals like Anjem Choudary, he conceded, was only part of the solution. British foreign policy in the Middle East remained a cause of genuine anger in Luton; the council needed to engage more, and better, with the town's vulnerable youth, while the government's counter-extremism policies had so far succeeded only in further alienating them.

'But you know what? We are still very lucky to live in this country. We are free to practise our religion and our culture – and in return, we should respect the law.'

Samia took me back down Dunstable Road to chat to the shopkeepers. With its grocery displays of okra and chilli, its Haji & Sons halal butchers, a fashion shop called Memsaab and money shops offering to turn gold into cash, it was an uncompromisingly Asian market street, reminiscent of Southall or Manningham. It was not difficult to see why Muslim radicals

239

might view it as a promising recruiting ground – and not difficult, either, to see why it might attract the attentions of the far
right.

We spoke to a jeweller, Bill Kumar, an Indian Punjabi who had
been trading in the area since 1965: the founder of a family business, now in its third generation. He was old enough to remember
the National Front, who were frequent visitors to Luton in the
1970s and sometimes smashed in shop windows. Britain First,
their ideological heirs, were also regulars in Dunstable Road
and had mounted one of their 'Christian patrols' there only two
months previously, leafleting and accosting passers-by right
outside Kumar's shop.

'They are idiots. I am not even Muslim,' Kumar observed.

He whipped out a smartphone and logged on to YouTube.
Paul Golding and Jayda Fransen leapt to life on the small cracked
screen, still carrying their absurd white crosses.

'This isn't about ethnicity,' I heard Jayda say. 'This is about
religion. Britain is a Christian country.'

Bury Park didn't take this provocation lying down.

'Fuck you,' shouted a white-coated vendor outside the Deshi
Mass Bazzar. 'This is our country. It's not a Christian country.
Are you jealous we're taking over?'

'Ooh, taking over, are you?' said Jayda, for the camera.

'We've already got it, mate,' said the vendor, a little strangely.
'We're loving it here.'

Knots of young Asian men began to gather. There was some
shoving and more bad language. An egg was thrown. Britain
First beat a retreat.[5]

Golding and his twenty fellow patrollers had overstepped the
mark in Bury Park. Unlike in Dewsbury, they were all identi-
cally dressed in olive green fleeces and hats badged with Britain
First insignia. *Rule Britannia*, the badge read, beneath a lion, a
crown and a Union Jack, and their slogan *Taking Our Country
Back*. They looked like a militia – and the following month,

Bedfordshire police arrested Golding for 'wearing a uniform with political objectives', an offence under the Public Order Act of 1936, which was originally passed to curb the activities of Oswald Mosley's Blackshirts. Both Golding and Jayda Fransen ended up with fines for their clothes. Fransen was later additionally found guilty of 'religiously aggravated harassment' for telling a niqabi – Sumayyah Sharpe, out shopping with her four young children – that Muslim men forced women to cover up to avoid being raped 'because they cannot control their sexual urges'. In a Facebook video afterwards, Fransen commented: 'It was just absolutely absurd in the court. It was just a really clear display of Islamic appeasement . . . We have an establishment that is against anything patriotic in this country.'

Golding added: 'The fact of the matter is, it's one rule of law for Muslims, the protected species in this country, and another for British people.'[6]

I later went to meet Ashfaque Chowdhury, the head teacher of Al-Hikmah, an independent faith school on Dunstable Road outside which Britain First had also demonstrated. I had seen no support for Golding and Fransen in the YouTube footage Bill Kumar showed me, but you didn't have to walk far to see where they might have found some. Immediately behind the school was an end-of-terrace house that had been turned into a fortress, with heavy grilles on all the windows, a burglar alarm and a CCTV camera to the side, while up above a cross of St George hung limply from a flagpole. Tucked in next to the house was a big white van, of the type known as a Luton High Top because so many of them were once manufactured at the vast Vauxhall motor plant on the edge of town. As a symbol of local white pride the van was actually ambiguous, since it was jobs at the plant that had drawn so many Asian workers to Luton in the first place, turning the town into the ethnic hodge-podge it has become. I took a surreptitious photograph of the house anyway. Visually, at least, it was a parody of the Britain First demographic.

I waited for Chowdhury in a reception area prominently decorated with Ofsted-friendly posters that spelled out all the Home Office-defined fundamental British values beneath another Union Jack. This building, too, was protected by CCTV cameras. Under a welcome sign reading *Hola! Bienvenu! Benvenuto!*, the receptionist watched a bank of sixteen different screens showing all the approaches to the building, as well as an empty car park.

There was a pronounced atmosphere of discipline and calm at Al-Hikmah. Through the open door of a staff office I spied a 14-year-old boy in the school's uniform, a flowing white shalwar and kufi cap, cross-legged on the floor and facing a wall: a miscreant, I guessed, awaiting sentence when his teacher returned. Ashfaque eventually appeared and, it being Friday, invited me to observe the school at prayers. I sat at the back and watched a hundred teenage schoolboys bow and prostrate themselves, their close-packed forms resembling furniture under dustsheets, then a mogul field in a ski resort.

'So, what do you think?' said Ashfaque afterwards. 'Do you see any extremism here? Do you see anything wrong?'

He took me for coffee at Jimmy's, a multi-cuisine self-service restaurant in the town centre, whose owner he knew and who didn't charge him. We were joined by Inspector Hob Hoq, the head of the community policing team, a jovial Bangladeshi with a 'Luton in Harmony' badge shaped like two musical notes pinned to his tie. He was keen to tell me that Bedfordshire police had 'learned a lot' since the poppy-burning incident in 2009.

'It hasn't been repeated. al-Muhajiroun's ringleaders have all either been arrested or are awaiting trial.'

They were just as tough on extremists from the other side. After the Britain First patrol, Hoq had spent eight hours with Ashfaque going through CCTV footage from the school, looking for any material that might be actionable. Bedfordshire police these days, he said proudly, were a 'flagship force' for the National Community Tension Team, to whom they reported weekly; the NCTT reported upwards in turn to the Cabinet Office. He added that South Yorkshire police, the unfortunate force blamed for the Rotherham grooming scandal and its fall-out, not to mention Hillsborough and Orgreave, were due to visit Luton soon to see how community policing should be done.

He shrugged when I ask why Luton has produced so many actual or suspected terrorists.

'It's not a rich town. There's a lot of deprivation. Then again, I came from nothing myself. And Luton is no different to, say, St Albans or Harpenden.'

At the same time, he acknowledged that Luton was a 'diffi-cult' town to police, with a level of gun and drug crime so high that Channel 4 made a programme about it as part of their series *24 Hours in Police Custody*. He told me about a recent spate of 'Asian gold' burglaries, targeting the dowry gifts and heirlooms typically amassed by traditional Asian families. When one suspected case ended in the murder of Saima Khan, a mother of four, a local vigilante patrol sprang up, organized through Facebook.

'It was getting out of hand. There were thousands of people out on the streets after dark,' Hoq recalled – although things calmed down again when the culprit turned out not to be a gang of outsiders but Saima Khan's younger sister.

As a Muslim brought up in Luton, Hoq said he got 'real intel' from the community.

'There was an honour-based job not too long ago – I got involved in that,' he said.

But it was startling to learn that he was the only Muslim among Bedfordshire's 1,000-plus police officers, and that the community cohesion team he headed numbered just five.

'It's the government's austerity cuts. We used to have a dedi-cated schools officer, who built relationships with the kids. We need that back or we'll be in trouble. You've got to get to them when they're young.'

In the absence of more Inspector Hoqs, Luton's Muslims perhaps had no choice but to continue to police themselves.

My guide, Samia, took me to the Nadeem Plaza to meet Abdul Majid Ali, who turned out to be another British Muslim first for me: a TV imam in the style of an American network evangelizer. He was as flamboyant as a gameshow host, a huge man with a booming laugh, white teeth flashing in a luxuriant black beard and a bouffant, centrally parted hairdo. He was also wearing an immense silver three-piece suit.

'There's a girl coming to see my son today,' he explained with a wink, 'and this is what I wear on my TV show. It's how her parents know me.'

Majid Ali is a Bombay Gujarati who moved to Luton ten years ago from Dubai, where he worked for the Ministry of Religion. He hadn't always been an imam. Until the mid-1980s, he said, he had been an atheist who wanted to become a scientist. He was also a former Shotokan karate cage fighter – one of the top ten in the UAE, he said. 'I only weighed twelve stone then. Now I weigh twenty, ha-ha!'

His confident, self-deprecating humour made him hard to dislike.

'I know Bollywood stars who love to come here for hair plantation, but it never works and they are jealous of my hairstyle, ha-ha!'

For the last eight years he had appeared every Saturday evening on the London-based Islam Channel as one of the stalwarts of *IslamiQa*, the channel's longest-running and best-known series, in which Muslim scholars answer phoned-in questions from viewers. Majid Ali, whose TV personality name is Babu – Father – claimed that his audience numbered 'in the millions'. This wasn't implausible: although aimed at British Muslims, *IslamiQa* attracts satellite viewers from as far away as Nigeria and Uganda. When he wasn't preaching on TV he taught Islamic classes at his curiously named Islamwood Foundation Centre.

'It's not Hollywood, it's not Bollywood. It's Islamwood!' he roared, with a flourish of his meaty hands.

Like the American TV evangelists he seemed to emulate, he knew his holy texts by heart and spat appropriate religious quotes with staccato efficiency. He was also an irrepressible spouter of jingly aphorisms.

'Have your plans for life worked out? No? That's because someone else is making plans for you!' he said, pointing a finger at the ceiling.

His theology was Salafi-Wahhabi, although he didn't admit to it, not even informally over lunch. As a Gujarati married to a Pakistani wife, by whom he had eight children, Majid Ali was a cheerful but fervent non-sectarian.

'The Prophet was clear. Koran 3,103: "Hold fast to the rope of Allah all together, and do not separate. Let there be a community among you." I am just Muslim. We are all just Muslims.'

His non-sectarian style had not endeared him to everyone in Luton. As a blow-in from Dubai, he was perhaps an awkward fit. He once preached at the Salafi Islamic Centre but that association came to an end because, he said, he had been 'too lenient'. Luton's Salafis, he observed later on, refused to pray behind the Barelwi imams at the Central mosque. But if anything he seemed to relish his outsider's status, supported as it was by his success as a TV personality, his charisma, and of course his faith.

'I support the public, not the leaders, because they play divide and rule,' he said. 'Being a Gujarati is sometimes a problem. There is a perception that Indian Muslims aren't "proper" Muslims. But I don't get racist abuse because I'm a huge guy! And people like my smile. There is a hadith: "Greeting your brother with a smiling face is charity."'

In the end he felt not just comfortable in his adopted town but proud of it.

'Bury Park is a peaceful place and the people are lovely. Its bad reputation is grossly overblown. Muslim people sometimes contact me and ask, "Where should I live in Britain?" And I always tell them, "Luton!"'

He made a point of holding his doors open to everyone, including the extremists.

'Tommy Robinson is a young boy who needs guiding. Koran 3, 64: "Invite the non-believers to discuss the similarities." But Rome wasn't built in a day.'

He quarrelled also with hardline Islamists, including some of the children of the town's al-Muhajiroun activists, whom, very interestingly, he had taught in his religious centre for the last four years.

'These kids are not welcome anywhere else and their parents have been banned from all the mosques. But they are only children and they are part of our community. There is a hadith: "Humanity is like a body; if your finger hurts, all the body feels it."'

There were, he thought, at least eighteen families in Luton who had been ostracized by the Muslim mainstream. Some of their children had dangerous ideas, such as believing it was haram to have any dealings with the kuffar.

'I tell them to take a coin out of their pocket and I show them the Queen's head on it and I say, "So what's this?" Their parents might disagree with my teachings, but they haven't got the guts to argue with me, except at election time, ha-ha!'

These children sounded precisely the sort who should have been picked up by the Home Office Channel programme for 're-education'. Perhaps they had been: Majid Ali declined to confirm or deny that he cooperated with the authorities when I asked him, although it didn't seem at all likely. I looked him up online afterwards and found that in 2010, following a complaint by Quilliam, he had been censored by Ofcom for an Islam Channel broadcast in which he advised that it was permissible for a husband to physically punish his wife. He also described women who wore perfume in public as 'prostitutes'. Neither position was remotely acceptable or compatible with the mores of modern Britain.[7]

I found the Ofcom charges hard to square with the man I had met, jovial, sociable, impatient with dogma, and entirely comfortable in my and Samia's company in the Nadeem Plaza. The thrust of his message, like the man himself, seemed shot through with common sense and a forgiving faith in humanity, which is surely precisely what is needed to draw the poison of extremist ideology. Whatever his faults, I thought it was better by far that al-Muhajiroun's children should receive Islamic instruction from someone like him than to receive none at all, or else to hear it only from their parents at home.

'Koran 2:78,' said Majid Ali. '"Some of them are illiterate, knowing nothing of the Book but wishful thinking. They only speculate. Woe to those who write the Book with their own hands and then say, 'This is from Allah' to sell it for a paltry price."'

In a complex, roundabout way, Majid Ali was yet another example of Luton Muslims' ability to police themselves, as well, perhaps, as their ballsy insistence that they could manage without interference from outside.

In November 2016, Luton Muslim impatience with outsiders reached a new level, when twenty-six local mosques and Islamic centres – that is, almost all of them – wrote to Trevor Holden, the Chief Executive of Luton Borough Council, announcing that they were formally withdrawing their support for the 'ineffective' and 'unjust' Prevent programme until it was fully reviewed. The government, they said, appeared to have 'genuinely misunderstood' Islam and the point that extremism violated its basic principles.

'Followers of Islam are known as "the middle nation" due to their adherence to God's path of balance and justice,' said the letter, which continued:

'We have consistently and unequivocally spoken out against terrorism and violent extremism. However, we believe that the Prevent strategy is counter-productive and cannot work in any shape or form. We cannot lend our support to policies which have damaged our communities.'[8]

Was the government's counter-extremism strategy unravelling? It seems unlikely to succeed without the support of communities that loom as large as Luton's in the national Muslim psyche. Without partnership and trust, it is useless. The government, I suspect, will soon be forced to think again about its approach. What race relations model might it follow in the future? There is one place where the relationship between Muslims and the authorities appears healthier than anywhere in England, a place that surprised me not least because it concerns the community nearest to my own home – in Scotland.

10

Asians in Kilts

Glasgow

ONE SUNNY SATURDAY IN Glasgow in 2014, not long before
the referendum on Scottish independence, I stumbled across a
Scotland Says Yes rally in full swing in George Square. As it was
through much of the Yes campaign that summer, the atmosphere
was triumphalist, so certain were its supporters that they were
going to win – at least in Glasgow. The crowds wore blue and
white paint on their faces and waved the Saltire flag or the Lion
Rampant in red and yellow. Rousing speeches were bookended
by snatches of tunes by The Proclaimers. Two lads in tails and
monocles posed for photographs, one with a sign around his
neck that read, *Lord Snooty and his chums. END TORY RULE FOR
EVER!* It all seemed like business as usual for the Scottish
National Party, until I saw this: a posse of bearded young Asians,
all wearing kilts, marching purposefully towards the square
from Buchanan Street, pumping their fists in unison to a chant
of 'Free-dom'.

It was a novel take on *Braveheart*. I had always viewed the SNP
as an essentially indigenous movement, a club for people who
considered themselves to be 'true Scots', as defined by their colour, their accent, their dislike of the English and their surnames
beginning with Mc. The SNP, surely, was for people of heritage,
hefted to the braes and glens, whose veins ran not with blood
but with pints of heavy or Barr's Irn Bru. These Asians, it was

true, spoke in the right accent but the rest didn't fit at all. What were they doing in George Square?

Later, on the train home to Edinburgh, I felt disquieted. As an English-born half-Scot I was wholly against the notion of Scottish independence. I disliked vacuous political slogans – who didn't? – yet I really did agree with the one adopted by the No Campaign: 'Better Together'. I defined myself as, and still feel, British. I cared about that concept and didn't want England and Scotland to be driven apart in any way. I was also sick of the referendum campaign, which had dominated all conversation for months, polarizing opinion everywhere. The SNP leader, Alex Salmond, called the public debate on independence a 'joyous festival of democracy', but I knew of a woman who had been punched in the face for disagreeing with the Nats, and another with a NO sticker on her car whose tyres had been slashed. For the first time in ten years of living in Edinburgh, my English accent felt like a liability.

The Asians in kilts, however, had shaken my unionist convictions. I had the ignoble thought that their support for the Nationalists was somehow disloyal. These young Glasgow Muslims were the sons or grandsons of migrants who had come to make a new life in a country called *Britain*. Did they have no conscience? A nice house-guest does not threaten his host. How dare they join in – and so passionately and colourfully – with those chauvinists in George Square who wanted to break the country up? Besides, they weren't *from* here and had only lived in Scotland for about five minutes. What right did they have to question the 300-year-old Act of Union that underpinned our country?

This was all nonsense, of course. Emotions ran high in those pre-referendum days and I too had been spell-struck by the malevolent spirit of the day. Anyone resident in Scotland had the right to vote. Furthermore, they were 'from here': that was what they were demonstrating with the kilts. I could trace my Scottish ancestors on my father's side back for centuries, but that was only part of the definition of Scottishness, and not necessarily the paramount one. As second- or third-generation Asians they had likely been born in Scotland, on which measure they were more Scottish than me.

I saw that I might have underestimated the SNP. Until this moment I had dismissed their talk of forging a new kind of Scotland, modern, diverse and inclusive, as so much nationalist cant. Their supporters' vision of independence seemed a backward-looking one driven by nostalgia and victimhood; their antipathy towards the English suggested they wanted a society based on a very narrow ethnic identity. But those fervent kilted Asians showed that the rhetoric about inclusiveness was not empty after all. Their confidence and enthusiasm for the cause were breathtaking. They were engaged in the domestic political process in a way that I had seen nowhere else in Britain, not as passive, biradari-style block-voters, but as equal participants in a popular revolution, shouting as loudly as everyone else. It was actually heartwarming, thrilling, to watch. I wondered, later, if it could even be a model for the rest of the country to follow. The government in Westminster wanted British Muslims to integrate. Maybe political enfranchisement of this sort, the offer of a genuine stake in a different kind of future, was the way to achieve that. The SNP had promised those Asians a chance to reset the old status quo and they had grabbed it. The irony was not lost on me that it was at a rally for the break-up of Britain that I first and most clearly saw al-Britannia in the making.

The Asians I saw were no anomaly. Exit polls when the referendum finally came around suggested that 64 per cent of Scotland's 90,000 Asians had voted for independence. They had, traditionally, been strong Labour supporters. Persuading so many of them to switch allegiance was quite a coup for the SNP. I was curious to know how they'd done it, and in the late summer of 2016 I got a chance to ask Alex Salmond himself. He had resigned as Scotland's First Minister in 2014 and become a Westminster MP again, so it was in London that we met, over glasses of white wine on the terrace of the House of Commons overlooking the Thames. He was, as I had suspected, very proud of his party's appeal to Asian Scots.

'It was always our policy to welcome all minorities into the community,' he said. 'There's something good about a people claiming their rightful place in society.'

The allegiance of Asian Scots, he explained, was the fruit of a long and carefully thought-out campaign. The key moment came in 1995, when Salmond was invited to address the biggest grassroots Muslim organization in Scotland, the Pakistan Welfare Trust. Not everyone at the PWT was keen to have him: the perception in those days was that the SNP were at bottom a party of racists, like the BNP – unlike Labour, who were seen almost axiomatically as the party of immigrants. Salmond shared the floor that night with the senior Labour MP Donald Dewar, taking the floor immediately after him.

'I made a point of addressing them in a different way,' Salmond said, drilling me with his intense brown puppy eyes; his famous eyebrows, thick and curiously short, were like a pair of dancing inverted commas. 'Donald's speech was all "We're pleased you work so hard and keep your shops open so late" – the usual. But I compared the Scottish people to a great tartan, in which the Muslims were a key coloured thread. They loved that.'

Salmond had an important ally at the PWT: its SNP-supporting president, Bashir Ahmad, who deliberately put Salmond on after Dewar in order to highlight the difference in his approach. Soon afterwards, Ahmad founded a new organization, Scots Asians for Independence. The text of his inaugural speech was remarkably similar to the words used by Prime Minister David Cameron ten years later, when he was obliged to defend his status as an Old Etonian.

'It isn't important where you come from,' said Bashir. 'What matters is where we are going together as a nation.'

In 2007 when Bashir became the first Muslim and first non-white member of the Scottish Parliament, he took his oath of allegiance at the parliament in Edinburgh in both Urdu and English.

The start of the Iraq War in 2003 provided another important boost for the SNP. The war was supported by all the major parties but was implacably opposed by Salmond, who tried to have Tony Blair impeached. As elsewhere in Britain, a great many Muslims in Scotland were troubled by Iraq and knew then that they had found an Establishment voice for their concerns. Then, in 2007, came the failed suicide attack on Glasgow airport – to date the only Islamist terrorist attack launched on Scottish soil. Salmond went straight to the airport and from there to the Central Mosque where, against the wishes of the Home Secretary in London, Jacqui Smith, he made a point of revealing that the perpetrators were outsiders: Bilal Abdullah, an Iraqi doctor born in Aylesbury, and Kafeel Ahmed, a Saudi-raised engineering student from Bangalore.

'Sometimes you've got to get across the road and give them a hug,' Salmond said. 'Meeting them half way isn't always enough.'

He made the display of public solidarity even more explicit soon after, when he ordered that the 'Welcome to Scotland' sign at the airport be changed to incorporate a large photograph of a young Asian draped in the Saltire.

'I was idolized after that,' Salmond noted.

His gesture also helped to head off any anti-Muslim sentiment among the wider Scottish population following the airport attack, just as it was designed to do. Glasgow's outrage did not express itself on that occasion in the usual wave of Islamophobic abuse, but remained focused on the perpetrators themselves. What every Scot now remembers about the 2007 attack is the role played by a baggage handler, John Smeaton, who assisted the arresting policemen by kicking Kafeel Ahmed as hard as he could in the groin. As he told the media: 'Glasgow doesn't accept this. This is Glasgow; we'll set aboot ye.' Even in their response to terrorism, it seemed, the Scots were somehow different to the English. While Kafeel Ahmed died of self-inflicted burns, 'Smeato' was awarded the Queen's Gallantry Medal, and was so lionized that two years later he stood, albeit unsuccessfully, as an independent candidate in the Glasgow North East by-election.

Salmond's successor as SNP leader, Nicola Sturgeon, continued the tradition of showing solidarity with local Muslims when, following the Paris attacks of 2015, she too immediately visited Glasgow Central Mosque, where she observed a minute's silence for the victims.

'England's politicians could have done the same, but they didn't,' Salmond said, with a subtle toss of his head at the building behind him. 'Our position on Muslim minorities has always been positive. Down here it's the precise opposite.'

There are other reasons for the relative tranquillity of Scotland's race relations. For one thing, Muslims make up less than 2 per cent of the Scottish population, compared to the British national average of 5 per cent. Salmond acknowledged that the competition for places in schools, hospitals or for welfare services is therefore not as intense, even in those parts of south Glasgow with the densest Muslim communities, Pollockshields and Govanhill. In the words of Dr Nasar Meer, a social scientist at the University of Strathclyde, the Scots 'are yet to be really stress-tested by, say, if communities wanted to open sharia councils in Scottish cities, or even a Muslim school. There aren't any currently in Scotland. Then it would be interesting to see the colour of public debate, we may start to see a shift.'[1]

Salmond, nevertheless, maintained that the Scots historically have a much deeper experience of emigration than the English – 'Every Scot you meet has got a distant cousin living somewhere like America or Canada' – and that this had created an intrinsically different attitude to foreigners.

'Scots don't fear immigration because so many of them have been immigrants themselves.'

I thought this was only partly true. I had read a report of how, following the Paris attacks, the Muslim MSP Humza Yousaf received so much hate-mail on social media that the police were called in.

'Humza Yousaf,' said one post. 'Good Scots name. I am sure he is 90% backing Muslim killers. Be having a whip round for terrorist families soon.'[2]

On the other hand, on a recent trip to Glasgow I had fallen into conversation with a local white taxi driver – he was in his late fifties, from the East End, and very old school – who did illustrate what Salmond was getting at.

'When I was growing up, everyone around me was white,' he said. 'In my street, at my school, at the football. They say these Asians don't integrate, but why should they? I don't mind; I've never had any hassle from Asians. My sister lives in Australia, in a neighbourhood packed out with Scots like her. It's natural for people to group together when they're abroad, and if we do, why shouldn't they?'

We were briefly joined on the Commons terrace by another SNP MP, Tasmina Ahmed-Sheikh, a former model and actress who founded the Scottish Asian Women's Association.

'You should ask Tas about Scottish Muslim identity,' Salmond said.

Ahmed-Sheikh, who is half Pakistani, quarter Welsh and quarter Czech, was born in Chelsea, but grew up and was educated in Edinburgh.

'I'm a Scot, first,' she said. 'Then I'm a Scots-Asian Muslim.'

'Scottishness is a very unthreatening identity, easy to adopt,' Salmond went on. 'We've got a lot of Somalis in Glasgow, and Iranian Shia. Sikhs, too. And they've all bought into Scotland's special sense of place. You remember Norman Tebbit's "cricket test" of English citizenship? Well, we don't have that in Scotland.'

I took his point: no one had forced the Asians I saw in George Square to wear kilts. Indeed there is much evidence to suggest that Scottish-Asians have enthusiastically embraced all the overt paraphernalia of being Scottish and ingeniously fused it with their own. The Primark chain does a steady trade in tartan hijabs. In 2012, Scottish Asians even struck their own 'Islamic tartan', with blue checks to represent the Saltire, green ones for the colour of Islam, a black square for the Kaabah in Mecca and five white lines for the pillars of their faith. Best of all, a group of Scottish Asians have turned the annual Burns Night celebration in January into a combined 'Burns-Iqbal Supper', where readings from the works of Pakistan's national poet, Sir Muhammed Iqbal, are heard alongside those of the Scottish bard.

It helped, no doubt, that so many trappings of Scottish identity have been assimilated around the former British Empire. The formal regalia of the Indian army, for instance, includes a tartan; armies all over the world have adopted, and retain, a pipe band for ceremonial occasions. Salmond recounted how in 2007 he went to Colombo in a bid to secure Glasgow as the venue for the 2014 Commonwealth Games.

'We were up against Abuja,' he recalled. 'We pulled every sentimental argument in the book.'

The negotiating team had a lucky break when they heard a performance of the Sri Lanka navy pipe band.

'They were frankly not very good,' he said, 'so I arranged for pipers with two bands from home, the Peat Bog Faeries and the Red Hot Chili Pipers, to come out and teach them, ahead of a Remembrance Day service. The improvement was *dramatic*.'

The poster child of the SNP Muslim scene was Humza Yousaf, who described himself as 'hailing from a bhangra and bagpipes tradition' and who, in 2011 aged 25, became the youngest ever member of the Scottish Parliament. Like his mentor, the late Bashir Ahmad, he took his swearing-in oath in English and then Urdu, as he did on his re-election in 2016. Dressed in a kilt and an elegant dark *sherwani* (a garment based on the nineteenth-century British frock coat, traditionally associated with the Mughal aristocracy), he swaggered down the aisle of Holyrood's debating chamber with the confidence and style of a Vivienne Westwood model on a catwalk.[3] Young, good-looking and married to a white law PhD (and Muslim convert), Gail Lythgoe, Yousaf is the conscious embodiment of the new Asian-Scottish identity.

I went to meet him in his office at Holyrood, a small room with a spectacular view of Salisbury Crags, a map of Scotland on the wall behind him and an almost empty box of chocolates on the table between us.

'Help yersel',' he said. 'Ah'm sorry ah've ate all the guid'ains.'

He explained how both his grandfathers had come to Glasgow to work in the 1950s. Like the vast majority of Scotland's 80,000 Muslims, perhaps three-quarters of them, both were Punjabi. Humza's maternal grandfather, a former railway conductor, found work as a bus conductor in Glasgow. His paternal grandfather, a tailor, worked at the immense Singer sewing machine factory in Clydebank, something of a Glasgow Asian tradition. Punjab, he explained, was 'the affluent, middle class' part of Pakistan. The first migrants were therefore relatively skilled, which meant they found it easier to find work, and therefore integrated faster and perhaps more willingly than elsewhere.

'The experience of people from Mirpur or Baluchistan or Sindh is very different.'

Yousaf confirmed Alex Salmond's story about addressing the annual Pakistan Welfare Trust meeting in 1995 and how the audience there had been 'mesmerized'. The dominance of Punjabis in Scotland, he said, gave the Muslim community a homogeneity unusual in Britain, which made it much easier for non-Muslim politicians to address.

'There were maybe 40,000 Muslims in Scotland by the 1990s but it was still a very, very tight-knit community where everyone knew everybody.'

Some of Glasgow's Muslims were also wealthy, representing another opportunity for a cash-strapped young movement like the SNP that they did not pass up.

'When I was a kid in the late nineties, I remember going to Asian funerals and weddings and seeing Alex and Nicola [Sturgeon] and the party's Chief Executive Mike Russell, and wondering what on earth they were doing there. But they came so often that you'd almost expect it, you saw them just about everywhere.'

Almost every Asian corner shop and restaurant in Pollockshields, he said, still had an old photograph over the till of the owner shaking hands with one or other of the SNP hierarchy.

'You see that and think, blooming heck, how many miles did these guys cover?'

Yet he did not think their gladhanding was entirely cynical.

'I think they genuinely fell in love with the community. It's so hospitable . . . Bashir was famous for feeding the living daylights out of you at his house. You'd almost be physically sick before you left. They had and still have a genuine affection for that community – and it's reciprocated.'

Their groundwork paid off in 2003 when the Iraq War broke out.

'That was the game-changer. Because then you had a second or third generation of Muslims who are more educated, who were born and brought up here, questioning why we blindly voted for Labour just because our mums and dads did it. And now they're attacking another Muslim country, with all the sexed-up dossiers, all the claims about WMDs . . . Iraq completely changed the way I thought about politics.'

It wasn't only Salmond's criticism of the war that chimed with Scottish-Asian sentiment. The SNP waded into the 2006 row over the niqab, started by Foreign Secretary Jack Straw when he revealed that he preferred visitors to his constituency surgery not to wear it.

'It would have been easier for Alex to keep quiet, because many of the public thought Straw had a point. But we opposed it. Alex said, "No man has a right to tell a woman what to wear, period."'

The SNP also made a point of standing up for migrants and refugees, striking a tone 'very different to what you get down south. It's not always popular on the doorstep – and God knows I've had enough doors slammed in my face for it – but we took a stand.'

Glasgow is, in fact, one of Britain's few designated 'reception cities' for refugees. I had seen what this meant for myself in early 2015, when I interviewed a group of Syrian Kurds in a spartan, government-funded flat in the Parkhead area of the city's East End. They were new arrivals, still traumatized by their experiences in Syria and by their journey here. One of them had been whipped by the Shabiya, the Assad regime's feared secret police, who then rubbed salt into his wounds. Another had survived a terrible migrant boat sinking in the Mediterranean in which eighty-one people drowned. They were, naturally, grateful for the safe haven they had been given, and said they had been treated with kindness by Parkhead's locals. On the other hand, life on society's bottom rung in the alien environs of Glasgow was not easy.

'There was no orientation when we arrived, no introduction to your country's laws, so we felt very lost at first,' said Bilal, who had been a trainee nutritionist in Damascus.

One new arrival from Syria had been given an on-the-spot fine of £80 by an environmental health warden for tossing a cigarette butt on the pavement: a near-disaster for a refugee dependent on a job-seeker's allowance of £70 a week.

I wondered if the appeal of Scottish independence was a specifically Pakistani thing. Pakistan, after all, knows a thing or two about decoupling from a larger and older territorial entity. Maybe Scots Asians had unconsciously recast Alex Salmond in the role of Pakistan's founding father, Muhammad Ali Jinnah. But Yousaf said that if anything, Pakistan's history worked against the SNP's campaign, particularly among his grandparents' generation, who remembered Partition as a period of indescribable violence and bloodshed.

'There were some older folk who lived through 1947, and even some of their children, who told me before the referendum, "We support the SNP but, sorry, we're not voting Yes because we don't want to go through that again." I told them it would never happen like that here but they weren't having any of it.'

Yousaf conceded that there were other obstacles to his modernizing agenda, some of them serious. In this, perhaps, Scotland was no different from anywhere else. In March 2016, the police announced they were investigating the management of Glasgow Central mosque for their alleged links to Sipah-e-Sahaba, a Sunni extremist party long proscribed by the British government as a terrorist organization. There was further controversy the same month when the source of a WhatsApp post, which described the recently hanged murderer Mumtaz Qadri as 'a true Muslim', was revealed to be the mosque's senior imam, Maulana Habib Ur-Rehman. Qadri had been the bodyguard of Salman Taseer, the reform-minded Governor of Punjab, who wanted to repeal Pakistan's harsh and archaic blasphemy laws. This was too much for Qadri, a devout and Prophet-worshipping Barelwi, who turned on his employer and shot him twenty-eight times. Yet a great many Barelwis, including British ones, viewed Qadri as a martyr for the faith. His funeral in Rawalpindi was attended by 30,000 people.

While all this was going on, a well-liked newsagent in Glasgow's Shawlands district, Asad Shah, was stabbed and stamped to death outside his shop for the crime of 'disrespecting Islam'. Shah was an Ahmadi, a Sunni sect regarded as heretical by purists, who had overstepped the line with his eccentric assertion, posted on Facebook, that he was the Prophet. It was the third time in a month that the savage sectarianism of the homeland had crept into the SNP's Muslim Eden. It came as scant relief to the shocked residents of Shawlands that the unrepentant perpetrator, taxi driver Tanveer Ahmed, was not a local but had driven all the way from Bradford specifically in order to kill Mr Shah.

'What you are seeing here is a tension between a Pakistani version of Islam conflicting directly with the values we have in Scotland,' said Yousaf. 'I've said before that the politics of home have no place here.'

It was tempting to see the conflict as a straightforward generational split. Younger Glasgow Muslims were forever challenging their elders for control over the Central Mosque, just as they were in cities around England. But Yousaf thought it was more complicated than that, because there were many young Muslims with exactly the same conservative mindset as their elders.

'It's fine to be conservative in your religious practice,' Yousaf went on. 'It's just that it's not always applicable to the circumstances we live in. I get pounded on a regular basis for asking, for example, why on earth we don't have any women on our mosque committees . . . I think it's a disgrace, and if it were up to me I would change it tomorrow. In fact I think there has to be a frank discussion. In my opinion, the reason Islam has survived for 1,400 years is that it has been able to adapt. In Muslim Spain, al-Andalus, there was a Spanish version of Islam that fitted round the context of that country. The same here, I think there has to be a Scottish Islam. That doesn't mean you abandon the tenets of the faith – the belief in one god, the finality of the Prophet – but to think somehow that Pakistani Islam can be replicated here is foolhardy.'

Proportionate to their numbers, Scotland's Muslims have produced notably fewer ISIS jihadis than similarly sized communities in England. Yousaf gave a politician's explanation for that.

'People here are genuinely closer to politics and politicians, so they are better able to vent their anger and frustration,' he said.

Many Muslims I had spoken to in England cited British foreign policy as a major cause of discontent but they seldom did in Scotland, where the hot issues of the Islamic world were often viewed through a very different lens, above all when it came to Palestine. Dundee, after all, is twinned with Nablus, and even Glasgow is twinned with Bethlehem. In 2014 the Labour leader of Glasgow Council, Gordon Matheson, was forced to apologize to the local Jewish community for flying the Palestinian flag above City Chambers in solidarity with the people of Gaza and the West Bank. It was a far cry from English towns like Luton, where the wearing of a 'Free Palestine' badge to school could get a teenager referred to the Home Office under Prevent Duty.[4]

Yousaf nevertheless acknowledged that Glasgow was not immune to Islamist extremism. As everyone knows, radicalization often happens over the Internet, and there was no magic filter for Scotland. The most notorious case was another Shawlands Muslim, the teenage Aqsa Mahmood, who absconded from her well-to-do parents in 2013 to become a jihadi bride in Raqqa, where she became a senior officer in ISIS's feared all-female al-Khansa police force. Mahmood was also implicated in the online radicalization of the Bethnal Green schoolgirls who travelled to Raqqa together in 2015.

Something, clearly, had gone wrong with her religious education. As Yousaf said, the mosques 'don't cater very well for women'. At his suggestion, therefore, I later went to inspect the community's most conspicuous remedy: the al-Meezan Islamic

Centre, an educational institute catering exclusively for girls and young women. I was surprised by the smartness of its neighbourhood when I got there, a moneyed enclave of mansions surrounded by large walled gardens, just across the M8 from the Rangers Ibrox stadium. The centre operated from a former College of Accountancy, whose motto – *Dum Spiro Spero*: While I breathe, I hope – is still emblazoned on a stained-glass window above the grand staircase. Al-Meezan had put up their own motto in the entrance hall: *Balancing Life with Islamic Learning*. Al-Meezan, I Islamically learned, means 'The Scales'.

'We teach Koranic recitation, but we are not a madrassah,' explained the director, Aisha Omar. 'We are not muftis. For definitive answers on matters of Islam, we advise our girls to ask their local imam. We like to think of ourselves as paramedics and them as the surgeons. Our focus is on ethics, morals, values, manners – the foundations you need to be a good Muslim in a non-Muslim land.'

'Sort of life classes, then,' I said.

'Yes. Because Islam is a way of life.'

The centre administered to over six hundred girls from the cradle to the teen years, and had a long waiting list for places. It started in 1998 as a 'travelling circus' of ladies who went around Glasgow's schools teaching girls after-hours classes in the basics of Islam, before expanding into dedicated Sunday classes, and eventually into this building, bought and extended at a total cost of £3.7 million, all raised from the community itself. Aisha led me around classrooms and lecture halls, a soft play area, a canteen, all clean and modern and brightly lit, with a certificate of carbon neutrality up on the wall. Its fifty volunteer staff ran mother-and-toddler sessions, provided food for new mothers, taught young children to read English, and raised a great deal of money for charitable causes, both local and international. A rack of lending books in the reception area gave a flavour of their mission to build pride and confidence in an Islamic identity, with titles like *1001 Inventions and Awesome Facts from Muslim Civilization*, or *A Picnic of Poems in Allah's Green Garden*.

I wondered what Aisha thought about the SNP. Part of the reason Humza Yousaf had suggested I come here was that his mother, Shaista, sat on al-Meezan's board of directors, where she shared responsibility with two others for the centre's education policy. But Aisha wouldn't be drawn: 'We leave politics at the door here,' she said.

She didn't quite give the answer I expected on Scottish identity, either.

'Do I feel Scottish? I don't know what the question means,' she said.

'You've got a Scottish accent.'

'There is a connection, of course. But if I lived in Timbuktu I would have that accent, wouldn't I? It is an outward thing. It doesn't matter where I am "from". What is important is that we are all creatures of God.'

The SNP agenda of inclusiveness, the idea behind Alex Salmond's Great Scottish Tartan, did not strike her as particularly new or revolutionary, however attractive it might be to Scottish Muslims. As she pointed out, the principle of equality was a core Islamic value long before the SNP started promoting it. She did, however, recognize that the Scottish way of life was different to the English one. People were better mannered here, she thought, with more time for one another. Her 21-year-old son had recently visited a family member in London, who reported back that he had driven her crazy with all his pleases and thank-yous.

'She told him, "Stop apologizing for everything, you're not in Glasgow now!"'

I asked about the doctrinal shenanigans at the Central Mosque that she knew I knew had electrified every Glasgow Muslim, but again she refused to comment. Al-Meezan, she insisted, was open to *all* Muslims; when I asked what school of Islamic thought it favoured, she wouldn't, or possibly even couldn't, say.

'We are just Muslims,' she shrugged.

Her own creed, nevertheless, was on the traditionalist end of the spectrum. She personally did not celebrate Mawlid, the Prophet's birthday, which purists (but not Barelwis) disapprove of as a form of *bid'ah*.

Al-Meezan, I understood, was in the business of moral rearmament. Resolutely orthodox, it saw itself as a reassuring bulwark against the more corrupting influences of Western life. Aisha tutted at the 'sexualization' of the state school system; her girls were taught that there should be no free-mixing out in town on Saturday nights. Her line on homosexuality was particularly uncompromising: 'That is a difficulty for Muslims, because the text says it is forbidden and we follow our text. But the problem here is not us – it is that you no longer follow *your* text,' she said. This was not the sort of response, I knew, that would please the last prime minister, who counted the legalization of gay marriage among his government's proudest achievements.

Even so, as a charity dedicated to the development of healthy and confident women, secure in their Muslim identity, I felt sure that al-Meezan was a force for good. It promoted integration but did so on its own terms, not the London government's; and like the taxi driver from the East End who brought me here, I couldn't see much wrong with that. By its own lights, and by the light of Islam, al-Meezan was a model of civic responsibility.

And yet. As I was leaving, Aisha disappeared for a moment before returning, beaming, with two presents: a translation of the Koran and a copy of *Let Us Be Muslims* by Abul A'la Maududi.

'Do you know his work?' said Aisha, when I raised an eyebrow. 'He is very good.'

As the founding father of political Islam in south Asia and a key influence on the tenor of the modern Pakistani state, Maududi's writings still sell by the million and are utterly mainstream. But he is also a well-recognized influence on terrorist organizations like al-Qaida and thus regarded with suspicion by many governments, including some Muslim ones. In 2016, following a British government review of prisons, a similar book by Maududi was withdrawn from prison libraries on the grounds that it was 'extremist literature . . . in opposition to core British values'. The author of the review, the former prison governor Ian Acheson, said that its 'free access to vulnerable and suggestible prisoners is an obvious security risk'.[5] A certain kind of tabloid journalist, therefore, might well have described Aisha's kind goodbye present as a jihadist training manual – and might have made a story, too, out of al-Meezan's connection to the Scottish government via Humza Yousaf's board director mother.

There was more. After I left, I realized I had forgotten to ask what Aisha thought of Glasgow's own jihadi bride, Aqsa Mahmood, and phoned her back for a comment. There was a long pause.

'Maybe you should come in again and speak to our chairperson about that,' she said.

I was puzzled by her reticence. Even MI5 agree that a solid grounding in the traditions of the faith is often the best antidote to Islamic extremism. All I wanted from Aisha was a line on where she thought Aqsa's religious education had gone wrong and how she might never have been radicalized if she had only had the benefit of after-hours classes at al-Meezan. But perhaps I should have guessed: Aqsa Mahmood had, in fact, briefly been a student there.

'Of course we were very shocked,' Aisha eventually admitted. 'What she did was wrong, as well as Islamically incorrect. But Aqsa was an occasional student, not one of the regulars, and she wasn't with us for long . . . We can't possibly know what is in all of our students' minds. And look at the ratio. We have taught hundreds of girls here over the last ten years. To condemn a whole institution by association with a single student would be very unjust.'

I had heard that defence often before, from the imams of

mosques frequented by suicide bombers to the vice chancellor of Westminster University, the alma mater of Jihadi John. It was a fair one. By common consent, Aqsa was groomed for jihad not by al-Meezan but online, over many years, by a boyfriend in Nottinghamshire called Adeel ul Haq, who was jailed in 2016 for his role in assisting a group of young jihadis from Cardiff.[6] As usual, not even Aqsa's parents realized what their 'model child' was planning until it was too late.

'Aqsa had her own wrong ideas about Islam, which she never discussed with us,' Aisha went on. 'Of course it is tragic, but you can't reach everybody. All of the girls are bombarded with wrong ideas all the time. All we can do here is to teach what is correct.'

The emergence of a new Scots-Asian identity, she left me thinking, was wonderful in many ways – in its pride, its confidence, its bold embrace of the outward tropes of Scots culture along with its inner values such as fairness and social equality. Perhaps it even points the way to a different future for all of British Islam, the longed-for sunlit uplands where Muslims and non-Muslims might co-exist in mutual respect, affection and admiration. It seemed a brave and even noble project, but one that was also fraught with risk and difficulty for its political sponsors, the SNP.

11

Another British Religion

ONE SUNDAY MORNING IN Bradford, towards the end of my
year's travels around Muslim Britain, I stopped by the cathedral,
curious to see how the established church was doing in the middle of one of the most Muslim cities in Britain. I arrived too late
for the Sunday service, but the dean, Jerry Lepine, was still there
in a side aisle, delivering a PowerPoint lecture in a snowy white
surplice on the use of the word 'Allelujah' in the Book of Psalms. I
sat at the back and listened in, thinking how similar the word
was to its Islamic equivalent, 'Alhamdulillah'. One is Hebrew,
the other Arabic, but both mean Praise the Lord.

It was yet another #moreincommon moment, of a type that
I had experienced so often over the previous months that I
almost no longer registered them. If my immersion in British
Islam had become a kind of catharsis, this was, I supposed, a
sign that the process was nearly complete. My travels through
al-Britannia had changed my perception in quite a fundamental
way not just of Islam, but of what it meant to be British. The latter
alteration was disorienting. Britishness was a part of me. It went
to the core of my identity, my sense of self; it was not something I expected to find myself questioning when I started out
on my project.

Britishness is, of course, a nebulous concept, a historical construct suited to the unifying ambitions of past kings and
politicians. My own sense of Britishness had always been more

of a feeling than anything else. I knew it when I saw it; the feeling was strong. But I was also aware that it defied accurate definition, and now that I had begun to scrutinize it, it was disturbing to find how quickly it fell apart. The government couldn't tell me what it meant. Their best shot, the 'fundamental British values' identified by the Home Office, are not fundamentally British at all but universal.

When I tried to visualize Britishness I came up with Britannia, the helmeted goddess who still rules the waves with her trident and pet lion on older 50-pence pieces. Yet Britannia was a Roman invention; while the eighteenth-century tune that accompanies her, Arne and Thomson at the Last Night of the Proms, had always sounded to me like joke jingoism, good fun for the tourists, no doubt, but nothing a patriot would choose to die in a ditch for. What else was there? Cool Britannia, the Blairite rebranding exercise of the 1990s? That was just Geri Halliwell in a Union Jack dress. Not even Wikipedia knows what Britain is. The term, it says, requires 'disambiguation': it may refer to 'the United Kingdom, a sovereign state'; or to 'Great Britain, an island'; or to 'national sports teams of the United Kingdom'. It seemed that Britain, and therefore Britishness, meant different things to different people, depending on the time and place and context. The need for disambiguation was permanent.

That was not the case, though, with Christianity. Gazing up at the gilded angels beneath the fine hammer-beam roof of Bradford Cathedral, I could understand why Britain First had co-opted the crucifix as the symbol of their unpleasant campaign. The Anglican Church, with its centuries-old beliefs and traditions, was a rare fixed point for a society in flux, an anchor to cling to in a world roiled by tumultuous seas. Christianity, according to Britain First, is the mainstay of Britishness; it follows, for them, that non-Christians are by definition not British and cannot belong. But the kilted Asians I had seen showed that it was possible to belong to a nation without the bonds of a

Al-Britannia

common faith. Christianity was clearly not an identifier of the new Scottishness – and I no longer believed that it was an identifier of the new Britishness, either.

The emptiness of Bradford Cathedral this Sunday morning seemed to prove it. There was no one here apart from the dean and his audience, who numbered precisely fourteen. Was this where I belonged? The dean's slide show was not displaying correctly: *This computer has been scheduled to go to sleep in two minutes*, it said on the screen behind him.

'Oops! Forgive us our technology,' he chuckled, as he paused to fiddle with his keyboard.

We chatted after his lecture and he admitted that his job was hard at times. Originally from Nottingham, Dean Jerry had been in Bradford for three years.

'We don't do evensong at the cathedral because I've found that people won't come out at night. There's a perception that Bradford is too dangerous after dark, although actually I've found it to be really quiet. It's part of Bradford's massive PR problem as a city. When I told my friends that I was coming here as dean three years ago, they all said, "What? Really?"'

His potential parishioners were few in number. The cathedral, he said, was the only Church of England church remaining in the inner-city area. There was, unsurprisingly, an emphasis on interfaith work: the north transept was given over to a multi-faith rug exhibition organized by the local Methodist association called *Weaving Women's Wisdom*. It was not always so easy to bring people together, though. Fifteen years ago, with help from the Millennium Fund, the cathedral had set up a Museum of Religion in the old town post office just down the hill. But the visitors obstinately refused to come, leaving the diocese so deep in debt that there were periods when the cathedral had to be shut for lack of any staff at all. The cathedral had survived that crisis, but as an institution it still felt like it was hanging by a thread. Christians had worshipped on this spot since the eighth

270

century, yet these days, even on a good Sunday, Dean Jerry admitted that the seats were never more than a fifth full.

What did it mean to be a Christian in the twenty-first-century West? Around Muslim Britain I had sometimes been asked if I believed in God, to which I usually mumbled something about the strong evidence of intelligent design in the universe. But the truth was that I didn't know what I believed. At home, I felt compelled to attend a church from time to time without being fully able to explain why, beyond a conviction that a life without a spiritual dimension is a shallow life. The church I preferred, the Canongate in Edinburgh's Old Town, could be a good place in which to contemplate the spiritual. Its Sunday service provided a valuable breathing space in which to meditate without the usual distractions of children or television or iPhones. I liked my church.

At the same time I knew how fortunate I was to have found it, because I had been in many others in my life that I did not like. English country churches, particularly, often have tiny regular congregations of frail old people with voices too weedy to do anything but mouth the words to hymns that are themselves archaic. Such places can feel as cold and depressing as mausoleums. The surrounding empty pews evoke not the spiritual or ethereal but, for me, the slow death of Christianity as an organized state religion. Even the Church of England admits that it loses 1 per cent of its membership every year through natural causes, because the deceased are not being replaced. In 2015 the number of people attending its services each week dropped below 1 million for the first time – less than 2 per cent of the population – with Sunday attendances falling to 760,000.[1]

People who identify themselves as having no religion in England and Wales now outnumber those who call themselves Christians of any denomination, a state of affairs not seen since the seventh century. The new godlessness has implications beyond the risk of personal hellfire. Its obverse is secularism and, it appeared to me, a creeping intolerance of those who stubbornly cling to any faith.

In contrast to the emptiness of Bradford Cathedral, I had visited dozens of mosques in the preceding months – including, tellingly, several that had been converted from old, unwanted parish churches – and invariably found them packed with worshippers on Fridays, the Muslim Sunday. It was impossible not to notice the youthful energy on display, the vibrant sense of belonging to something bigger than the sum of their selves. A strong community spirit was surely part of the definition of religion, a word said by some etymologists to come from the Latin *religare*, to bind fast, the verb the Romans used for the mooring up of a ship. Part of me still greatly envied the strength of that bond between Muslims, as well as the ease with which they seemed to connect to the spiritual through their many rituals and the unwavering certainties of their belief. These were aspects of Islam frequently ignored or overlooked in the furious public debate over extremism and immigration – though not by me.

I thought it was just my hard luck to belong to a culture that had so obviously lost its religious moorings. And yet there was really no reason, other than habit and loyalty to my heritage, why I should not embrace Islam for myself if I chose to. Islam, after all, professes itself constantly to be a faith open to anyone. White non-Muslims convert all the time: at the rate of about 5,000 a year, according to one survey, which estimated that there were 100,000 converts in the country, 70,000 of them white.[2] A white English childhood friend of mine, Salih Brandt, converted many years ago to a Moroccan brand of Maliki Sufism. The suggestion that Islam was a foreign religion, and therefore somehow intrinsically 'unBritish', cut no ice with him at all.

'Where do you think Jesus came from?' he liked to say. 'Bournemouth?'

White conversion had been stigmatized by its association with extremism. All that most people knew of it came from media stories about people like Thomas Evans from Wycombe. But of course the vast majority of converts were not extremists. They had merely chosen to worship God – the same God that Christians worship – in a different way. And as I had discovered, there was no reason at all why being a Muslim should affect one's sense of Britishness.

Salih Brandt's long-time mentor was another convert, Sheikh Abdalhaqq Bewley, a noted Islamic scholar who with his wife Aisha had translated the Koran into English. He belonged to that 1960s hippy generation who went seeking existential truth in every corner of the world. In 1968, as the Beatles were learning transcendental meditation techniques from Maharishi Mahesh Yogi in the foothills of the Himalayas, Bewley went to Morocco, where he fell in with a charismatic Ayrshire Scot, Ian Dallas, who had recently converted to Islam in Fez. This was, as Bewley recalled, a heady era of 'sex an' drugs and rock'n'roll'. Dallas's circle of friends included Eric Clapton, who was in love at the time with George Harrison's wife Pattie Boyd. Clapton's rock classic 'Layla' was inspired by the narrative poem *Layla and Majnun*, a tale of unrequited love and madness from twelfth-century Persia, a copy of which Dallas had given him.

Abdalqadir as-Sufi, as Dallas became, went on to form his own offshoot order, the Murabitun World Movement, the earliest British manifestation of which was a converts' commune in Bristol Gardens near Little Venice in west London: the first truly indigenous Muslim community in the country. Abdalqadir had long since moved his headquarters to South Africa, but Abdalhaqq was still here, indeed right here in Bradford, running a *zawiya*, a small religious school, from a terraced house on a hill opposite a tyre shop on the city's western outskirts.

I couldn't wait to meet Abdalhaqq Bewley. His zawiya sounded improbably exotic; cultish, even. But he turned out to be disarmingly normal, with a gentle, understated manner that was also quintessentially, reassuringly English. With his white hair and glasses, his sensible V-neck sweater and checked shirt and tie, he looked more like a friendly university tutor than a guru. We sat in armchairs by a library fire, drinking tea from proper cups and saucers, a plate of digestive biscuits on the table between us.

'I became a Muslim because I wanted a better way to worship God, and Christianity didn't give me the access I needed,' he explained. 'I don't feel any less English for it at all.'

Abdalhaqq described his zawiya as a spiritual clinic, a religious retreat as much as a school. There were a handful of students staying at the house, some of them from abroad – two young Spaniards, a Frenchman – one of whom had politely served the tea. On Thursday nights, he said, a group of up to forty people gather in the sitting room next door for a *qasida*, the ancient Moroccan Maliki tradition of sung prayer recital. It was, however, a Tuesday morning, and I found this ceremony quite hard to imagine. The shelves of his library were filled with novels by Joyce and James, Huxley and Hesse, and books of poetry by Dylan Thomas and T. S. Eliot. If Muslim Britain sometimes seemed a foreign country, Abdalhaqq's house felt like home.

He saw Islam as part of a historical continuum, the latest in a series of waves of spiritual regeneration to break over Britain from abroad. As he pointed out, Christianity was brought to England by monks from Italy or France or Ireland, all of whom were members of religious orders that were foreign. He saw himself and his life's work as part of the same missionary tradition.

'I'm actually descended from one of the original followers of George Fox,' he said, referring to the seventeenth-century English Dissenter who founded the Quakers, a movement that he called part of the 'yeast' of religious fermentation and renewal.

'[Archbishop] Rowan Williams worried about the lack of spirituality in our national life,' he went on. 'Wouldn't it be wonderful if that aspect of Islam could somehow be transferred, shared? I'm not trying to convert anybody. I've got nothing against

Christianity at all, when people actually practise it. But spirituality could be Islam's great gift to British culture.'

It was quite a startling concept, but he didn't regard Islam as an 'alien' religion. To him, rather, it had become 'another British one'. Englishmen like him, after all, had been converting to Islam since Victorian times – a point proven by another book I spotted on his shelves, *From Drury Lane to Mecca*, an account of the life of Hedley Churchward, a theatre set designer from Aldershot who converted and became, in 1910, the first known Muslim Briton to make the *hajj*, the pilgrimage to Mecca. However, it was not Churchward or even the high conversion rates of modern times that have established Islam's Britishness, but inward migration. It was simply a fact of life, Abdalhaqq said, that Islam was the fastest-growing religion in the country, practised by 5 per cent of the population, a percentage that had doubled in a decade. And it was, he thought, folly to think such a process could be manipulated or reversed.

'This idea persists that Muslims are from somewhere else, and therefore don't belong here, or could even be sent back. But we *invited* them here in the 1950s and '60s, and their children and grandchildren were born here. Of course they are a part of our society now.'

He had, he said, been waiting all his life for a distinct British Muslim identity to emerge from the UK 'soup'.

'Islam isn't a culture: it's a *filter* for culture. That's why so many discrete but recognizable versions of the faith have evolved over time. It has taken longer than I hoped to arrive in Britain, but perhaps it is coming now that we are on to the fourth generation of Asian immigrants.'

His words paraphrased a saying I had heard, that Islam is like a river that takes its colour from the bed over which it flows. Abdalhaqq gave the example of a new mosque in Wakefield, built to an unusual architectural design using local English stone, which he called an 'exciting' departure from the usual gaudy Arabic pastiche using imported materials. His enthusiasm again revealed his innate Britishness. I could imagine him looking forward to the Wakefield mosque's inclusion in some future edition of Pevsner's *Architectural Guides*.

His intellect, the depth of his knowledge, was occasionally mesmerizing. He argued that Muslim and Western values – the deeper, underlying ones – had far more in common than was usually supposed, and he did so with reference to St Thomas Aquinas, to the political scientist Joseph Schumpeter, to the moral philosopher Alasdair MacIntyre. He quoted from Harold Laski's commentary on the sixteenth-century Huguenot tract *Vindicae Contra Tyrannos*. He argued that the UN Charter of 1945, the Universal Declaration of Human Rights, was not just foreshadowed by but was fundamentally the same document as the Constitution of Medina of 622.

His was an unusual voice with, I thought, the rare potential to bridge the gap of understanding between Muslims and non-Muslims. It seemed a pity that his views were not sought out more often by people who mattered in London. Recent visitors to his zawiya did at least include Dame Louise Casey, in the course of a major review into integration commissioned by David Cameron. Her report, published in December 2016, argued that rates of integration in some communities, including Bradford ones, had been undermined by high levels of transnational marriage – a practice, she argued, that had created 'a "first generation in every generation" phenomenon, in which each new generation grows up with a foreign-born parent'.[3]

Abdalhaqq also thought that maintaining an umbilical cord to the subcontinent in this way was a custom 'well past its sell-by date'.

He had useful things to say, too, on how Islam could be harnessed to combat religious extremism.

'The Prophet constantly preached the importance of achieving balance in all things: the *opposite* of extremism,' he said. 'Not one of Islam's so-called radical leaders today is classically trained. Zawahiri [the leader of al-Qaida] was a GP! The solution to radicalization, I maintain, is a solid Muslim education. That is why, by going after madrassahs, the government has chosen *completely* the wrong target.'

He was equally scathing of the targeting of the Trojan Horse state schools in Birmingham, which he insisted had only been trying to 'reinforce children's identity as Muslims': the key, he believed, not just to the defeat of extremist ideas, but to the creation of self-confident young Asians who would in turn lead to a better integrated British society.

His goal in that respect was the same as Dame Louise Casey's. And yet Abdalhaqq was also a Muslim traditionalist, with some views that did not chime at all with the assumptions underpinning her report.

'The government keeps talking about fundamental British values as if these were ancient and immutable, when the reality is that some Western values, on things like sexual morality or homosexuality, have changed hugely since the 1950s. The problem is that the values of Muslims have not.'

That was the rub. He was, in the end, an old-school conservative; if he had been a Christian, I suspected he might have been a very orthodox one, the kind who lamented the Church of England's constant modernizing reforms. Islam's attraction, to him, was precisely that its values *are* immutable, not least because he believed, as devout Muslims do, that they had been handed down directly by God. The Prophet, he explained, declared that he had 'only been sent to perfect the noble qualities of character'. In Abdalhaqq's view, Islam offered society a precious chance to reclaim the better side of human nature, a tool for a kind of permanent moral rearmament, with the Prophet – whom Abdalhaqq described as 'a man unlike other men, a flawless ruby among pebbles' – setting the best and only example to follow.

I liked and admired Abdalhaqq, and respected and

understood the logic of his message. But for all the undoubted good in Islam, I remained wary of its prescriptive nature, the accompanying rules and regulations that seemed to govern every aspect of daily life. I doubted I could ever embrace a fourteen-hundred-year-old moral code if it meant forfeiting the right to challenge it. I fell down at the first pillar of the faith, the sincere recitation of the shahada according to which one accepted without question that there was no god but God, and that the Prophet was his messenger. I was not, finally, looking for a better way to worship God, and I was not about to convert.

And yet, I did not wish to close myself to Islam with such finality. I had warmed to the religion and its many followers whom I had met around my country, and felt reluctant to abandon it, or them, after an experience so immersive.

British Muslims have many peculiarities and problems. In Dewsbury, Wycombe and London, I had seen how Islamic ideology can be stolen and twisted into justification for violence. In Oldham, Bradford and Rotherham I had encountered the dark side of Asian culture: the domestic abuse, the grooming gangs, the casual violence and drug crime attendant on high rates of unemployment and urban poverty. As if that were not enough, Britain's Muslims dealt every day with a hostile press, a resurgent far right, and an uptick in xenophobic hate crime following the vote for Brexit. In Birmingham, Luton and Leicester, they were grappling with a government strategy that had mistaken religious conservatism for extremism, and community spirit for isolationism. The core of their identity, Islam itself, was in many cases demonstrably under attack.

Yet they mostly dealt with this pummelling with an inner strength and dignity that I found immensely appealing. Beneath the masking noise and fury of the public debate, I kept hearing the quiet but unmistakable murmur of prayer, sustaining the faithful through the hardest of times. Muslims were always quoting the Koranic verse about holding fast to the rope of Allah, and there was something magnificent in the way that they actually did. I admired, too, the courage and determination of the many political activists I had encountered, their refusal to be bullied and their insistence that Muslims should be treated the same as anyone else. There was an emerging self-confidence about communities like Luton that suggested that British Islam will prevail; while what I saw in Scotland showed not only that co-existence with Muslims is possible, but that their talent and values can be harnessed to fashion a different and perhaps better kind of society – a new version of Britain, my country, al-Britannia.

Islam is not a pick'n'mix religion. I didn't think it possible to be some kind of Muslim Lite. But I still wondered if there was a way to get closer to the experience of being a British Muslim without actually becoming one, and in the spring of 2016 I thought I had hit upon one: the fourth of the five pillars of Islam that all good Muslims are obliged to live by, known as *sawm*.

Sawm means fasting. Every year during Ramadan, the ninth month of the Islamic year, Muslims refrain from all food, drink, tobacco and sex during daylight hours. They are also supposed to think only good thoughts. Great claims are made for this famous practice, a tradition started by the Prophet himself. Fasting is an exercise in self-discipline designed to turn one's thoughts away from the material towards the spiritual, and therefore closer to God. It teaches the rich what it means to be hungry, and thus empathy for the poor, as well as the true value of generosity and charity. Practised each year by a billion Muslims, the Ramadan fast is a giant affirmation of the ummah, and an expression of religious fellowship every bit as impressive as Christmas.

Because Islam follows a lunar calendar, the beginning of Ramadan moves back by eleven days each solar year. In 1999, when Ramadan fell over the winter solstice, the fast for Muslims in northern hemisphere countries like Britain was as easy as skipping lunch. In 2016, however, Ramadan was scheduled to fall in June, right over the summer solstice. The days would be challengingly long in Edinburgh where I lived. In fact there wouldn't be a Ramadan fast as arduous as the 2016 one for another thirty-three years. What might it be like to share in such a rare bonding experience – and what might I learn, not just about Islam, but about myself?

What follows is an account of my experience of Ramadan 2016, presented in the form that it was first written, a rough and contemporaneous diary. Peace be upon you, reader – and *Alhamdulillah*.

My Ramadan Diary

Thursday 2 June

Ramadan is five days away – or possibly four, depending on the sighting of the new moon – and Edinburgh is enjoying an uncharacteristic heatwave that I hope isn't going to last. It's typical, after last summer's washout. Everyone else is going round with grins on their faces and telling each other how lovely it is. At lunch hour yesterday the crescent of grass by the tram stop on Shandwick Place was crowded with semi-clothed, picnicking office workers: a spot I'm going to avoid from next week.

The prospect of going hungry doesn't trouble me so much, but I'm starting to worry about thirst, and the headaches that I know I'm going to get when I'm dehydrated. The clue is in the name: *Ramadan* translates as 'scorching heat' or 'dryness'. It's just so impractical. I've got a couple of big DIY jobs at home that I need to finish: clearing out a coal cellar, and stripping the paint and pointing off the back wall of our house. Both are the kind of hot, sweaty tasks that I usually quite enjoy, but they are going to be difficult without water. Or indeed Nurofen. I doubt I'm even going to be able to go on cycling to the office I'm borrowing at the moment. At least I'm not in Mecca, where the forecast for the whole of next week is 47°C. Do the purists, like the Salafis whose aim is to live as the Prophet did, allow themselves air-conditioning?

Scotland might be cooler than Arabia in summer but I suspect the long days might actually be tougher than fasting in extreme heat. A late dinner – *iftaar*, the evening meal is called – doesn't sound too bad. I'm more worried by the other meal, *suhur*, taken before dawn. It seems that the latest time for suhur – quaintly translated by the hadith scholar Bukhari as 'night tiffin' – is not at the last moment before dawn, which would seem sensible, but up to two hours earlier, according to your Islamic affiliation or tradition. I wonder how much night tiffin I am going to feel like at 2.30 in the morning after a big iftaar meal at 10.

Ramadan isn't supposed to be easy, but still: nineteen and a half hours of fasting. I bet the Prophet never envisaged Islam spreading to Scotland. At what point does the exercise spill over into masochism? It is said that some Salafists will not even swallow their own spit. The Prophet, to be fair, didn't want anyone to overdo Ramadan.

'Allah intends for you ease and does not intend for you hardship,' it says in the Koran.[1] Children and pregnant women are exempt from the fast, while anyone who falls ill or who has to travel during the month is permitted to skip a day or two and make them up later.

Friday 3 June

I've never been to Friday prayers in my hometown. The eve of Ramadan seems a good moment to put this right, so today at noon I go to Edinburgh Central Mosque, the city's biggest, by the university complex around George Square.

I know a bit about the Central Mosque from Kate, a parent at the state primary school my children attend, who is a Muslim convert, married to Jim, a Djembe drum instructor from Senegal. They send their nine-year-old daughter to Koran classes here, and she says there is an element of conservatism about these that she is unsure about: a blanket disapproval of rock music, for instance. It's hardly surprising if there is a whiff of Wahhabism about the place, because the mosque, built in 1998, was paid for by King Fahd of Saudi Arabia. Its formal name, the Mosque of the Custodian of the Two Holy Mosques, is proudly inscribed on a plaque by the main entrance. And so I am expecting a bit of old-style Koran-bashing from the imam's sermon, the khutbah.

I settle down at the back, cross-legged on the big green carpet, and watch the prayer hall fill up. I am surprised to see how ethnically mixed the congregation here today is. There are Punjabis, certainly, but also North Africans, Turks, Syrians, Palestinians, Sudanese. I spot Malays, and a family who I take to be Uyghur Chinese. No one looks at me twice for the colour of my skin. In such a diverse crowd, all differences are levelled. Islam's colour-blindness strikes me as one of its most attractive features. It makes the brotherhood of man seem not just possible, but real. Malcolm X was similarly struck on his first pilgrimage to Mecca in 1964, when he wrote: 'During the past eleven days here in Makkah, I have eaten from the same plate, drunk from the same glass, and slept on the same rug – while praying to the same God – with Muslims whose eyes were the bluest of blue, whose hair was the blondest of blond, and whose skin was the whitest of white. And in the words and in the deeds of the white Muslims, I felt the same sincerity that I felt among the black African Muslims of Nigeria, Sudan and Ghana.'

The imam, Yahya Barry, is dark African black – he is a Fula-Wolof, from the Gambia – and looks blacker against the dazzling white of his thobe and kufi cap. His sermon, in Arabic first then repeated in English, is only mildly puritanical. Ramadan, he says, is a time for activity, to make a mark in the world, because it might be your last; sleeping through the long fast, however tempting, or treating the month as a holiday, is cheating. Fear God and be strong, he tells us. Pure thoughts at all times.

Afterwards, on the sunny steps outside the mosque, I fall into conversation with a bearded volunteer, a Pizza Express chef from Algeria, who is handing out prayer timetables for the coming month at this and three other mosques in the city. I am puzzled to read that *fajr*, the official start of dawn and therefore of the daily fast, is listed slightly differently for each mosque, and I ask the Algerian why.

'I know,' he shrugs. 'Everyone is talking about that.'

Disagreement over when dawn really starts goes back centuries. The Koran stipulates that the fast begins 'when the white thread of dawn appears to you distinctly from the black thread', which sounds straightforward. However, the hadith warn that 'there are two dawns . . . one is called the tail of the wolf, which is the false dawn that appears vertically, not horizontally. The other appears horizontally and not vertically.' If this was confusing in seventh-century Arabia, it is worse in twenty-first-century Scotland, where in the 'abnormal summer months' it never gets truly dark, and night is one long wolf's tail. The start of fajr thus has to be extrapolated. Some mosques, particularly Deobandi-influenced ones, push the time back in order to be on the safe side: no one wants to be responsible for the sacrilege of eating and drinking after sun-up.

My daughter Amelia, who is 11, keeps asking how a Muslim would fast at the North Pole in summer, when it never gets dark. Or, indeed, at the South Pole in winter. The Prophet can hardly have imagined Muslims living at the extremities of the world, several centuries before these were even discovered. I discover online that the world's most northerly mosque is in Tromsø, Norway, where the locals have been granted special dispensation to choose between following Mecca time or that of the Muslim country nearest Tromsø – which I think must be Bosnia. It is still unclear, though, how far north one has to be before the dispensation kicks in. It doesn't apply in Oslo, for instance, where the local Muslims sneer that the Tromsø brothers have gone soft.

Saturday 4 June

The Central Mosque has a restaurant operation, very popular with students, called, unimaginatively, the Mosque Kitchen. During Ramadan they put up a couple of marquees where anyone turning up at iftaar or suhur time can eat for free – a Muslim tradition that will be replicated at most large mosques in Britain this month. The Koran enjoins Muslims to be especially kind, patient and hospitable at Ramadan, and I am hoping these meal times will be a good opportunity to talk to them in their mosques.

They were asking for volunteers yesterday to help put the tents up, so today I go along for an hour. There are ten of us, a mixed crew who speak mostly in Arabic. There is, inevitably, no instruction manual, and with no one discernibly in charge it takes some time and several false starts to get the first tent up, a Krypton Factor puzzle of swivelling joints and tubes. But the camaraderie is jolly.

I chat to Radwan Al-Zidan, a pharmacologist studying for a PhD in medical bio-tech at Napier University. He is from Nineveh, the ancient capital of Assyria, now a suburb of Mosul, a city under occupation by ISIS. I ask how the ruins are doing and he pulls a long face. 'Mostly gone,' he says. He used to commute to work through a monumental city gate carved in the shape of a winged lion, 'like the one in the British Museum,' but Da'esh, ISIS, has destroyed it. He shows me a picture on his smartphone of his one-year-old son, still in Nineveh with his wife.

'I'd like to get them out but it's too dangerous to even try because of Da'esh.'

He's worried by the fighting in Fallujah, where thousands of civilians are trapped as the Iraqi military closes in to liberate them. The liberation of Mosul is said to be next.

In the evening I take my wife Melou to a 'Welcome Ramadan' nasheed concert charity fundraiser (with dinner) in a hotel in a business park in Bellshill, ten miles southeast of Glasgow. I love nasheed, a devotional, a cappella artform that, at its best, can put the hairs up on the spine, and am hoping that Melou, who has never heard it before, might like it too. The 150-strong audience is predominantly Asian. Most of the tables in the convention hall have been taken by extended families on a big night out. There are no other white Brits in attendance, but the organizers are very welcoming and no one seems to find our presence particularly odd. We get put on a table with three pre-teen Pakistani girls whose parents appear to have abandoned them for the night, and two student dentists who have come over from Edinburgh University, one an Indian root-canal expert from Lucknow, the other a Syrian from Homs who specializes in false teeth.

'What am I doing here?' Melou whispers at me.

The Bellshill evening, unfortunately, turns out to be a bit of a con. The opening act is promising: a Saudi, Sheikh Saad Nomani, who is a sort of Islamic Rory Bremner, famed for his ability to mimic ninety-nine of the world's leading Koran reciters. But after twenty minutes he is replaced by a compere with an aggressive fundraising pitch for the charity of the night, Human Appeal, which wants to provide safe water to villages in Pakistan. The audience clearly isn't wealthy, yet he starts in with a plea for £10,000. The dentist from Lucknow clucks his tongue in disapproval. Generosity to the poor is a key part of Ramadan, but eliciting charity in such a public way, he thinks, is a distasteful business, a sullying of the pure spirit of the season: a Muslim version, perhaps, of the commercialization of Christmas. Proper *sadaqah*, charity, should be done selflessly and without fanfare. Here, instead, he worries that richer diners will be tempted to show off in front of their peers, while poorer ones will feel pressured into giving more than they can afford. The compere's pitch lasts for an hour nevertheless, the amount solicited dropping as the big sums fail to materialize. Eventually one of the parentless teenagers on our table shyly raises a hand, a pledge for £100, to half-hearted cries of *masha'allah* up and down the hall. I ask her how she intends to raise the money.

'I don't know,' she says. 'Sell cupcakes?'

Sunday 5 June

In the afternoon, humping rubbish to the council wheelie bin at the end of our street, I bump into our Asian neighbour-but-one. We are on slight nodding terms, but in the nine years we have lived here have never actually spoken. I know him to be Muslim from the hordes of friends and extended family members who descend on his house every Eid. I wish him a *Ramadan Mubarak*, and when I add that I am preparing to fast too this year, the barriers instantly tumble. His name, I discover, is Shaukat, and he runs several corner shops in a nearby part of town called Jock's Lodge – so many shops, in fact, that the locals jokingly refer to the area as Shauk's Lodge.

Originally from the northern Punjab near Islamabad, he has been in Edinburgh for over twenty years, although he was brought up in Rotherham, which explains his accent, a strange Yorkshire-Scottish hybrid. We talk about Ramadan, and he tells me that the new moon has already been spotted in Saudi, triggering an early start to the fast, at least for him. I check the Edinburgh Central Mosque website and find that their start date has indeed moved forward by a day. I say I find the uncertainty around the start of Ramadan rather charming in this day and age, but Shaukat says I'd be surprised how much friction it causes. Later I find that Twitter is indeed alight with the controversy – the 'calm before the sawm' as someone jokes. In

2014 the Saudis, perhaps too intent on reminding the world's Muslims of their authority over Islam, reported seeing the new moon when they hadn't and were later forced to apologize. Starting Ramadan with the new moon is supposed to be about connecting humans with the natural rhythm of life, not Saudi Sunni hegemony. Have the authorities in Mecca made the same mistake again?

A hashtag is trending called #MoonWars. The new moon has yet to be detected in Pakistan, Morocco, South Africa or Britain, according to the Central Moonsighting Committee of Hizbul Ulama UK, the West Ham-based Society of Muslim Scholars. Yet, not all Muslims in those countries are delaying until Tuesday – not my neighbour Shaukat, and not the main mosque in Edinburgh, despite the online sneering of one tweeter who dismisses Monday starters as 'Saudi lapdogs'. I decide to join the lapdogs and to follow the Central Mosque from tonight.

Monday 6 June

The first of Ramadan! I stagger out of bed with the alarm at 2.05 and into the kitchen for a big bowl of porridge and a pint of banana smoothie. I think of Shaukat and Shaheen two doors up, doing much the same: Shaukat said yesterday that he swore by porridge. His friends, he said, all preferred the traditional Pakistani suhur of flatbread parathas – 'because it's a luxury thing, you know?' – but he finds the slow-burn carbs of porridge stave off hunger pangs for longer.

To set the atmosphere I turn on Radio Ramadan, 87.9FM at the bottom of the dial, a special programme for Edinburgh. The fajr call to prayer soon joins the hum of the fridge. Both seem unnaturally loud at this hour, especially in our kitchen, which is usually filled with the day-to-day clatter of a large family. The signal comes out in a muted crackle, giving it an austere, oddly old-fashioned feel. The transmitter, barely a mile away in the town centre, is evidently not powerful. Yet the medium suits the message. The static that fills the long pauses between the muezzin's phrases is suggestive of space, maybe even of eternity. 'Allahu akbar!' sings the muezzin. 'God is greatest! Hasten to prayer! Hasten to success! Prayer is better than sleep!'

Unlike me, Shaukat has to pray at 02.29, after his porridge, and again at 04.27 when the sun comes up. He says that as a corner-shop owner he has to leave for work at five o'clock each morning anyway, so it isn't worth going back to bed. Impressed by his fortitude, I intended yesterday to stay up after suhur and write, but in the event 02.45 feels just a bit too early and I go back to bed and sleep until it's time to get the children off to school.

By lunchtime I have a headache and a very dry mouth. Bad breath, I have read, is a common complaint during Ramadan. I check a website, islam21c.com, and find that mouthwash, although considered *makruh* by some authorities (the word means 'frowned upon', a sort of haram lite), is nevertheless permissible so long as you don't swallow. The liberal application of a *miswak*, the traditional teeth-cleaning twig cut from the branch of an arak tree, is also recommended. Popping a couple of headache pills, though, is definitely out.

Back from school, the children think this fasting business is hilarious. There is a stream of impish questions about what my favourite food is, and they keep saying 'yum' while waving biscuits under my nose. Muslims, of course, welcome such trials of patience. It is one of the religion's most important virtues, mentioned in the Koran ninety times.

> If something good happens to you, it galls them.
> If something bad strikes you, they rejoice at it.
> But if you are patient and god-fearing,
> Their scheming will not harm you in any way.[2]

By 3 p.m. the headache permeates everything. I try to do some DIY, a simple B&Q kit for a bedroom shelf, but end up screwing its two parts together the wrong way round, permanently damaging its top surface. Twelve hours into the fast, just as Humza Yousaf warned, my brain is turning to mush. By 6 p.m. I have become completely taciturn. It is difficult to articulate anything much, and when I do speak my voice sounds thick, like the precursor to a cold. My children are puzzled when my answers to their questions tail off, unfinished, into silence.

An old friend comes to supper, up from London to raise capital from Edinburgh's private banks for his booming electricals wholesale business. I watch, drooling, as he and Melou sit down to a pair of steaks at 9 o'clock.

'You mean Sadiq Khan does this?' he says. 'For a month? You're joking. Don't they just sort of pick and choose?'

My brother-in-law Rupert texts. 'Peckish?' it says.

But then at 9.50 p.m., when it is at last about to be my turn to eat, the doorbell rings. It is Shaukat's wife Shaheen, shyly grinning in her hijab and proffering a tray of homemade samosas, pakoras and spring rolls. She has also brought a side-order of dates, the traditional way to break the fast. I feel indescribably touched by this proof of the brotherhood of Islam.

I eat three dates in quick succession, chased down with a pint of water, focusing mindfully on the *essence* of the date, as you're supposed to do. They are delicious, and I feel my equanimity start to return, along with the ability to speak. *Hahab az zamaa'u wab tallatil urooqu wa thabat al-ajru Insha-Allah*, it says in the hadith. 'The thirst has vanished, the veins have been wetted and the reward is established – God willing.'[3] It is a good end to the first day of Ramadan.

My Ramadan Diary

Tuesday 7 June

I had not fully appreciated before how important food and drink are to the structure of an ordinary day. Not just meal times but snacks, tea breaks, a beer after work: the punctuation marks of our waking hours. All of this grammar has disappeared, making my day disconcertingly formless.

For Muslims, the normal day is demarcated not just by meal times but by the five daily prayers, fajr, zuhr, asr, maghrib and isha, which in Ramadan become doubly important, stepping into the breach left by the fast. This is what Ramadan is about: a turning away from the temporal towards the spiritual, from the gratification of the body to that of the soul. I'm not used to the disciplined self-denial this exercise requires. We don't get to practise it much in the modern West, where all is geared to convenience and ease. When I'm working at home, I tend to wander into the kitchen on autopilot to make a cup of tea or steal something from the biscuit cupboard. This fast is making me realize how ingrained the habit has become. It is slightly appalling that the kitchen, the natural centre of the household, has become a room that I need consciously to avoid.

My non-Muslim friends and family are reacting to my fasting in interestingly varied ways. Most are amused and interested, but others have been strangely hostile, bordering on the racist – for instance, in the surprisingly common assertion that 'Muslims don't lose weight during Ramadan because they stuff their faces at sundown', which manages to disparage both Ramadan and Muslims. Why do they say it? The Prophet expressly warns against overeating. Allah, he says, 'does not love the profligate'. In any case, an empty stomach contracts. Forty-eight hours in, my daytime hunger pangs are already diminishing. It is as though my appetite has been ignored for so long that it has given up; and at iftaar when food does reach the gut, it hardly knows what to do with it.

This of course is the point of starting iftaar with dates. Even modern doctors acknowledge that the fruit is an excellent restorative for an empty stomach, because the sugars travel to the liver, kick-starting the metabolism and rapidly producing the energy the digestive system needs to cope with the meal to come.

The Prophet himself liked to break his fast with dates, ensuring that Ramadan is to date-growers what Christmas is to turkey-farmers. This year, a campaign run by an online activist group called Inminds has been warning Muslim shoppers to check that their dates are not grown in Israel, one of the world's biggest producers. Most Israeli dates, they claim, are grown on illegal settlement plantations.[4] I check the box of medjools in my fridge and find they were grown in Iran.

Wednesday 8 June

The children have barely got into their stride with their teasing.

'Are you hungry yet?' says my eight-year-old brightly as she arrives home from school. 'What happens if you eat before it's dark? Does God kill you?' There are, in fact, quite a few places in the world where flouting Ramadan might get you killed.

My Somali journalist friend Ridwaan calls from London. He's a correspondent for Voice of America, although until six months ago he was the chief government spokesperson in Mogadishu. He is still badly shaken by news of an al-Shabaab suicide attack on the Ambassador Hotel that has killed sixteen people, including two MPs who were close friends of his. Like Ridwaan they were Somali Londoners who had gone back to Mogadishu to help rebuild their shattered country, as so many diaspora Somalis do. Ridwaan is just back from paying his respects at the Willesden family home of one of the MPs, Abdullahi Jama

Kabaweyne, where he found a bereaved 12-year-old daughter offering up special Ramadan prayers for 'the best Dad in the world'. Kabaweyne had apparently tried to barricade himself in his hotel room but the gunmen broke down the door and killed him. Ridwaan says that hotel room, Room 78, had been his home in Mogadishu for two years; Kabaweyne had taken it over from him on the day he left.

Today is our youngest child Robbie's fourth birthday party. Eighteen of his friends come to tea. We've hired a magician for an hour and soon the house is filled with joyous shrieking. At tea I notice, with a jaundiced eye, how much food these little people waste. At 10 p.m., the kitchen long since quiet again, I defiantly eat their reheated sausages and the remains of the birthday cake.

Thursday 9 June

I am getting tired of porridge at night. And I am missing eating with Melou and the children during the day more than I expected. Eating alone is a joyless business, with a perfunctory quality that I dislike. Meanwhile I've started feeling very cold in the afternoons, and can't warm up again even when I put on three jumpers. It's a natural consequence of calorie deficiency, but it's still a surprise in the middle of June. On the plus side, Shaheen came around again just before ten with another meal: a parcel of spicy bajis, a stack of parathas, dahl made with two kinds of lentil, even a fruit and yoghurt pudding. This charming neighbourliness is a Ramadan tradition that even the disgruntled whites I met in Dewsbury admitted they liked. Is she going to keep it up for the whole month?

Friday 10 June

To the mosque on Annandale Street, the main Pakistani one in Edinburgh. I know it well from the outside: a crumbly old building of cream-coloured brick, a hundred yards up the road from our children's school. The impressively turbanned imam, Hafiz Abdul Ghafoor, is often to be seen about the neighbourhood. The mosque was, famously, firebombed in the wake of 9/11. No one was hurt, but the legacy of those fraught days is still seen and felt in Edinburgh – for example, in the bollards erected on Calton Hill Terrace that still protect the American consulate from car bombs, or in more recent acts of Islamophobia, such as an incident in 2013 when the door handles of Edinburgh Central Mosque were draped in bacon.

It being Ramadan, the mosque is packed – perhaps 800 people, almost all Pakistani. The khutbah is in Urdu only. I let the words wash over me for a bit, then read the copy of the Koran I have brought along. The man sitting next to me tells me off when I put the book down on the floor: an act of sacrilege even in a mosque, apparently.

I am uncertain of the Annandale's affiliation. One online mosque directory says it is Deobandi, but it seems to be more of a classic Sufi Barelwi establishment. The clue is in the mosque's name: the Anwar-e-Madina, 'The Light of Medina', one of the many synonyms for the Prophet. One of the peculiarities of Barelwis is their belief that Mohammed was created from light. I introduce myself to the imam after the service and ask for confirmation: is he Barelwi or Deobandi? He smiles thinly, and I wonder if I have been too blunt. The Barelwis and Deobandis disagree on several points of theology. Instead of answering he goes to fetch an old man in a suit.

'I do the interfaith bit,' says the old man, whose name is Bashir Malik. 'How can I help you?'

I repeat my question.

'Oh!' he says. 'There's no problem asking the imam about *that.*'

The imam, however, has retreated into his corner office. We knock and poke our heads around the door, to find him ensconced in an armchair, surrounded by five other men in their Friday-best kufi caps and shalwar kameez: the mosque committee, as I take them to be.

'We are . . . a Sunni mosque,' he says with a steady look.

'Sunni . . . Barelwi?' I push him.

He holds my gaze and eventually concedes, with an exaggerated nod: 'Yes, Barelwi.'

The imam's reticence is perplexing. There is nothing controversial per se about the Barelwis, who number perhaps 200 million on the subcontinent, and who control around 500 mosques in Britain, a quarter of the national total.[5] On the other hand, the management of Scotland's Pakistani mosques has been under quite serious media attack recently, for alleged links to extremists back in the homeland. In the current climate of intolerance, it may not be so surprising that Imam Ghafoor doesn't want to talk.

Saturday 11 June

England drew with Russia in the first round of the European Championship in France today. Before the competition the papers were predicting the tournament would be wrecked by violent extremism, and it looks like they might be right, although not in the way they meant. Marseille old port is full of tear gas as the police try to separate battling hooligans: English, Russian and North African French.

The last time England played in Marseille was in 1998, in the first round of the World Cup against Tunisia. England fans fought their rivals around the old port then, too. It emerged afterwards that al-Qaida had plotted to attack England fans and even their team during the match, using gunmen posing as stewards. The attack was reportedly ordered by Osama bin Laden, who personally identified which players among Glen Hoddle's side were to be singled out for execution, in front of an estimated television audience of 300 million.[6] The England fans who provoked local North Africans today with chants of 'ISIS, where are you?' should be careful what they wish for.

Sunday 12 June

Word that I am fasting has spread, and a rumour has taken hold among some of our Edinburgh friends that I am about to convert. I wonder if it might be entertaining to wear a shalwar kameez the next time I do the school run. Or else to get the children to wear niqabs and to tell their teachers: 'Daddy said we had to.' Subversion has never felt so easy, or so cheap.

The truth is that Islam and its practices are not nearly as strange and alien as non-Muslims suppose. For instance, the Prophet's habit of fasting every Monday and Thursday, as well as throughout the month of Ramadan, is very similar to the fashionable 5:2 Fast Diet. This is not coincidence: the 5:2 diet was popularized by a BBC *Horizon* documentary in 2012, in which its presenter, the science journalist Dr Michael Mosley, specifically acknowledged the 5:2 diet's debt to Prophetic tradition.

We Westerners may have stopped going to church, but the appetite for a spiritual dimension to our lives has not diminished. On the contrary, the shallow materialism of so much of modern life seems to be driving many of us to search for deeper meaning – which may be why, as the *Evening Standard* columnist Richard Godwin recently put it, 'the rituals of religion are being repurposed for the modern world'. The example he gave was mindfulness, a modish meditation technique taught at my elder daughter's school, which Godwin describes as 'a corporate cult . . . Buddhist meditation minus the Buddhism'.

At home, Melou and I are regular listeners to Jarvis Cocker's music show on BBC Radio 6, which he archly calls his *Sunday Service*. Are rock and pop songs the new hymns? Cocker's show attracts an audience of around 2 million, which is significantly larger than the audience for the real thing, BBC TV's 55-year-old flagship religious programme *Songs of Praise*. There was a quasi-religious quality to the public response to the death of David Bowie at the beginning of 2016. It was as though one of our Prophets had just died. In the Middle Ages, the public would probably have demanded his canonization.

Traditional Muslims, of course, do not feel the need to repurpose any religious rituals because they have their Islam. As the literal gift of God, and therefore perfect, their religion has proved peculiarly resistant to reform and innovation. As God tells the Prophet in one of the Koran's most famous verses:

> This day have I perfected your religion for you and
> completed My favour unto you,
> and have chosen for you as religion AL-ISLAM[7]

Monday 13 June

Terrible news from Orlando, Florida, where an Afghan-American has gunned down sixty people in a gay nightclub. The liberal left, and indeed the gunman's own father, are predictably insisting the tragedy 'has nothing to do with Islam' and everything to do with the availability of assault weapons in America; while the right, equally predictably, are saying the opposite. My assumption is that Islam probably does have *something* to do with what happened – as does the availability of guns. What certainly would not have prevented the massacre is @realDonaldTrump's proposal, now repeated, to ban Muslims from entering the US, since the shooter, Omar Mateen, 29, was a US citizen born in New York. But this hasn't discouraged Trump, who tweets: 'What has happened in Orlando is just the beginning. Our leadership is weak and ineffective. I called it and asked for the ban. Must be tough.' Trump also wants Obama to resign for refusing to use the phrase 'radical Islamic Extremism'. But what does that phrase even mean?

Trump is by no means the first American populist to target an ethnic minority. In the 1850s, the raison d'être of the so-called American Party, also known as the 'Know Nothing' movement, was to limit the influence of German and Irish Catholic immigrants. In the 1880s, President Chester Arthur passed a Chinese Exclusion Act in response to blue-collar anger at the cheapness of immigrant Chinese labour. On TV, Obama looks uncharacteristically rattled:

'We now have proposals from the presumptive Republican nominee to bar all Muslims from emigrating to America ... suggesting entire religious communities are complicit in violence. Where does this stop?'

Tuesday 14 June

Bashir from the Annandale mosque invites me to iftaar. He greets me in a shalwar kameez instead of a suit this time, and takes me into the prayer hall where I watch the preparations for the meal with interest. A stout drum of transparent plastic, 50 feet long and 3 feet wide, is rolled out to form a picnic mat, and pinned down with water jugs, plates and beakers. Tonight's dinner is yellow lentils, which are put down in three steam-wreathed tureens as the diners file along to their places either side. Dates are distributed, and thick rounds of nan are tossed down like Frisbees. The process is slick and practised. With no furniture and no cutlery, it has taken less than ten minutes to lay up for and serve over sixty people. The mosque provides food to anyone who turns up, at no charge, every night of Ramadan. Sixty people is about the average; Bashir tells me that on Fridays and over the last ten days of the month, the numbers can triple.

He invites me to sit with him at a table reserved for those too old or disabled to squat on the floor, a gesture of kindness to a Western guest that I recognize as belonging to their home country. We are duly joined by four rheumatic codgers with not much English and fewer teeth. As we slurp our lentils, Bashir recounts how he came to Britain in 1961. A former textiles inspector, he settled first in Birmingham as a shop-floor manager for Lucas Industries. He moved to Edinburgh in 1974 when, he recalled, there were only five Pakistani families in the city. These days the city's Pakistanis number 7,000.

As in Glasgow, the core of the community is Punjabi, typically from the Faisalabad area. This makes them more educated and more mercantile than the rural Kashmiri Mirpuris who predominate in Bradford or Birmingham. Britain's original Mirpuris, Bashir asserts with barely concealed disdain, were stokers for the East India Company who jumped ship when they reached an English port. The mainstay of Edinburgh's Pakistanis was never lowly factory work, as it was for Mirpuris elsewhere. Edinburgh never had that kind of industrial base. Instead they thrived on that British Asian classic, the corner shop industry. Like my neighbour Shaukat, Bashir and all of his colleagues here followed that path, shopkeepers in a nation of shopkeepers. Bashir's generation, he tells me, worked long hours to build up their businesses to make the money necessary to educate their children for something better. His own grandchildren are studying to be solicitors.

After supper, Salim Irshad, the chairman of the Edinburgh Pakistani Association for which the mosque doubles as headquarters, calls me over to a corner of the hall where he is holding court with his other old shopkeeper friends, distributing sweet cardamom tea from a big silver flask. Imam Ghafoor flutters on the margins, getting ready for another round of prayers. His status here, I now see, is more one of employee than community leader. The imam takes care of spiritual matters; Salim runs the place. At one point, someone approaches and hands him a fat wad of banknotes wrapped up in an elastic band.

'Ah: the money arrives!' he laughs. 'A donation from the community. To pay for all the iftaar meals, you see?'

There is a flash of green as he tucks it away in an inside pocket of his waistcoat: the notes are all 50s.

There aren't many young Pakistanis around tonight. This mosque, the entire operation, looks and feels like a club for old men. When Imam Ghafoor is out of earshot I ask Salim if he worries about this, and whether he thought young British-born Pakistanis were turned off by sermons delivered only in Urdu. The men all glance at each other.

'It's important to us Pakistanis to maintain a link with home,' Salim begins.

'But it's true that there is a lack of appeal to the next generation. Some of whom, it's true, barely understand a word of Urdu,' interrupts a colleague. 'We feel it. And we are addressing it.'

Next Friday, he explains, a British-born imam from Glasgow has been invited to give the Friday khutbah in English; an innovation that, he hints, could become a permanent fixture if it works out. It is the clearest indication yet that the old order is changing at Annandale Mosque.

Wednesday 15 June

The Orlando shooting is still making headlines, despite stiff competition from the British Euro-referendum, where the Remain campaign is faltering. The latest twist is that the shooter,

Omar Mateen, was a regular at the nightclub that he attacked, who even posted photos of himself on a gay dating website called Grinder. This makes a nonsense of the simple narrative still being pushed out by Donald Trump. Mateen dedicated his murders to ISIS in a 911 phone call from the nightclub, but that justification now looks bolted on; the real cause looks less like Islamist ideology than his own repressed sexuality.

This is not to say that Islam played no role. The Koran and hadith are unequivocal in their disapproval of homosexuality. 'When a man mounts another man, the throne of God shakes,' says a hadith – which to a pious Muslim might be reason enough to repress his natural inclination. But still: was this hate crime actually a self-hate crime, committed by a man described as mentally unstable by his ex-wife, whom he used to beat? What was lacking here was not stricter border controls but a psychiatrist.

Our own security services have known for some time that mental instability is an important factor in radicalization. In a police study of 500 referrals to Channel, the Home Office's multi-agency counter-radicalization support programme, 44 per cent of them were assessed as being 'likely to have vulnerabilities related to mental health or psychological difficulties'.[8]

'There comes a point when you have to stop pulling people out of the river and you have to find out who's pushing them in,' said Chief Constable Simon Cole, the police lead on Prevent. 'You're not going to arrest your way out of a terrorist crisis, it is not possible to do that. So how do you identify who might be about to fall in?'

Michael Adebowale, one of the men who almost decapitated Drummer Lee Rigby in Woolwich in 2013, was a diagnosed psychotic who believed djinns made him do things and were 'playing with him'. An examining psychiatrist reported that he felt that his religion, far from driving him to murder a kuffar, had actually lessened the effects of his psychosis. Could better pastoral care have prevented the Orlando nightclub massacre?

Shaheen from Number 29 knocks on the door with rice, paratha and a Tupperware box of yellow lentils. It's lucky that I like yellow lentils.

Thursday 16 June

The Batley-born Labour MP Jo Cox was murdered in Birstall today, shot and stabbed outside her constituency surgery. Tommy Mair, a loner with mental health issues, is said to have shouted 'Britain First' as he went at her with a foot-long hunting knife. She was pro-refugee and pro-Europe, and far-right organizations like Paul Golding's have done much to stoke the ugly nationalist mood against both. UKIP and other Brexiteers say they 'want our country back', a slogan that suddenly sounds uncomfortably like the sort of rhetoric I heard in Dewsbury at the beginning of the year.

Jo Cox once ran a camp for the orphans of Srebrenica, and was so affected by the experience that she named her daughter Leija, a Bosnian name. Andrew Mitchell MP says she was 'a force of nature, a five-foot bundle of Yorkshire grit and determination absolutely committed to helping other people'. It's hard to imagine what terrible misplaced passion drove Tommy Mair to kill her. The police who searched Tommy Mair's house found Nazi regalia, copies of a pro-apartheid magazine called *SA Patriot* and a manual explaining how to build a handgun. If true, this murder looks a big failure for Prevent. In Yorkshire, half of all Channel programme referrals are about far-right extremism, the highest proportion for any region in the country.[9] How was Mair overlooked?

On LBC, James O'Brien fulminates on the 'politics of hate' that, in his view, are behind what happened:

'If I was to be reading my newspaper every single morning and be told that my very existence was under siege from people I've never met and never seen but keep getting told are coming here in their hordes. If I was to open my newspaper or turn on my radio or TV to hear that everybody who is coming here is a rapist and they've got their eyes on our women and we've got no chance whatsoever of protecting ourselves. And unless we do this or do that, or treat them like this or treat them like that, then we're all doomed, we're all going to hell in a handcart. If I was being told it's time to reclaim our country every time I got out of bed in the morning, I'd begin to believe it, I think, if I didn't have the knowledge and the insights and the education to know that it is not true. We want our country back from whom? We want our country back from when?'[10]

Friday 17 June

To Annandale Mosque for Friday prayers, to hear the new English-speaking imam from Glasgow. To Bashir and Salim's embarrassment, he fails to turn up. Back at home a supper party is under way for my friend Fo Neill, up from London with her son Felix, who is having a look at the university with a view to studying medicine here. It is difficult watching them eat. The questions I field have become irritating in their familiarity. Why are you doing this, what happens if you cheat, has Ramadan Man lost weight? I eat, finally, at 10, and my temper returns. Then I feel boiling hot, and have to take my jumper off. My thickened speech returns to normal, and I have the strangest sensation of hearing myself chatting again, as manic as a monkey.

'He's baaaack!' cries Fo, like Jack Nicholson in *The Shining*.

Saturday 18 June

With Edinburgh's Islam-discovering possibilities starting to thin, today I launched part two of my Ramadan plan – a short national tour – beginning with one of the most distant mosques of interest to me, the Manar Centre in Cardiff. I fly to Bristol, hire a car and reach the address, a grubby late-Victorian terrace in the Cathays district, at noon.

Al-Manar comprises two small houses knocked together and extended out the back. The sound of unruly children floats from an open upstairs window. From the paper darts scattered about on the pavement it seems the teacher of this weekend *maktab*, the equivalent of a Christian Sunday School, is running late today. I have an appointment with Ali, one of the mosque managers, but the lady who answers the door tells me he is on holiday until Tuesday and doesn't invite me in. I wait and wonder what to do next, studying the road sign opposite the entrance with the carcass of a bicycle chained to it. *Twmpathau*, says the sign. *Humps*.

Al-Manar was once considered the first and oldest mosque in Britain. According to many books and articles it was established in 1860 by Yemeni seamen working for the East India Company, whose ships from India terminated at Cardiff's port. But although there is indeed a sizeable Yemeni community still living in Cardiff, the story about their mosque turns out to be a myth. Al-Manar was actually founded in 1992; the oldest mosque in Britain is the Muslim Institute in Liverpool, which dates from 1887.

It doesn't matter. Al-Manar is interesting for another reason: it was the mosque favoured by three young Cardiff men who joined ISIS in Syria in 2014. One of the three, Nasser Muthana al-Yemeni, appeared in ISIS propaganda films, including one gruesome execution video where he stands in a line of sixteen jihadis, each of whom proceeds to cut the throat of a hooded captive kneeling before him. The knifeman standing next to Muthana in the video is the infamous Jihadi John. The mosque's leaders denied any involvement in the radicalization of the Cardiff boys but that hasn't stopped the media from pestering them ever since, so it is not entirely surprising that I'm not being invited in.

I'm about to give up when a builder pulls up in his van, delivering a box of bananas and his eight-year-old daughter to the maktab. We end up chatting for some time. He's an Algerian called Abdul-Fatah who works as a shopfitter for Aldi. He used to live in Cardiff but recently moved to Walthamstow when he separated from the girl's mother, who is Irish. Walthamstow, he says, is the undisputed centre of Britain's Algerian community. He doesn't much like Cardiff, which he says is a racist city; he only comes now to visit his daughter.

'I don't like these people,' he says, in French-accented English. 'They are rude to me because of my colour, and I was attacked once. Look!'

He pulls out his phone and, after much scrolling, produces a photograph of himself with a big black eye.

'I tell the police, but what do they do? Nothing. It is not at all like this in London.'

We talk about ISIS. He says that there are hardly any Algerian volunteers in Syria, because Algerians understand better than anyone the futility of war. He himself came to Britain as a refugee from his country's bloody Islamist insurrection in the early 1990s. I tell him I know all about it, that actually I covered it as a cub reporter for the *Daily Telegraph*, and he says, 'Then you will understand how we Algerians *learned*.'

As zuhr, the noon prayers, approaches, Abdul-Fatah sneaks me inside to watch. The congregation is an ethnic hodge-podge, not the predominantly Yemeni one I expected, although the service is all in Arabic. There is no pulpit at the front, not even a lectern. Instead the imam preaches cross-legged on the floor at the same level as his congregation, a headscarf draped modestly across his head. Some of the congregation pray with a little wooden screen placed in front of them, which I've not seen before. Called a *sutrah*, it is designed to prevent any visual distraction from the task in hand. It all looks and feels more austere and puritan than usual: a Salafist mosque, in a word.

In the evening I visit another mosque nearby, the Dar ul-Isra. A local group called Bridges for Communities is holding one of its regular interfaith iftaars, and I tag along. The group is run by a husband and wife team, Mark and Sarah, who lived in the Middle East for a spell, and have made it their mission to break down the prejudices about Muslims that, they say, they themselves harboured before they moved there.

The Dar ul-Isra is bigger and more relaxed than Al-Manar. One of the eighty or so mosques that took part in the Muslim Council of Britain's 'Visit My Mosque' open day in February, it has made community relations a speciality. The mosque committee even includes a white Welsh convert called Amanda. This is the public, most easily acceptable face of British Islam. A billboard by the entrance boasts half a dozen thank-you letters from charities, the causes ranging from refugees in Palestine and Syria to a local Muslim primary school. It also carries a Ramadan greeting from the prime minister, on Downing Street letterhead.

There are forty of us visitors and we form a peculiar group. There is a large contingent of teenagers, girls and boys in ill-fitting white shirts and ties, who turn out to be Mormons from the School of the Latter Day Saints. There are two state school teachers who want to understand their Muslim pupils better, and an 86-year-old Methodist lay preacher called Jim. We sit in a circle in a hall full of murmuring reciters. Two committee members take us through the five pillars of Islam. There is a step-by-step demonstration of prayer technique, and a *qari* who gives a short but beautiful recitation of the Koran, the famous verses about holding fast to the rope of Allah.

Jim the Methodist asks about prayer. For him, he explains, it's often like an ad-lib conversation with God: a spontaneous dialogue, not a scripted one. In Islam, he wants to know, how do you ask God a question – and where in their prayer system is the moment to listen, the opportunity to hear His reply? Our lecturer doesn't properly understand the question. Because the Koran is the literal word of God, he says, you are hearing his voice every time you read or recite the Koran, so you always have a direct line to the divine. Amanda the convert adds that your 'chi' realigns if you 'settle' as you prostrate yourself, and that this creates a connection to God. Jim is polite but isn't persuaded.

'I've always felt friendly towards Islam, but I don't think I'll be converting any time soon,' he confides to me afterwards. 'Certainly not at my age.'

Methodism, I learn, is holding up pretty well in Cardiff, with seventeen chapels still active in the city, down from twenty-five when he started forty years ago.

Sunday 19 June

Baroness Warsi announces that she is switching her support from Brexit to Remain, explaining that the former's campaign has become too racist and negative on immigration.

'The Leave Line Up – BNP, Le Pen, Geert Wilders, Farage, Gove. I wouldn't get on a night bus with them would you?' she tweets.

It is front-page news in some newspapers, who call her a 'leading Tory' who is 'defecting'. Farage, in damage-limitation mode, responds that he wasn't aware she had been in his camp in the first place. He has had to withdraw his infamous 'Breaking Point' campaign poster, though, which Remainers are likening to Nazi propaganda from the 1930s. Launched the day after Jo

Cox's murder in Birstall, the poster's timing is certainly unfortunate. Will it tip the balance for the Remainers in next Thursday's vote? Remain have inched ahead in the polls, which some pundits are putting down to a 'Jo Cox effect'. A hashtag campaign, #moreincommon, is trending on Twitter, in commemoration of her inaugural speech to Parliament: 'We have far more in common than that which divides us.'

Monday 20 June

It's the summer solstice tonight, so tomorrow's fasting hours are the longest possible. To mark the occasion I invite myself to iftaar at Britain's most northerly mosque, in Inverness. Their iftaar is at 10.23, with suhur at 1.30: almost 21 hours of fasting.

The community is tiny, and seems genuinely pleased to see me. The mosque secretary is a hospital doctor, Wahid Khan, who explains that there are no more than 500 Muslims in the whole Highlands region. In Inverness they prayed in a two-bed council flat until two years ago, when the community got together and bought the present premises, a former Rangers FC supporters' club – which explains why the arched prayer-box shapes on the carpet that point towards Mecca do not run parallel to the walls. Wahid and his friends converted the old club themselves. He shows me a photograph of doctors, dentists, taxi drivers and curry-house owners, all side-by-side in dust masks, sledgehammers over their shoulders.

Alan, a convert who works in the Citizens' Advice Bureau, says being Muslim in Inverness is easier than it was. He used to have to go to Aberdeen to find halal meat, but these days it is stocked by the local Cash & Carry. Islamophobia isn't an issue, he says, apart from a few teenagers on laptops in their bedrooms.

'Inverness has always been a churchy sort of place. It wasn't that long ago that you couldn't go out on Sundays. So people here sort of respect us. We're a faith-based community just like they used to be.'

There are about sixty people in the hall tonight, including a handful of women, imperfectly screened off by a curtain across a section to the side. They are mostly Asians but there are others here too, from Egypt, Algeria, Mauritius. I meet a jolly, portly man in a kufi cap and a gold shalwar, I guess a Bangladeshi, who is one of the city's curry-house owners. He says there are ten such businesses in Inverness, which together sell £200,000 of curry every week.

'Everyone likes curry,' he beams.

News and greetings are swapped, mostly in strong Scottish accents. One man's wife has just had a baby. Tired but glowing, he is congratulated all round. Someone else has just opened a new fish and chip shop in Drumnadrochit, half way up Loch Ness.

'Now, that's a proper village,' he says. 'It's so beautiful. Like Swat.'

These Muslims are becoming Highlanders. An Egyptian oilrig engineer's contribution to the iftaar meal yesterday was a large, freshly caught brown crab. Many Muslims won't eat shellfish – it is generally considered makruh – but Wahid insists that all seafood is fine. I also notice that the new, Indo-Saracenic plasterwork above the chimneypiece in the prayer hall is sur-rounded not by the traditional arabesques, but by tiles in sludge-brown tartan.

The imam, Hafiz Ibrahim, is a smiley-serious Bangladeshi who grew up in Lossiemouth. Aged just 24, he turns out to be a scion of the Islamic Institute in Dewsbury, one of four main sat-ellite schools of the Deobandi Darul Uloom in Bury: a classic example of the new breed of British-born clergy. He sits me down next to him at iftaar, and insists that differences of doctrine among Muslims are unimportant. His congregation, he says, includes people from many Islamic traditions. There are even a couple of Shi'ites: the equivalent, perhaps, of Catholics and Protestants worshipping together.

'Yes, I am Deobandi. But we are all Muslims here, and we are Muslims first. Islam stresses the importance of unity, and makes it very easy to find the commonalities. And it is easier to find unity in a small community like this one. I love it here.'

Ibrahim is not a worldly person. Politics leave him cold; he has no idea which way to vote in the upcoming Euro-referendum, and plans not to vote at all. His interest is in the spiritual. He tells me how, just before his ninth birthday, his father sent him to a madrassah in Sylhet in Bangladesh, where the Koran was the only subject. It took him two years to memorize every surah and become *hafiz*, rocking back and forth cross-legged on the floor in the traditional way, for up to eight hours a day, six days a week.

'Sylhet was tough,' he recalls. 'I got very sick. And then I got migraines. And the mosquitoes were terrible. It was just Bangladesh.'

I think about his achievement, the application it must have taken.

'Some parts of the Koran are easier to remember than others,' he goes on. 'And the rhythm of its poetry helps. Allah said, "I have made it easy for you to remember." But you have to keep practising, otherwise it all starts to drift away. It's like learning a foreign language.'

I stay at the mosque long after iftaar, to see what he can do. The Koran is traditionally recited in its entirety over Ramadan, in thirty prescribed sections, with each nightly section taking about an hour. Tonight's section is to start with Surah 15, *Al-Hijr*, The Stoneland. The other men assemble before Ibrahim in two long lines on the misaligned carpet. He opens with a short homily, in English, on the sin of arrogance. Next is the regular isha night prayer, and then the *tarawih*, a special Ramadan one.

Finally the verses come. Ibrahim's singing voice is high and clear, more incantation than recitation. He is not absolutely word-perfect, but there is a trick to his trade: there is another hafiz in the congregation, who instantly prompts Ibrahim from his own memory at the rare moments that he stumbles. The two of them spent the afternoon rehearsing tonight's recitation, and the spell is never broken. Like most of the worshippers here I can't understand the Arabic, but the music of it is obvious as it echoes from the walls of the calm, still room. I get out my Koran and try to follow along in translation, but I am too drowsy from the food and the lateness of the hour. The words blur on the page and I fall into a kind of trance, in thrall to the power and beauty of Ibrahim's magic, foreign, 1,400-year-old words.

> Alif. Lâm. Râ.
> Those are the Signs of the Book
> And a clear Qur'an
> It may be that those who disbelieve
> Will wish that they had been Muslims.
> Leave them to eat and enjoy themselves.
> Let false hope divert them.
> They will soon know![11]

Tuesday 21 June

In Edinburgh again. I weigh myself and find I am literally as well as spiritually enlightened: half a stone lost in a fortnight. I haven't yet spoiled my fast with any liquid or food, nor smoked, either – unlike the Pakistani lad in our local newsagent, who I catch with a cigarette on his shop doorstep.

'This Ramadan is just so loooong,' he says, rolling and then crossing his eyes. 'But it's OK, I can make up for the broken fast later.'

With a fortnight still to go, it seems best not to ask how many fast days he is planning to add on.

> O Allah, veil my weaknesses and set at ease my dismay. O Allah, preserve me from the front and from behind and on my right and on my left and from above, and I take refuge with You lest I be swallowed up by the earth.[12]

Wednesday 22 June

A train track problem near Doncaster makes me an hour late for the annual interfaith iftaar at the East London Mosque in Whitechapel.

It is not my first time at the ELM, the spiritual heart of east London's Bangladeshi community, but I hadn't appreciated before how enormous it is. It's an ordinary Ramadan weekday but there are hundreds of people milling about, with more arriving all the time. It's like being in a busy airport. Its five prayer halls are designed to accommodate 7,000 people, although on important Ramadan nights 10,000 or even 12,000 have been known to squash in. Dumping one's shoes by the door in the usual way would lead to chaos in such a place. Instead the new arrivals are issued with little plastic bags so that they can carry their shoes in with them. The building's empty spaces are covered in the same Mecca-aligned fitted carpet as the prayer halls, to accommodate the overflow. Tonight there is already a line of worshippers prostrated in the reception area bookshop.

I head for the seminar hall I am supposed to be in, and join a crowd dotted with clergy in dog collars and *kippot*, the traditional Jewish skullcap. I am placed at a table next to two Bangladeshi women and chat to Mahera Ruby, one of the mosque's trustees. The director of an organization called Blooming Parenting, and with a PhD in Education, she is interesting about the social cost of dysfunctional families. Life in too many homes, she says, is dominated by electronic screens. Many Asian families see television as a means of keeping in touch with home, with sets permanently tuned to satellite stations broadcasting soap opera from the subcontinent. The consequence is a collapse of proper communication between parents and offspring, and a 'lost' generation of children prone to go off the rails as they grow up.

Blooming Parenting, with support from Tower Hamlets Council, aims to address this through back-to-basics workshops with titles like Nurturing Positive Discipline. It sounds the sort of thing the security services would be interested in, another means of nipping extremist tendencies in the bud, and I ask if she's ever been offered funding by Prevent.

'Yes,' she says, 'but I wouldn't touch *that*, thank you very much.'

When it's time to leave I absentmindedly offer my hand in goodbye. She clasps her hands to her chest in decline, but does so with such charm that I almost laugh.

It has been a sultry evening and a storm breaks just as I emerge on to Whitechapel Road. I run for the cover of a Shell garage opposite where a snappily dressed young Bangladeshi man is also sheltering. He laughs when I say it's like Dhaka in the monsoon.

'It is as God wills,' he says.

The deluge intensifies, thundering on the metal roof above the pumps and cascading off the edges in sheets. Other Bangladeshis hoot and shout as they splash past on their way to the mosque, defiant or past caring, some in flip-flops, some in bare feet, their sodden shalwars clinging to their bodies.

The man sheltering with me is from Stepney, with an accent to match. He tells me that he works for the council, and that he is getting married soon but is worried about the expense. He has already paid £20,000 in dowry money and entertaining his in-laws, with about another £10,000 to go. Then, in an apparent non-sequitur, he confides that today he got into a fight with a white non-Muslim, like me.

'It was road rage,' he says. 'This cyclist ran into my car, but would he say sorry? So I says, I'm calling the police. So he starts pulling my windscreen wiper off, and then we start fighting, fists and everything, right in the street. I feel really bad about it now cos he probably went away feeling bad towards Muslims. I know I felt bad towards non-Muslims,' he adds, with a sideways look.

'Oh dear,' I say. 'It's not really in the spirit of Ramadan, is it?'

'Yeah, and that. I'm worried I've spoiled fifteen whole days of fast. In me head, if you know what I'm saying. I prayed for forgiveness today. What's your name?'

I tell him.

'Dalal,' he says, shaking my hand. 'Nice to meet yer.'

The rain eases and he stalks off into the night.

Thursday June 23

To Woking in Surrey, the unlikely site of the first purpose-built mosque in Britain. It was built, entertainingly, by a Jew, the Orientalist and languages scholar Gottlieb Leitner, in 1889, for the benefit of students at the Oriental Institute that he founded nearby. The spot where the institute stood is now a supermarket car park, but the mosque remains, surrounded by Scots pines, tulip trees and a well-tended rose garden. Named the Shah Jahan after its principal benefactress, the scholarly Begum of Bhopal, it was built in the same Indo-Saracenic style as the Royal Pavilion in Brighton and immediately strikes you as a product of its age, an architectural mishmash reflecting the Victorian era's fascination with its exotic imperial possessions.

Mohammed Habib, a former cashier for the security company

G4S, now a heavily bearded mosque committee member with a salary from English Heritage, produces a big iron door key and lets me in. It's a tiny building with room for perhaps eighty people – a reflection, Habib says, of the number of Muslims in Britain when it was built. Today there are 9,000 of them in Woking alone, part of a community in Surrey that numbers 120,000. The Shah Jahan is still used for special occasions but is essentially a museum piece now. For everyday worship, the locals use a converted plastics factory just beyond the rose garden.

The Shah Jahan's proportions are perfect but miniaturized, giving it the gem-like quality of a Wendy house. The interior is being refurbished and is full of dustsheets, scaffolding and the smell of fresh paint. The restorers from English Heritage, who have gone home for the day, have left off retracing the Arabic script that decorates the corners and runs around the base of the ceiling dome. Habib spots a piece of used tracing paper on the floor and scoops it up, tutting. The words spell out one of the hundred synonyms for Allah found in the Koran and should not be so sullied.

The committee have been reorganizing the mosque's archives in preparation for an exhibition about the beginnings of British Islam. Despite its toy-like size, the Shah Jahan was for many years the focal point for Islam not just in Britain but in northern Europe. The religion's main propagators, furthermore, were not foreigners but native whites. Habib lists their names with something like pride. Marmaduke Pickthall, the first modern translator of the Koran, was briefly an imam here. Lord Headley, Lord Stanley of Alderley and Charles William Buchanan Hamilton, a deputy surgeon general of the British army, were also all converts closely associated with the mosque, as was William Quilliam. It is not a narrative often heard in these Islamophobic times, but before World War Two, fully one-tenth of the estimated 10,000 Muslims in Britain were native converts.

'Some of the lads who go off to fight for a caliphate in Syria say it's impossible to practise their religion properly in this country, but how can they say that when this mosque has been here for 127 years?' says Habib. 'The truth is that it's easier to be a good Muslim in the UK than it is in some supposedly Islamic countries.'

There follows a paean of praise for British tolerance and freedom that I have heard many times before. Habib points out that in the two world wars, over a million Muslims sacrificed their lives for the UK. London's Central Mosque at Regent's Park was built and paid for by a grateful government, on the orders of Winston Churchill. The way Habib sees it, the Muslims who died for Britain were not cannon-fodder vassals of a colonial empire but men fighting for a set of values much closer to traditional Islam than many native British realize.

'The British benefits system is an *Islamic* system,' he says. 'It would be recognized by Omar, the second rightly guided caliph, who led his servant on a camel when he was ill, and whose cloak was held together with seventy patches. Can you imagine any modern Muslim leader wearing such a cloak? They are all sitting on toilets of gold.'

We go for iftaar in the ex-plastics factory. We sit with perhaps two hundred others at a trestle table running the length of the former machine hall, a cold, cavernous space with a pronounced 1950s feel that echoes with the chatter and scrape of diners and metal chairs. Woking's Muslims clubbed together to buy the factory years ago, but haven't yet saved enough to do it up as they would like. The prayer hall next door was flooded by a big rainstorm a few weeks ago and still smells appalling. After the salat, over coffee in the little library adjacent to the mosque, I chat late into the night with Habib and the mosque handyman, Asif, who says in a rich Yorkshire accent that he is 'from Halifax – or Sunnifax, as it's known. I moved down here to keep meself out of trouble. I were going off the rails up there, like.'

He offers no further details other than that he has recently regained his driving licence, allowing him to go back to his second job as a cab driver. There is surprisingly little talk about today's referendum on Britain's membership of the EU – it is ideology and faith that fires them up, not politics – although Asif does mention that he voted Leave because he wanted to give the Tories a kicking. Their insouciance doesn't augur well; and, sure enough, by the time I get back to London at 2 a.m., the TV pollsters are in meltdown. I stay up all night to watch, aghast, as Britain votes to leave the EU.

Friday 24 June

To 'The Big Iftaar' community event in Luton with Ashfaque Chowdhury, the shrewd and watchful head of Al-Hikmah School. I'm so tired from last night and addled from lack of food that I accidentally get off the train too early, at St Albans, and arrive in Luton only just in time.

Ashfaque is aflutter with Cameron's resignation. The frontliners to replace him do not bode well for British Muslims: Boris Johnson, who once called black people 'picaninnies'; Theresa May, the Home Secretary overseer of the Prevent programme; and Michael Gove, the neo-con bogeyman viewed by many Muslims as the government's Islamophobe-in-chief. Ashfaque predicts that Theresa May will prevail.

I had assumed that the Muslim vote would be solidly for Remain, in opposition to the awful racism in the UKIP campaign particularly, but it seems this was not the case and that Muslim society is as split over Europe as everyone else. The big Muslim centres outside London all voted Leave, with the exceptions of Manchester and Leicester. In Luton, Ashfaque is blaming the result on older white people, but I doubt it's as simple as that.

There are 1,500 people in St George's Square, and big queues for the free food. Ashfaque and I have to shout to hear one another over a speaker system on which the results of a raffle are being announced. Most but not all of the crowd here are Asian. In amongst the families with children is a group of crusty-clothed homeless people swigging cider. They are also smoking dope, which seems risky as well as inappropriate, since there are several uniformed policemen in attendance tonight. The police, however, ignore the unmistakable smell and don't even move them on. I presume this is because tonight is a *community* event, designed to spread happy feelings of cohesion, so all must be made welcome.

Ashfaque introduces me to a lady who runs a church-funded community cohesion programme called Near Neighbours, and to two Anglican vicars. They are keen to tell me about their projects: a tile-making project, a peace garden, an interfaith solidarity march from a church to a gurdwara to a mosque. One of the vicars, David Kesterton, is from All Saints Church in the middle of Bury Park, once a white working-class neighbourhood, now the Muslim heart of Luton. His regular Sunday congregation, he says, numbers about thirty. I ask him how, in that case, he thinks he can speak for the non-Muslim community, although it is difficult to put the question without seeming rude. He replies that it would be a mistake to count Luton's Christians by church attendance. It doesn't sound much of an answer to me.

Saturday 25 June

I give a talk at the Hammersmith Literary Festival, at the Godolphin & Latymer school in west London, on 'My Journey Through Muslim Britain'. Unfortunately the organizers haven't advertised the event enough. Or possibly at all. Nothing feels emptier than a big school on a weekend, when the silence echoes down the long classroom corridors. I get an audience of seven that includes my sister Lucy and her daughter Iris, and quickly abandon my plan to ask for a show of hands in illustration of London's ethno-religious diversity.

We discuss the fallout from Brexit, which has begun in earnest for Muslims. The police say that reported hate crime has risen fivefold since last week. It's unlucky timing perhaps, but many pubs were already full of England flag-wavers thanks to the European Cup, and now the nationalist chanting has spilled out into the street. Is bigotry becoming socially acceptable?

The xenophobia has a frightening craziness to it. In Birmingham, a young Muslim girl was cornered by a group of white lads shouting, 'Get out, we voted leave.' Two other men were arrested outside a mosque where they were demonstrating with a poster reading 'Rapefugees not welcome'. As Baroness Warsi told Sky News, this abuse is being directed at people who have lived in Britain for three, four, even five generations. It's not just the result but the purpose of the referendum that has been misconstrued here. Even white Remain campaigners have been attacked for 'bringing sharia'. The *Guardian* writer John Harris yesterday quoted George Orwell: 'The gentleness of the English civilization is perhaps its most marked characteristic. You notice it the instant you set foot on English soil', but added: 'Not now, surely?'[13]

He is right: not now. Britain at the moment feels more like the fascist land described by Pink Floyd's 'Waiting for the Worms', a track from their 1979 album *The Wall* that I listened to a lot as a teenager, and which seems weirdly prescient now. There really are people out there who think Britannia could rule again, if only we sent our 'coloured cousins' home. With Trump proposing to fence off Mexico, and borders being reinforced all over Eastern Europe, walls have come back into fashion.

I tell my tiny audience in Hammersmith that I think this madness is temporary and that normal British service will resume soon. I have faith in our mongrel nation's innate qualities – our phlegmatic dislike of authority, our suspicion of cant and dogma, our sense of humour and appreciation of the absurd – that have prevented far-right politics from ever taking hold in Britain as they have in, say, modern France or Austria. We grumble at queue-jumping immigrants but stop short of wanting to criminalize or kill them. We might sneer at Johnny Foreigner but we tolerate his differences in the end. It is not always easy to see the end of a tunnel when you are in it, though – especially if you are a Muslim on the end of a hate crime.

Sunday 26 June

Iftaar tonight in London W10 with Mujib Gallagher, a protégé of Abdalhaqq Bewley's. Mujib is an ex-Radley schoolboy who fell in love with Islam on his gap year in Pakistan in 2001. He had just started his Classics degree at Edinburgh University when 9/11 happened and found himself telling anyone who would listen that 'the Muslims I met were not like that'. His interest in Islam deepened, he switched his degree to Arabic and Persian, studied the Koran in Egypt and Iran and, in 2006, to the initial outrage of his Northern Irish, lay-preacher father, converted. He later became a solicitor specializing in Muslim rights and moved to Norwich for a spell, where he was appointed an imam.

We meet at a Moroccan restaurant on the Golborne Road, the Zayane, and order the 'Ramadan special': sweet sesame biscuits called *shubukir*, a lamb tagine, mint tea in a tiny silver pot with a tasselled velvet cosy over the handle, all served by a man in a fez and a long stripy djellaba. Although next door to Notting Hill, the Golborne Road has somehow resisted the northward creep of white gentrification and remains an important centre for London Moroccans.

'There's a café at the bottom of Trellick Tower where it's all tea and spliff and gambling. Step inside and you are *in* Morocco,' Mujib enthuses.

Before we eat, Mujib leads me across the road where we duck into a doorway beside a travel agent's. Up a narrow staircase is a tiny mosque that was set up years ago by Abdalqadir as-Sufi, Abdalhaqq Bewley's friend and mentor, whom Mujib still refers to as 'the big boss'. It is a damp summer's night and the room, which is crowded with Moroccans, reeks of sweat and wet shoes, mixed with the smell of rice and chicken from a basement canteen two floors below. Mujib is well known here: it is where he learned to recite the Koran, Maliki Sufi-style. The imam greets him warmly.

Back in the restaurant, the portrait of the community he paints is not an entirely happy one. The root of the trouble is that the older Moroccans, who are typically 'very traditional, very devout, the sort who like to dress up in djellaba and fez to celebrate Ramadan', have lost control of their young. It's the classic 'big fight' between generations that he has seen replicated elsewhere – among the Somalis of Harlesden, for instance. The W10 Moroccans, he says, are blighted by a 'huge' drug problem. Another mosque nearby, the Manaar on Acklam Road, attracted the attention of the police when it emerged that Moroccan youths were hiding their drugs and guns on the premises. Just as bad, many young Moroccan men have embraced a kind of street Wahhabism – what Mujib calls 'punk Islam' – and keep going off to fight in Syria and Libya.

'It's a completely open secret. Everyone gossips around here about who's gone, who's about to go, who's just come back. The authorities must know all about it. At least, I assume they do.'

They clearly know about some of it. Al-Manaar, which was opened by Prince Charles in 2001, was described in the media in early 2016 as a 'focal point of a network of ISIS extremists', and the place where Jihadi John first met other members of his ISIS cell. At least nine terrorists, including the failed 21/7 bombers who tried to attack London Transport in 2005, are reported to have attended the mosque. The exodus to Syria, Mujib says, has slackened significantly since its peak in 2014, when ISIS emerged as the dominant jihadist force and word began to filter back that life in Raqqa was not all it was cracked up to be.[14]

Monday 27 June

To the Old Bailey, for the much-delayed start of the trial of Anjem Choudary, the poppy-burning former al-Muhajiroun leader accused of encouraging terrorism online. As the subject of numerous TV documentaries he is probably the best-known extremist in the country, so it's no surprise to find a gaggle of pressmen loitering outside. They are not the only ones waiting for him: across the street is a shaven-headed man in combat trousers and a 'British Pride' Union Jack T-shirt imprinted with the words *Patriotism is not a Game*. The photographers size up the aggressive set of his shoulders and wink at each other: there's a good chance of a photogenic street scuffle outside court today.

It's a long wait and conversation is difficult thanks to the amplified sound of drilling from a building site across the road, an office block draped in a tarpaulin that reads 'Redefining London'. I pass the time interviewing 'Brabs', a willowy Sikh from Hounslow queuing for the court appearance of his brother, who is in trouble for 'sorting out' a local Polish drug-dealer of whom he disapproved.

'Unfortunately he sorted him out a bit too much. But when a *drug-dealer* calls the police, and they charge my brother with a crime . . . know what I'm saying?' he says.

Vigilantism sounds the norm in his neighbourhood. He has never heard of Anjem Choudary, but has plenty to say about Muslims in general.

'To be honest we have a lot of fights with them. They're always hitting on girls outside the tube and whatnot. I've got this friend, a Sikh girl, it happened to her. I only live two minutes away, and when it happened she called me and I went straight out. I said, do that again, mate and I'll break your legs, all right?'

I wander back to the press pack and chat to a photographer, Rebecca, who works for the London bureau of Breitbart, the 'alt-right' American news organization whose CEO, Steve Bannon, is running Donald Trump's election campaign. Rebecca's job seems to be to tour the country photographing the downside of immigration. Real or perceived, it's all the same to Breitbart, whose London operation she herself describes as 'basically Pravda for UKIP'. She has been in Dewsbury recently, where she somehow managed to visit a sharia council, and is a regular in places like Bradford and Luton. Rallies and demonstrations, like the highly politicized memorial for Jo Cox in Trafalgar Square last week, are a speciality. She says she doesn't much like being a cog in the Islamophobia industry but that working for Breitbart pays the bills.

Choudary, she goes on, is bread-and-butter to an organization like Breitbart because he actively courts notoriety.

'He's a master puppeteer. It's all Punch and Judy to him, and he just loves it.'

I see what she means when Choudary finally appears at the top of the road. His sandals slap the pavement as he strolls nonchalantly towards us, his hands thrust deep into the pockets of a billowing white thobe, grinning smugly at the line of photographers blocking his way. He pauses as he reaches us and preens like an actor at a movie premiere. It is probably just as well that Mr Patriotism across the street has unaccountably abandoned his post just at the wrong moment. Choudary seems to ooze sanctimony.

He has been on bail for several months ahead of this trial, living at home in east London under a court injunction not to talk to the media, but this didn't stop him from talking to Breitbart when they phoned him last week to ask how he would be voting in the referendum.

'I'm for Remain,' he said, 'because EU laws make it harder for the UK to deport Muslims.'

The story duly made headlines in the pro-Brexit *Sun*.[15]

'So, what do you think of the referendum result now, Mr Choudary?' shouts Rebecca.

'I'm delighted,' he beams. 'Brexit weakens Europe and weakens the British state, and that is to the advantage of all Muslims.'

'So, er – the opposite of what you said last week?' says Rebecca.

'What you reported last week is not what I said,' Choudary replies, wagging a finger and smiling still. 'I said that *either* result, exit or remain, would be to the maximum advantage of Muslims.'

And with this confusing utterance he disappears through the door towards his trial.

*

I catch a train to Birmingham to spend the evening with Amir Ahmed, one of the Nansen primary school parents I interviewed last winter. He and his wife Rubina live with their seven children in a small terraced house in Alum Rock, the most solidly Mirpuri urban district in Britain. Unusually among the Mirpuris I have met they describe themselves as Ahl al-Hadith, the 'People of the traditions of the Prophet', a Salafist, south Asian offshoot of Arab Wahhabism. As Amir explains in painstaking detail, they do not blindly adhere to any single mainstream school of jurisprudence, as most Muslims do. Their beliefs and practices derive instead from rigorous personal examination of the Koran and the hadith. Amir likens the Ahl al-Hadith to Jesuits. They are very conservative but not stick-in-the-muds.

'It's important to keep one's mind open to reason and truth,' Amir says.

But I am still surprised when, after dinner in his front-room *majlis,* we are joined by the cooks, Rubina and their eldest daughter, Samaya, 28. I remark on this later to Amir, who confesses smilingly that he had not expected them to do this either. It is a reminder that it is not only men who observe and uphold patriarchal tradition. In this Asian home as in others I have visited, there is a strong sense that it is the women, not the men, who make the rules.

I wonder if this confidence and openness in the home is a function of education. Amir is a physics graduate and a former IT consultant for the accountancy firm KPMG. Samaya, an accountancy clerk, wears a niqab outside the home, but has no difficulty chatting to me without one now. Her father voted Leave in the Euro-referendum, attracted by the promise of 'taking back control', and on the assumption that the UK would stay in the single market. Samaya, on the other hand, voted Remain, on the sophisticated grounds that the economy is 'too stormy' at the moment to handle the shock of a Brexit. I find myself umpiring a family discussion that never happened before the referendum.

'I didn't know you were so interested in all this,' Amir says to Samaya.

Wives and daughters voting independently of the patriarch is not something I had expected in Alum Rock, but this is, I can see, entirely in keeping with the tradition of their brand of Salafism, in which truth is arrived at not by diktat but via careful individual analysis of the facts.

Alum Rock, Amir acknowledges, is a strange place, semi-insulated from the world by its mono-ethnicity.

'A lack of education makes people cluster together . . . they are happier like that if they don't speak English.'

The locals are typically not just from Mirpur but, in many cases, from the same small communities within that region. Many of Amir's neighbours are from Didyal, a village on the north bank of the Mangla reservoir. Both he and his wife's families are from Panyam, a former hill town to the south. The upside of Alum Rock, Amir says, is that it is a safe place to live, in the way that rural villages are safe. The papers are full of stories of Islamophobic abuse, but the Ahmed family have experienced none of it. When everyone knows or is related to one another, the community polices itself.

We talk late into the night, discussing the shortcomings of the English state school system, the *ishtihad* tradition of consensus decision-making, Barelwi dogma, eclecticism, Birmingham reformism. At two o'clock Amir proposes to take me to Green Lane mosque, a five-minute drive away in Small Heath, where his son Othman works as a volunteer, and whose IT system he set up. It is a rambling complex with room for 5,000 worshippers, converted from a disused municipal library and swimming baths. Amir says it is 'very old', by which he means not that the building is Victorian, but that it has been operating as a mosque since the 1980s.

I'm keen to see this supposed den of super-Salafists. In 2007, a Channel 4 *Dispatches* programme aired secretly filmed footage of one of its imams, Abu Usamah, apparently denigrating women, attacking homosexuality and lionizing the killer of a British soldier in Afghanistan. The old men of the mosque committee, Amir says, were 'spooked' by this adverse publicity and have since been replaced by a younger generation of managers, who have enforced a change. The mosque's six imams all preach in English now. Unauthorized discussion groups are strictly forbidden, and any sign of radicalism is jumped on and neutralized by a mosque-run mentoring team.

We arrive to find the mosque's halls swarming with people, and very hot. We are into the last ten days of Ramadan, the most sacred of the month, when attendance always spikes. The congregation is far more ethnically mixed than I had expected. There are many Somalis here, and Arabs, black Africans, whites.

I am introduced to the mosque manager, Amer Ijaz, who is over-seeing final arrangements for another suhur breakfast for 1,500 people. A dozen stewards run about wearing supervisor bibs and carrying walkie-talkies. Trestle tables are loaded with tureens of baked beans, boiled eggs, nan and curry. The logistics of mass catering is a mosque speciality. In a week's time, Green Lane will be the lead organizer of the Eid celebration in nearby Small Heath Park, which is expected to be attended by 90,000 people. I'm amused to hear that it will be sponsored by that charity with the sharpest eye for an opportunity, the people behind the nasheed concert in Glasgow, Human Appeal.

Ijaz is Birmingham through and through, with a homely out-look on life and the Black Country accent to match.

'Did you hear that England lost 2–1 to Iceland tonight?' is the first thing he says. 'Roy Hodgson's resigned. I'm gutted.'

He looks frazzled with tiredness but is friendly and proud of his work, which includes a lot of charity fundraising for Syrians in the camps around the warzone, where he is a regular visitor. He views this work not just as effective humanitarianism but as a necessary counter to radicalism within the community.

'People see what is happening in the Middle East and they see the West's inaction and they get frustrated. So we have to refo-cus the energy of the youth into fundraising.'

This refocusing, he wants me to know, is central to the mosque's transformation since the old committee was replaced, and the seven-figure sums the mosque routinely raises for the causes it espouses are his evidence that the strategy is working. Green Lane is as much a community centre as it is a religious institution these days. Ijaz is a regular face at police forums, where he teases his opposite numbers that he gets 'more crime-reporting than the local police station . . . because many of the brothers here won't trust the West Midlands police'.

Despite the mosque's high profile, he says there has been little trouble from racists since the Brexit vote – thus far, at least.

'I've been telling people to tie up their camels because I think we are in for a rough ride.'

The irony is that, like Amir Ahmed, many among the Green Lane community voted for Brexit.

'You'd be surprised how many people here are true-blue Brits. I was stunned meself, but I'd say it was about 50-50 . . . One bloke told me he'd done it because he was worried about immigration. I said, whoa there – I'm a migrant, and so are you. And he goes, I know, but we've got the best benefits system in the world here and we don't want to break it. It's the numbers that are out of control.'

Tuesday 28 June

Edinburgh again. Bashir at the Annandale texts, asking me down to the mosque for iftaar to meet some 'special friends'. The Annandale Pakistanis are my new best friends: it's the second time he's invited me in a week. The trestle tables for guests are out again, but the friends, disappointingly, turn out to be two community policemen, both called David. It's their first visit to the mosque, and it's clear from the stiffness of their posture and the way they watch each other from the corners of their eyes that they are not iftaar-experienced.

One of the Davids, who has swapped his uniform for a shirt and tie – 'to show my other side,' he says – reveals that Lothian police are on the alert for hate-crime in Edinburgh, particularly in the wake of an incident in Walsall yesterday in which a Kashmiri butcher's shop was fire-bombed.

'The projectile was aimed directly at an employee,' he adds in policeman-speak, his eyebrows raised to express the notch up from the usual verbal abuse.

It is difficult to believe that such a thing could happen in Edinburgh. Yet last year, he says, he helped to police a demo on

Princes Street by a right-wing group in tight black masks and flags depicting a thunderbolt that neither he nor his colleagues had ever seen before.

Back home, Melou complains that I smell of curry, body as well as clothes. Listening to the radio as I brush my teeth, I hear that Istanbul airport has been assaulted by suicide bombers, killing forty and injuring hundreds: the worst terrorist attack ever on an airport. A Ramadan terrorism campaign is gathering pace. Suicide car bombers killed another forty-two in Yemen yesterday.

Wednesday 29 June

To another interfaith iftaar, this time in Batley with Mohammed Pandor, the mufti I met demonstrating against Britain First in Dewsbury in February. I've heard him on Radio 4 since then, a programme about British Deobandism, in which he was accused of calling Bonfire Night 'bidah', a heretical innovation. He is still cross with the presenter, the veteran Pakistan correspondent Owen Bennett-Jones, who he says misrepresented him by cutting out the context of his remarks. The programme was certainly highly critical of Deobandis, who came across not just as aloof from the modern world but, worse, fiercely resistant to integration. I can see why Pandor feels ill-treated. A stalwart of the interfaith scene, he has worked to improve community relations for years and is one of very few Deobandi clerics willing to engage enough to agree to go on Radio 4.[16]

I meet him outside an office in Leeds where he works on strategy and policy for the Department of Health, looking smaller and older without his trademark fan-shaped turban. We drive to his house in Batley where he changes back into the garb of a mufti, and then on to the Pakistani and Kashmiri Workers' Association for the evening's do. There is the usual assortment of Mormons, vicars and progressive council workers. There is a minute's silence for Jo Cox, who was scheduled to have been here tonight. The talk in the room is that far-rightists have been leafleting the area arguing that she got what was coming to her. The Dewsbury MP, Paula Sherriff, has raised the matter in parliament.

The evening is about one of Jo Cox's favourite causes, the plight of Syrian refugees, a handful of whom have been settled in the area by Kirklees Council. The local Muslims are huge fund-raisers for the refugee camps around the warzone. Arshad Patel, the co-founder of a charity called One Nation, has led several aid convoys there in the past, some of which comprised over sixty vehicles from Yorkshire. He tells me about Alan Henning, the regular mechanic on these missions, who was beheaded by ISIS in 2014.

'We called him Gadget because he was always fixing things,' he recalls. 'Brilliant bloke. Always making cups of tea.'

The star of the night is a refugee from Damascus, Razam al-Sus, who from her new home in Huddersfield has set up a halloumi cheese business, an award-winning artisan product that she markets as 'Yorkshire Dama' in honour of her home-town. Documentary-makers have been queuing up to film her inspirational story, which she is delighted to share with us again tonight, her face shining in the circle of her tight white hijab.

Mufti Pandor is an ebullient compere. He gives a slide presen-tation on Ramadan complete with a multiple-choice quiz sheet: *In which month of the Islamic year does Ramadan fall? Are injections permitted during the fast?* Half way through he hauls me to my feet and thrusts the microphone into my hand.

'James,' he says, 'please tell us what you've been doing this holy month!'

'I've, er, been fasting,' I stammer.

There is a round of wild applause, as if for a new convert to the Muslim fold. I sit down quickly, feeling a bit of a fraud.

He takes me later to the tarawih at Madni Mosque, formerly

a Victorian church in Dewsbury town centre, along with his Department of Health colleague Ann and her daughter Harriet, who have never been in a mosque before. Harriet is 20-something, pretty, and dressed in skin-tight jeans, which entirely negate the effect of the hijabs she and her mother have hastily put on, but there is no problem. Chairs are produced for the ladies, along with bottles of water and a plate of fruit.

The imam, preaching over the heads of two hundred people, and with Pandor acting as translator next to him, tells us we are children of Adam like them, and welcome here. Afterwards in his office I am introduced as a journalist who has spent time in Afghanistan. The imam's acolytes want to know what I think of the Taliban – followers of the Deobandi tradition, like them. I say they were never anything but kind to me when I met them, and that I found them to be Pashtun nationalists as much as Islamist ideologues, and nothing to do with al-Qaida. They listen intently, and when it is time to leave one of them jumps up and thanks me, pumping my hand. It is evidently not what they usually hear from non-Muslims in Dewsbury. We are barely a hundred yards from the spot where, in February, Britain First demonstrators were chanting 'Taliban scum'.

I spend the night at Pandor's house, in a borrowed sleeping bag on his sitting-room floor. The Deobandis, I discover, take suhur very early, at 1.30. Pandor says this is the correct interpretation of the scripture, but eating porridge at that hour, however delicious, feels to me like an act of puritan one-upmanship.

Thursday 30 June

It's a pleasure to return to Abdalhaqq Bewley's zawiya in west Bradford. The house feels even more than usual like an oasis of sanity and serenity after Batley; a unique outpost of native British Islam. The house is periodically filled with a monkish, monotone chanting as nine of his followers, all converts staying in the house, recite the Koran in congregation. They seem to be practising a form of *i'tikaf*, when some Muslims opt to seclude themselves in a mosque over the last ten days of Ramadan, the holiest of the month. The tradition of these Maliki Sufis is to recite the entire Koran over this period rather than over the whole month. Their chanting is very different to the usual solo recital by an imam or community hafiz. The company is a mixture of native Brits and foreigners, including even a Mayan from Mexico. One or two of the older men here are wearing stripy djellabas, showing that they have not lost touch with their movement's roots in 1960s Morocco.

Between recital sessions I go for a walk with Abu-Bakr Carberry, a herbalist from Guyana who lives in Burton-on-Trent and is a zawiya regular. Like the others in the house, his faith seems an intense and serious thing. There is a magnetic aura about him, a centred, meditative quality that you sometimes find in the very religious. We walk up the hill and around the Chellow Dene nature reserve where we pass three Asian lads on a bench, scoffing chips with guilty faces: sundown is still hours away. Abu-Bakr and I compose our faces and pretend not to notice. Further on we hear nefarious shouting from the bushes and scurry onwards towards the reservoir at the centre of the reserve, where we meet a Pakistani with an immense Akita guard dog on a chain. He has recently moved to Bradford from Northolt in Ealing but is finding life here difficult with the dog.

'Everyone is scared of him here,' he says.

His neighbours complain when he leaves the animal at home, and he can't find anyone to walk it for him while he is out at work. It is another measure of how Muslim Bradford is, how different to the rest of dog-loving Britain.

We retreat to the zawiya where I chat to Abdalhaqq and Ibrahim Lawson, who converted in 1976. He is the director of an Islamic Education Institute in Whitechapel, and very learned.

Islam, he theorizes, could be the spark for a second European Renaissance, taking intellectual thought back to the pre-Socratic age. He is on a mission to expand traditional Islamic teaching to include Western philosophy.

'I've got girls in niqabs at the institute studying Heidegger,' he enthuses. 'It's great. You should visit us.'

Friday 1 July

Tonight could be Laylat al-Qadr, the Night of Power, the holiest date in Ramadan, when the Angel Gabriel began to reveal the Koran to the Prophet in a cave near Mecca. The uncertainty of the date is curious. The scripture says only that the visitation was on an odd-numbered calendar day in the last ten days of Ramadan. Most but not all scholars say the twenty-seventh of the lunar month is the likeliest date, which is tonight, although only for those who started on 6 June; for everyone else, this is still the twenty-sixth.

Abu-Bakr told me that Laylat was a 'subtle' night and that I would know it when it came – although as a non-Muslim fasting for the first time, I rather doubt this. Back in Edinburgh for the weekend, therefore, I drive over to the Central Mosque at midnight and ask someone by the shoe pile what they think.

'It's a difficult call,' he says. 'This could be Laylat. Or it could be tomorrow. It's best to keep praying, just in case.'

Inside, the tarawih is in full swing. I settle down with my Koran, cross-legged with my back to one of the pillars, and dip in towards the back of it, where I find Surah 97:

Truly We sent it down on the Night of Power.
And what will convey to you what the Night of Power is?
The Night of Power is better than a thousand months . . .
It is Peace – until the coming of the dawn.

Laylat is certainly an important opportunity for the charity fund-raisers. There was another pushy email today from Human Appeal, calling tonight THE NIGHT YOU'VE BEEN WAIT-ING FOR, because generosity now is amplified in the eyes of Allah.

> Have all your previous sins forgiven. On this special night, Allah's Mercy will descend on those who maximise their ibadah. On every corner of the globe, there are people in urgent need, who are making intense dua for help. You can be there for them on this truly blessed night. You can be the answer to their prayers. You can open the gates of Allah's mercy and earn Jannah with one beautiful donation. Don't miss out!

Saturday 2 July

In Dhaka last night, a group of ISIS militants stormed the Holey Artisan Bakery, a café frequented by foreigners. A twelve-hour siege ended with twenty hostages killed, most of them Japanese aid officials and Italian workers in the garment industry. Hostages able to recite a verse or two of the Koran were spared, and even given a meal during the siege. The rest were taken upstairs and had bits cut off them with machetes until they were dead. In defiance of the stereotype, the assailants were all middle-class, well-educated locals. All were eventually killed, as they must have known they would be, by Bangladeshi commandos.

The Night of Power, the night worth a thousand months, is historically popular with wannabe martyrs. On this night in 2000, for example, al-Qaida tried to blow up an American destroyer, the USS *The Sullivans*, with a boat full of explosives off the coast of Yemen. (The boat was so full of explosives that it sank before it could reach its target.) One of the most shocking things about this travesty of Islam, to my mind, is how banal Islamic terrorism now seems. It's depressing to consider that today's suicide bombers were mostly still babies at the time of 9/11. Mass murder for Islam has been the backdrop to their whole lives: a hideous new norm for the millennial generation.

Sunday 3 July

Palestine. There is no other grievance like it for Muslims, which is no doubt why, in 1979, Ayatollah Khomeini inaugurated Al-Quds Day, an international day of protest against the Israeli occupation. In London today, as in previous years, there is to be a march on the US Embassy, organized by the Islamic Human Rights Commission, an outfit once described by Melanie Phillips in the *Spectator* as 'the most conspicuous promoter of Khomeini jihadism in the UK'. It promises to be a tenser affair than usual, thanks to a planned pro-Israel counter-protest by what IHRC calls 'a contingent of Zionists, racists and fascists' at Grosvenor Square.

I join the march at the start point on Portland Place. Posters are being handed out, one of them a close-up photograph of a semi-incinerated child's shoe, purportedly taken in Gaza. There are perhaps 2,000 people here, bussed in from as far away as Glasgow, chanting anti-Zionist slogans to a big bass drum.

> 1,2,3,4, Occupation no more
> 5,6,7,8, Israel is a terrorist state!

There is an earsplitting sound system mounted on gurneys, over which a long-haired compere makes a fiery speech referencing Michael Gove, English football fans and the 'pro-Zionist' BBC, which he says stands for the British Bullshit Corporation. He warns the crowd to watch out for 'infiltrators' and not to engage with anyone they don't know. I bump into Rebecca, the Breitbart photographer. Of course this is exactly her kind of gig. She takes a photograph of a demonstrator with a poster reading *We are all Hizbollah now*. It will appear online tomorrow above the caption, *Er, no we're not*.

The cavalcade moves off in a swarm of photographers, policemen and dazed tourists. The front row turns the standard view of the Palestine issue on its head. It comprises a dozen orthodox Jews, in their trademark black fedoras and *payot* sidelocks, marching shoulder to shoulder with a group of Shi'ite clerics in Iranian-style white turbans and brown robes. The Jews are Londoner members of Neturei Karta, the Guardians of the City, a Haredi offshoot dedicated to the overthrow of Zionism, on the basis that there can be no Israeli state until the coming of the Jewish messiah.

> Judaism here to stay,
> Zionism no way!

At one point they even hold up the green and yellow flag of Hizbollah, the Lebanese movement proscribed as a terrorist group by Israel, America and France, but whose political wing is tolerated in Britain. The flag's most prominent feature, it is impossible not to notice, is a large, stylized assault rifle.

We proceed down Regent Street beneath Union Jack bunting and turn west through the shopping hordes of Oxford Street towards Grosvenor Square, where the counter-demonstration awaits, corralled by many dozens of police.

The 'fascists and racists' turn out to be a well-heeled, middle-class crowd called the Sussex Friends of Israel, who wear the blue and white Star of David like a superhero cape and brandish placards declaring *PEACE NOT HATE*. There are shouts as the march approaches, and the pro-Palestinians shout back, a bellowed dialogue of the deaf.

> From the river to the sea
> Palestine will be free!

A dark-skinned lad who has evaded the security cordon suddenly unfurls an Israeli flag from a pocket and swoops at the IHRC stewards, goading them. I'm out in front taking photographs and, as the two sides close, find myself briefly kettled in a shrinking triangle of stony-faced policemen. The provocateur is there, his face still twisted with manufactured anger. He says his name is Ishmael, a Muslim who converted to Judaism. 'Believe it or not I spend a lot of time trying to bring people together,' he says. 'I think I'm going to die.'

The moment for violence soon passes, though. Al-Quds Day is a 30-year-old ritual, an exercise in venting steam rather than a genuine effort to force a solution to the old intractable conflict, and both sides secretly know it. The Neturei Karta pump their fists from the plinth of a statue of General Eisenhower but rocks and petrol bombs are not thrown. The picnickers on the grass in the square, although well within range of stray missiles, barely look up from their sandwiches. London's marvellous imperturbability triumphs. Eisenhower looks strangely camp with his arms akimbo on his high-waisted cavalry twills, and with the Jews, Old Glory and a monumental eagle on the embassy building all in shot, I take my weirdest photograph of the day.

We have been promised a speech by Leila Khaled, the legendary 1960s hijacker, via Skype video from Jerusalem, but the stage truck carrying the necessary equipment has got lost in London's traffic. Then the mobile sound system malfunctions, prompting some in the crowd to mutter about sabotage. With the audience unable to hear, the demonstration fizzles out.

Monday 4 July

The Iranian grocery around the corner from my father's house in west London has a half-price Ramadan special on watermelon. I ask the shopkeeper sunning himself on a stool if his business suffers with so many of his customers eating less, but he says not, because so many of them buy more than they strictly need for iftaar. Only about half of the grocery's custom is Muslim, moreover. The shop's lucrative sideline in Iranian caviar is entirely unaffected.

I have caught a cold, and am weary of Ramadan today and glad that it's almost over. I speak to no Muslims apart from the shopkeeper, and find I don't want to think about Islam at all. Instead, in a kind of defiant embrace of my own upbringing, I decide to break my fast in Sticky Fingers, Bill Wyman's rock-themed restaurant in Kensington, a place I used to visit often after it opened in 1989.

It's a mistake. I'd been looking forward to a beer and a burger and chips at my table for one, but when I sit down I find I have no appetite for meat after all. The restaurant is crowded with diners taking advantage of a half-price 'Monday madness' deal and their shouting over the blaring rock music feels like an assault. A month ago I'm sure I would have felt perfectly comfortable here. How has Ramadan turned me into such a delicate flower? Looking around, the diners themselves strike me as overfed and strangely gross. They seem to eat with the discernment of robots pecking at a conveyor belt. This sense of dislocation, of separation, is entirely unexpected. The overpriced three-bean jambalaya I eventually order is a bland vegetable porridge that I actually struggle to finish. Fasting, I conclude, has turned me into an ascetic, sensitized to consumption in general, and far more selective about what I eat. It has certainly physically changed me: later, before bed, I weigh myself and find I have lost 9lb since the beginning of the month.

An ISIS truck bomb killed 250 people in Baghdad last night – 250! – in the deadliest single attack in that city in years. The bomber blew up in Karrada shopping district, a Shi'ite area, which was crowded with families who had just broken their fast and were out buying sweets and the new clothes Muslims traditionally wear at Eid. Many of the dead are children.

Tuesday 5 July

The last day of Ramadan. It seems only fitting to break the fast for the final time with my Afghan Pashtun friend Mir, at his family's home in Dollis Hill. I've known Mir for almost half of my life, ever since he was my interpreter when I was reporting on the rise of the Taliban in northern Afghanistan in the mid-1990s. He was barely 20 then, and I was 30. He's still not married but the house is full of little nephews and nieces, all born in London to his brother and sisters. Mir is based in Muscat and Tehran these days and has only today come back to London for Eid.

The house, a detached 1930s villa, has been thoroughly Afghanized. Squeezed on to its weed-choked forecourt are four shiny Toyota Priuses. The cars are grey imports from Japan, so brand new they still have no number plates. Mir explains that his brother has recently gone into the minicab-leasing business. The rear of the house is no less startling. With the help of local Afghan builders, it has been extended by 8 metres into the back garden, the maximum allowed by the planning authorities, to create a richly carpeted and cushion-lined majlis so big that it contains two chandeliers. I imagine the formal objections this would prompt from the average native white neighbour in London, but there were no such neighbours in this case. The house on one side belongs to an Iranian politician, the other to a Moroccan businessman, neither of whom is often here. The majlis can hold perhaps fifty people, large enough for a *shura*, the gathering of elders at which important community decisions are taken, here among the British Afghan community as they are back home. It's needed because Mir's father is an elderly respected *alim*, an Islamic judge, who regularly receives delegations from Birmingham, Manchester, even abroad.

The judge is currently away on pilgrimage in Saudi, and Mir himself doesn't arrive from Heathrow until almost midnight. But I was warned nevertheless to expect a feast – and there certainly is one. Mir's nephew Mohammed, 10, with his cherubic five-year-old brother Ahmed on his wing, is fiercely proud of his traditional role as headwaiter. The boys are impeccably drilled, operating fast and in silence, only occasionally glancing at Mir to check that they are performing correctly. A plastic picnic rug is laid out beneath the chandeliers and is quickly covered by steaming plates of Kabuli pilau, boiled eggs, nan, all prepared by a sister and an in-law secreted in the kitchen. There is *mantu*, a stuffed pasta parcel delicacy, and *samanak*, Afghanistan's legendary slow-cooked wheat stalk porridge. The boys bring a metal ewer and basin for me to wash my hands in before we eat, a ritual that feels as old as the Hindu Kush. As ever in this household, there is no compromise in the preservation of the customs of the old country.

Mir is looking prosperous in his early middle age. He is working for an Omani consortium that exports luxury vehicles to Iran and is constantly on aeroplanes. He's effectively a sanctions profiteer; Oman functions as an unusually stable Arabian entrepôt for Western manufacturers forbidden from exporting directly to Iran, whose citizens will pay top dollar for almost any marque that isn't a state-manufactured ICKO Samand, the dreaded Iranian equivalent of the East German Trabant. Mir

is full of lurid tales of the corruption of Iranian society, particularly the hypocrisy of the religious elite. He describes an
ayatollah notorious for ordering beatings for women out after
dark unchaperoned or who expose an ankle in public, who is
nevertheless also famed for his alcohol-fuelled pool parties and
his taste for prostitutes. Apocryphal or not, his stories make Iran
sound ripe for another revolution.

I bed down for the night on the cushions in a corner of the
cavernous majlis. Mir even produces an old shalwar kameez for
me to wear as pyjamas. I fall asleep, feeling like I am back in
northern Afghanistan.

Wednesday 6 July

It's the first of Shawwal, the month after Ramadan, and the fast
is over. We breakfast in the majlis on mint tea, hard-boiled eggs
and nan. It is my first meal in daylight for a month. The boys, out
of school for the holiday, stage an egg fight, the Afghan version
of conkers and an old Eid tradition. Then Mir drives us to Glad-
stone Park in Dollis Hill, where the special short prayer, the Salat
al-Eid, is being staged out of doors.

Unfortunately we get stuck in a traffic jam and arrive too late
for the actual prayer, but it hardly matters. It's a sunny day and
the park is packed with 5,000 smartly dressed Muslims, all milling around the food stalls and fair rides that encircle the main
prayer area in the fenced-off tennis courts. Eid al-Fitr, the Festival of the Breaking of the Fast, is intended to celebrate 'the
happiness which man feels after successfully completing an
important task' – and it is good to be able to share the carnival
feeling now that I, too, have fulfilled one of the five pillars of
Islam.

We catch another Salat al-Eid at a mosque in Cricklewood, one
of three local mosques that Mir's family uses. There are so many

takers for prayers in the building, a tiny converted corner shop, that the imam, an engaging Yemeni-Somali, is obliged to hold three separate services. We squeeze into the second. His homily, delivered off the cuff, is rhetorical filler before the formal start at 10.30. Most of his material is unexceptional: don't underestimate yourself and your power to implement change; being a good Muslim is for all the year, not just Ramadan; be generous with your charity; thank and be kind to the sisters in your family, who have been working in the kitchen for you every night for a month. But then, suddenly, he is talking about 'bad habits in society' – by which he means homosexuality – and starts attacking sex education in state schools.

'We are not in control in this country,' he says, 'but in heaven you will be asked not if you followed local traditions, but whether or not you followed Islam. So, be sure to talk to your kids after school and explain what is going on – because otherwise they will grow up thinking homosexuality is normal. Because I am one hundred per cent certain that it is against our culture, our tradition and our *deen*.'

At this point an elder shuffles forward and whispers something to the imam, who abruptly changes subject. I look at Mir's little nephews sitting just in front of me, their backs impeccably straight, their eager faces radiating pride at being in this room full of grown-ups. I have just witnessed, I realize, the kind of car crash of values that Channel 4 likes to film covertly for its *Dispatches* documentaries.

The service is soon over and suddenly everyone is smiling, wishing one another *Eid Mubarak*, hugging and shaking hands. Mir pulls me forward through the crowd and introduces me to the imam.

'You've fasted?' he grins. 'And you believe in the divinity of God? Then you are Muslim. *Mubarak!*'

The mosque uncorks on to the street. Mir, the prodigal son returned from the Middle East, is clasped to the chests of a series of Pashtun elders in turbaned rig; he pushes his nephews forwards, who offer immaculate salaams. The warmth and sense of fellowship is wonderful and touching. But I can't quite put the sermon I've just heard out of my mind and afterwards, in the car again, I quiz Mir about it.

'James!' he says, almost testily. 'The gay thing is a black and white issue for Muslims. It's not me saying it, it's the Koran.'

I feel disquieted on the train back to Edinburgh. There is so much to like about Islam, but I know I could never submit to its unbending orthodoxy. I don't believe there are black and white answers to anything much. The Westerner in me, perhaps the journalist also, prefers questions to dogma. Eid has left me with a feeling of anticlimax, and an odd sense of foreboding, too, as a believer in mutual understanding and compromise. What does the future hold for Mir's young nephews – ambassadors for the next generation of British Muslims, born and bred in London yet each with one foot still held firmly in the culture of home?

Mir once told me of an east London Afghan he knew, a minicab driver from the eastern province of Paktia, who in the early 2000s used to commute back home each summer in order to fight for the Taliban. He avoided the potential paradox of killing soldiers from his adopted country – a country that he told Mir he respected and loved – by declining to take part in any operation against a unit known to be British. Soldiers from the US and all other Nato allies, however, were fair game. I have heard few starker illustrations of the fragile nature of Britishness, how perilously thin the line between belonging to a society and turning on it can be.

With unintentionally symbolic timing, the much-delayed Chilcott Inquiry into the Iraq War was published yesterday. Its conclusion is tougher on Tony Blair than the pundits anticipated and social media is full of gloating damnation. The man himself remains unrepentant in a TV interview, arguing once again that he thought supporting Bush's invasion was 'the right thing to do'. His voice, though, has gone all tremolo, and his puppy eyes seem to have lost their power to convince. Last week's bombing in the Karrada district of Baghdad seems verdict enough. The death toll is still being revised upwards and now stands at over three hundred.

At sundown last night, suicide bombers attacked three targets in Saudi Arabia, including the Mosque of the Prophet in Medina, one of the holiest sites in Islam.

'An attack in Medina in the final days of Ramadan? Almost literally unfathomable,' someone comments on Twitter.

'Like Frankenstein's monster, turning on its creator,' tweets someone else.

Mir reckons the target in Medina wasn't the mosque but the nearby court of the Mukhabarat, Riyadh's feared secret police. Either way, it is a sad finale to Ramadan, with the feel of a portent of trouble to come for Muslims everywhere, including here at home.

The last month has been every bit as interesting and valuable an experience as I hoped it would be. The fast has taught me new things not just about Islam but about myself. I wonder if I will ever do it again. For now, though, I am glad that it is over. Ramadan has thrown me out of sync with the non-Muslim world more than I anticipated, above all with my home life, and it is time to readjust. It will be good to focus on the children as they start their school holidays and to put thoughts of Islam to one side – at least for a while.

Glossary

adhan	Muslim call to prayer
Ahmadiyya	Islamic sect founded by Mirza Ghulam Ahmad of Qadian, India, in 1889
alim (pl. ulama)	Learned person, scholar
asr	Early afternoon prayer
Barelwi	Sufi-leaning, south Asian traditionalist movement founded in 1900s India
biradari	A particular style of south Asian politics in the UK; lit. 'brotherhood'
burqa	Full veil, commonest in Afghanistan, where the eyes are covered by a cotton mesh
chador	Body cloak, commonest in Iran, that leaves the face open
chowkidar	Urdu: a watchman, a gatekeeper
Da'esh	Acronym for the al-Dawla al-Islamiya al-Iraq al-Sham (Islamic State of Iraq and the Levant), also known as ISIL, ISIS
darul uloom	Islamic seminary; lit. 'house of knowledge'
da'wah	The proselytizing of Islam
deen	Creed
Deobandism	Sunni revivalist movement founded in Deoband, India in 1867
dua	Prayer of supplication
fajr	Dawn prayer

hadith	Report of the deeds or words of the Prophet, hundreds of which were collated long after his death; *cf* the Christian gospels
hafiz	One who has memorized the entire Koran; lit. 'memorizer'
hajj	Annual pilgrimage to Mecca at the end of the Islamic year; fifth pillar of Islam
Hajji	Honorific accorded to one who has completed the hajj
halal	Permissible according to Islamic law
Hanafi	World's most widely followed Sunni madhhab, named after the scholar Abu Hanifa (d. 767)
Hanbali	Smallest of the four orthodox Sunni madhahib (*qv*), named after Ahmad ibn Hanbal (d. 855), primarily found in Saudi Arabia and Qatar
haram	Forbidden according to Islamic law
hijab	Generic term for the headscarf
hudud	Punishment under Islamic law
ibadah	Worship; lit. 'obedience with submission'
iftaar	Breaking of the Ramadan fast at sunset
ijtema	Annual conference of the Tablighi Jamaat
isha	Night-time prayer
ISIL, ISIS	*See* Da'esh
i'tikaf	Period of religious retreat
jamiyat	Society, political party; lit. 'gathering'
Jannah	Paradise
jihad	The fight against the enemies of Islam; the struggle within oneself against sin
jumu'ah	Friday prayers
kafir (pl. kuffar)	Derogatory term for an unbeliever
keffiyeh	Traditional Arab men's headscarf
khatib (pl. khateeb)	Sermonizer
khutbah (pl. khutab)	The main Friday sermon
kippah (pl. kippot)	Skullcap worn by Orthodox Jewish men
kufi	Short round cap worn by men throughout the Islamic world

madhhab (pl. madhahib)	School of Islamic jurisprudence; lit. 'doctrine'
madrassah	School for Islamic education
maghrib	Sunset prayers; lit. 'place where the sun sets'
majlis	Public reception room found in traditional Muslim homes
makruh	Disapproved of in Islamic law but not quite haram (*qv*)
maktab	Elementary school
Maliki	One of the four Sunni madhahib, predominant in north and west Africa
maulana, maulawi	Senior Islamic scholar; lit. 'lord, master'
Mawlid	The Prophet's birthday
minbar	Mosque pulpit
miswak	Toothbrush made from the root of the arak tree
muezzin	The prayer caller, traditionally from the top of a mosque's minaret
mufti	Muslim jurist; canon lawyer
Muhajiroun, al-	Salafist extremist organization, proscribed in the UK in 2010; lit. 'the emigrants'
nasheed	Devotional musical art form usually sung a cappella and popular throughout the Islamic world; lit. 'a chant'
nikah	Marriage contract
niqab	Face veil that leaves only the eyes exposed
qari	Reciter of the Koran
qasida	Classical poetic form; an ode
Ramadan	Fasting month, the ninth of the Islamic calendar; lit. 'dryness'
sadaqah	Voluntary charity
Sahabah	Companions of the Prophet
salaf	Ancestor, predecessor
Salafism	Ultra-conservative Sunni reform movement developed in eighteenth-century Arabia, whose followers seek to emulate the Sahabah

salah, salat	Standard Muslim prayer ritual practised five times a day; second pillar of Islam
sawm	Fasting; fourth pillar of Islam
Shabaab, al-	Militant jihadist group in Somalia; lit. 'the youth'
Shafi'i	One of the four Sunni madhahib, predominant in east Africa and southeast Asia
shahada	Profession of faith; first pillar of Islam
shalwar kameez	Long flowing tunic, predominantly south Asian
sharia	Traditional Islamic law; lit. 'way' or 'path'
Shia	Branch of Islam who believe the Prophet was succeeded by his cousin Ali, not Abu Bakr, as the Sunnis believe
shura	Gathering of elders, council; lit. 'consultation'
Sipah-e-Sahaba	Pakistani Deobandi extremist organization, banned in the UK since 2001; lit. 'guardians of the Prophet's companions'
Sufism	Mystical dimension of Islam, organized into dozens of ancient orders around the world
suhur	Pre-dawn breakfast during Ramadan
Sunna	Record of the teachings, deeds and sayings of the Prophet, a source of Islamic law
Sunni	Followers of the Sunna
surah	Lit. 'Chapter', of which the Koran comprises 114
sutrah	Small screen placed before a worshipper as an aid to concentration
Tablighi Jamaat	Missionary offshoot of the Deobandi movement, established in 1920s India; lit. 'society for spreading faith'
talaq	Divorce
taqwa	God-consciousness
tarawih	Special Ramadan night prayer
thobe	Long white robe worn by men in the Arab peninsula; a dishdash

ulama	Plural of alim
ummah	The global Islamic community
umrah	The 'lesser' pilgrimage to Mecca, performed at any time of the year and non-mandatory
Wahhabism	Saudi brand of Salafism, founded by the eighteenth-century Arabian preacher Muhammad ibn Abd al-Wahhab
zakat	Compulsory charity; third pillar of Islam
zawiya	North and west African term for a religious school or retreat
zuhr	Noon prayers

Endnotes

Introduction

1   https://www.theguardian.com/world/2016/aug/11/britons-joining-
    isis-grown-to-850-100-killed-syria-khadiza-sultana
2   http://www.telegraph.co.uk/news/uknews/12132641/Number-
    of-UK-Muslims-exceeds-three-million-for-first-time.html; Office
    of National Statistics; Pew Research Center
3   http://www.telegraph.co.uk/news/religion/12000042/How-
    patriotic-are-British-Muslims-Much-more-than-you-think-
    actually.html
4   http://www.middleeasteye.net/columns/british-muslims-
    recognised-best-charity-givers-again-142522291
5   Mo Farah observed of Trump's infamous executive order:

On 1st January this year [2017], Her Majesty The Queen made me a
Knight of the Realm. On 27th January, President Donald Trump
seems to have made me an alien.

   I am a British citizen who has lived in America for the past six
years – working hard, contributing to society, paying my taxes and
bringing up our four children in the place they now call home. Now, me
and many others like me are being told that we may not be welcome. It's
deeply troubling that I will have to tell my children that Daddy might
not be able to come home – to explain why the President has introduced
a policy that comes from a place of ignorance and prejudice.

   I was welcomed into Britain from Somalia at eight years old and
given the chance to succeed and realise my dreams. I have been

proud to represent my country, win medals for the British people and receive the greatest honour of a knighthood. My story is an example of what can happen when you follow polices of compassion and understanding, not hate and isolation.

6 https://www.theguardian.com/society/2016/nov/01/call-for-action-to-tackle-growing-ethnic-segregation-across-uk
7 Al-Hujurat 49:13
8 https://www.chathamhouse.org/expert/comment/what-do-europeans-think-about-muslim-immigration#
9 https://www.theguardian.com/world/2014/dec/06/yusuf-sarwar-mother-british-jihadist-police-betray-syria

I Britain First

1 https://www.theguardian.com/uk/2008/aug/19/uksecurity.ukcrime
2 In the general election, to the Conservative candidate Simon Reevell, following significant boundary changes
3 http://www.mirror.co.uk/news/uk-news/gang-plotted-bomb-edl-rally-1861926
4 http://5pillarsuk.com/2015/12/01/the-need-for-grassroots-muslim-activism/
http://5pillarsuk.com/2014/09/12/september-12-2007-7-years-on-from-my-terror-arrest/
5 http://www.independent.co.uk/news/uk/home-news/britain-first-terrorist-organisation-listed-lousie-haigh-jo-cox-thomas-mair-labour-mp-a7439036.html
6 *Independent*, 24 July 2016

2 Converts to Terrorism

1 https://www.theguardian.com/uk/2008/aug/20/uksecurity.terrorism
2 https://www.youtube.com/watch?v=jGTn5yFNzp8
https://www.youtube.com/watch?v=VY0D1f40C3I

3 Literally, 'the Defectors', Muslims who rebelled against the Umayyad Caliphate in the seventh century

4 https://www.gov.uk/government/speeches/extremism-pm-speech

3 The Trouble with Prevent

1 https://www.theguardian.com/uk-news/2016/oct/19/muslim-leader-jailed-for-life-hiring-hitman-kill-mosque-rival

2 https://www.theguardian.com/uk-news/2015/mar/09/anti-radicalisation-prevent-strategy-a-toxic-brand

3 2000: The Terrorism Act first defines 'terrorism'. Introduces detention for questioning for up to 7 days, and Stop and Search powers
2001: The Anti-Terrorism, Crime and Security Act. Foreign terror suspects can be detained indefinitely
2001: Terrorism (UN Measures) Order
2003: The Criminal Justice Act. Detention increased to 14 days
2005: The Prevention of Terrorism Act. 'Control Orders' introduced
2006: The Terrorism Act criminalizes indirect incitement ('glorification' of terrorism) and the giving and receiving of 'terrorist training'. Detention without charge for up to 28 days
2006: Terrorism (UN Measures) Order (replacing 2001 Order)
2008: The Counter-Terrorism Act. Interpreted as banning the photographing of police
2009: The Coroners and Justice Act permits inquests to be held in secret
2009: Another Terrorism (UN Measures) Order (replacing 2006 Order). But voided by Supreme Court
2010: The Terrorist Asset-Freezing (Temporary Provisions) Act (replacing the previous Order)
2011: Terrorism Prevention and Investigation Measures Act 2011 replaces Control Orders with TPIMs
2012: Protection of Freedoms Act (Detention reduced back to 14 days, and a repeal of Stop and Search powers)

2015: Counter-Terrorism and Security Act: Prevent and Channel
become statutory duty
2016: New CTSA proposed; Extremism Disruption Orders

4   https://www.theguardian.com/uk-news/2016/jul/12/teachers-
made-one-third-of-referrals-to-prevent-strategy-in-2015
5   http://www.independent.co.uk/news/uk/home-news/four-
year-old-raises-concerns-of-radicalisation-after-pronouncing-
cucumber-as-cooker-bomb-a6927341.html
6   Rights Watch UK
7   https://terrorismlegislationreviewer.independent.gov.
uk/terrorism-acts-report-published-today/
8   https://www.gov.uk/government/news/pms-extremism-taskforce-
tackling-extremism-in-universities-and-colleges-top-of-the-agenda
9   http://www.islam21c.com/politics/dr-salman-butt-launches-legal-
case-against-uk-gov/

4 The Hunting of the Snark

1   https://www.theguardian.com/world/2015/dec/17/society-of-
mosques-to-boycott-anti-terror-prevent-programme
2   https://www.theguardian.com/uk-news/2015/dec/13/you-aint-
no-muslim-bruv-man-leytonstone-denounces-extremism
3   'Muslim extremists' campaign of lies to undermine the
government's fight against terror', *Sunday Telegraph*, 31 January 2016
4   https://andrewgilliganblog.wordpress.com/2016/10/30/ifhat-
smith-and-prevent-watch-the-facts/
5   http://www.telegraph.co.uk/news/2016/10/29/ifhat-smith--
an-apology/
6   https://www.theguardian.com/politics/2016/jun/23/michael-fallon-
damages-imam-suliman-gani-sadiq-khan
7   https://www.theguardian.com/world/2015/dec/17/uk-will-not-
ban-muslim-brotherhood-david-cameron-says
8   http://www.bbc.co.uk/news/magazine-33677946
9   HuT's attack looked prescient in October 2016, when MPs voted
to strip Green of his knighthood for his role in the collapse of
British Home Stores

10 *Kandahar Cockney*, pp. 205–9, Harper Collins 2004
11 https://www.theguardian.com/politics/2015/jun/29/cameron-backing-theresa-may-counter-extremism-strategy-fundamental-shift
12 http://henryjacksonsociety.org/wp-content/uploads/2013/01/HIZB.pdf
13 http://www.dailymail.co.uk/news/article-3389444/Fanatics-campaign-hate-campus-revealed-Islamic-zealots-backed-Jihadi-John-poisoning-minds-students.html
14 *The World's Most Dangerous Place*, p. 352, James Fergusson, Transworld 2013
15 Both quoted in *Jihadi John – The Making of a Terrorist*, p. 248, Robert Verkaik, Oneworld 2016
16 Source: http://news.sky.com/story/anti-extremism-prevent-scheme-referrals-reach-7500-a-year-10709045
17 https://www.theguardian.com/uk-news/2016/sep/29/academics-criticise-prevent-anti-radicalisation-strategy-open-letter
18 http://www.express.co.uk/news/uk/642878/Islamist-campaigners-CAGE-tour-universities-to-recruit-ARMY-to-fight-anti-terror-laws
19 http://www.bbc.co.uk/news/uk-england-birmingham-33507650
20 http://www.parliament.uk/business/committees/committees-a-z/commons-select/education-committee/news/extremism-in-schools-report/

5 Trojan Hoax

1 http://www.thetimes.co.uk/tto/education/article4488955.ece
2 Confirmed by Richard Adams in conversation with author
3 https://www.gov.uk/government/uploads/system/uploads/attachment_data/file/318392/Review_of_Park_View_Educational_Trust.pdf
4 https://www.gov.uk/government/speeches/birmingham-schools-secretary-of-state-for-educations-statement
5 Clarke was appointed HM Chief Inspector of Prisons by Michael Gove in 2016

6   For more on this allegation: https://coolnessofhind.wordpress.com/
    2014/07/21/youre-right-peter-clarke-there-is-an-orchestrated-plot/
7   http://5pillarsuk.com/2015/10/29/camerons-community-
    engagement-forum-from-the-irrelevant-to-the-toxic/
8   http://www.dailymail.co.uk/news/article-2652887/Five-Trojan-
    Horse-schools-placed-special-measures-c7mbat-Islamic-fanatics-
    Ofsted-chief-warns-children-risk-radicalisation-extremism.
    html#ixzz4OH9IOtjz
9   Andrew Anthony, 8 April 2004, https://www.theguardian.com/
    world/2004/apr/08/religion.race
10 https://www.theguardian.com/world/2016/aug/24/french-police-
    make-woman-remove-burkini-on-nice-beach
11 By self-proclaimed 'terrorist expert' Steven Emerson in January 2015
12 http://www.telegraph.co.uk/education/educationnews/
    10900955/Trojan-Horse-plot-driven-by-same-warped-Islamic-
    extremism-as-Boko-Harams-says-Tony-Blair.html
13 'The Coalition We Need to Defeat Islamism', November 2016,
    http://www.standpointmag.co.uk/node/6684
14 In fact, of 500 British Muslims polled by Gallup in 2009, *not a
    single one* thought homosexuality was 'morally acceptable'.
    http://al-bab.com/blog/2016/04/british-muslims-and-
    homosexuality%C2%A0-good-news-or-bad
15 http://www.thetimes.co.uk/edition/news/full-transcript-of-interview-
    with-donald-trump-5d39sr09d
16 http://www.mirror.co.uk/news/watch-butlins-race-hate-wrestling-
    7692301
17 http://www.bbc.co.uk/news/education-33520643
18 Mehmood Naqshbandi, quoted in *Medina in Birmingham, Najaf in
    Brent, Inside British Islam*, Innes Bowen, C. Hurst & Co. 2015

6 The Deobandis

1   http://www.englisc-gateway.com/bbs/topic/5975-is-it-too-late-
    for-britain/
2   http://www.leicestermercury.co.uk/census-2011-white-british-
    people-form-half/story-17558831-detail/story.html

3   https://theguardian.com/society/2015/dec/12/islamists-radicalise-
    convicts-prison-officers

4   https://www.gov.uk/government/publications/islamist-extremism-
    in-prisons-probation-and-youth-justice/summary-of-the-main-
    findings-of-the-review-of-islamist-extremism-in-prisons-
    probation-and-youth-justice

5   'Muslim chaplains working across most sectors learn new
    attitudes from their experiences,' it found. 'While they often tend
    to start with normative, didactic approaches that are directed
    towards their co-religionists, their experiences of working with
    all kinds of people in a multi-faith environment seem to inculcate
    within them attitudes of empathy, person-centredness, equality,
    broad-mindedness, openness, approachability, supportiveness,
    tolerance, non-judgementalism, non-directedness, compassion,
    patience and humility.' http://www.publicspirit.org.uk/muslim-
    chaplains-in-british-public-life/

6   http://www.thetimes.co.uk/article/prisons-chief-praises-islamic-
    sect-that-warns-of-repulsive-christian-women-srjb6cdc6

7   http://www.dailymail.co.uk/news/article-3440253/Muslim-man-
    fly-honeymoon-pregnant-wife-taken-plane-quizzed-terror-beard.
    html

8   For egregious example of profiling see: http://www.dailymail.
    co.uk/news/article-3755953/Three-British-siblings-kicked-easyJet-
    flight-fellow-passengers-said-d-seen-reading-ISIS-material-
    despite-none-able-speak-read-write-Arabic.html

9   http://www.thetimes.co.uk/tto/arts/film/article2469424.ece

10 https://www.youtube.com/watch?v=0_lzCTgMoCM
    https://mobile.twitter.com/TheLadBible/status/472069856658198529/
    photo/1

11 http://www.thetimes.co.uk/tto/arts/film/article2469424.ece

12 Riyad Mahrez and Islam Slimani from Algeria, and Ahmed Musa
    from Nigeria

13 https://www.theguardian.com/uk-news/2016/may/03/isis-mother-
    who-tried-to-move-family-to-syria-ordered-to-give-up-children

14 http://www.leicestermercury.co.uk/leicester-imams-use-friday-
    prayers-condemn-recent/story-28213121-detail/story.html

15 http://www.telegraph.co.uk/education/educationnews/12122713/
    Ofsted-to-mark-down-schools-if-wearing-the-veil-hinders-
    learning.html
16 http://www.dailymail.co.uk/news/article-3911470/The-
    extremist-schools-t-close-Four-Muslim-colleges-ordered-shut-
    Government-use-courts-defy-ministers.html

7 The Sisters Are Doing It For Themselves

1   http://www.independent.co.uk/news/world/europe/nigel-
    farage-claims-there-are-no-go-zones-for-non-muslims-in-french-
    cities-on-fox-news-9976907.html
2   https://fullfact.org/law/uks-sharia-courts/
3   http://www.ibtimes.co.uk/anjem-choudary-sharia-caliphate-
    west-478307
    http://www.dailymail.co.uk/news/article-1163510/All-
    homosexuals-stoned-death-says-Muslim-preacher-hate.html
4   ICM for the Channel 4 documentary *What British Muslims Really
    Think*, 13 April 2016. ICM's research was based on a sample of just
    1,000 people, which led to widespread questions about its accuracy
5   http://www.ibtimes.co.uk/sharia-law-britain-things-are-getting-ugly-
    british-muslims-says-islamic-court-scholar-khola-1539329
6   http://www.independent.co.uk/news/uk/home-news/sharia-
    courts-in-britain-lock-women-into-marital-captivity-study-
    says-a6761141.html
7   https://www.youtube.com/watch?v=KzemrlW0Nv4
8   Surah 4, Verse 282
9   http://www.telegraph.co.uk/news/uknews/terrorism-in-the-
    uk/12104556/David-Cameron-More-Muslim-women-should-
    learn-English-to-help-tackle-extremism.html
10 https://www.theguardian.com/politics/2016/jan/18/david-
    cameron-stigmatising-muslim-women-learn-english-language-
    policy
11 http://www.telegraph.co.uk/news/uknews/immigration/
    12105369/Are-David-Camerons-English-lessons-for-Muslim-
    women-simply-reversing-his-own-cuts.html

12 http://www.bbc.co.uk/news/blogs-trending-35403106
13 https://www.theguardian.com/commentisfree/2006/oct/06/
    politics.uk
14 http://www.standard.co.uk/news/london/i-only-wanted-to-get-
    a-packet-of-starburst-charity-worker-subjected-to-antimuslim-
    abuse-while-trying-a3217031.html
15 https://www.theguardian.com/commentisfree/2015/
    jul/24/david-cameron-radicalisation-speech-muslim-woman
16 https://www.theguardian.com/world/1999/oct/28/gender.uk1
    http://www.southallblacksisters.org.uk/campaigns/zoora-shah/
17 http://www.independent.co.uk/news/uk/politics/labour-
    antisemitism-row-naz-shah-israel-map-norman-finkelstein-
    obscene-a7012461.html
18 http://www.independent.co.uk/voices/you-wouldnt-be-
    surprised-by-naz-shahs-remarks-if-you-knew-more-about-the-
    town-she-came-from-a7005336.html
19 http://news.sky.com/story/1603061/where-is-the-uks-terror-
    arrest-capital
20 *Till Martyrdom Do Us Part: Gender and the ISIS Phenomenon*, Erin
    Saltman and Melanie Smith, Institute for Strategic Dialogue
21 'Don't laugh,' Bono told the senators. 'I think comedy should be
    deployed. It's like, you speak violence, you speak their language.
    But you laugh at them when they're goose-stepping down the street
    and it takes away their power. So I'm suggesting that the Senate
    send in Amy Schumer and Chris Rock and Sacha Baron Cohen.
    Thank you.'

8 Men Behaving Badly

1 http://www.yorkshirepost.co.uk/news/crime/keighley-grooming-
   case-arrogant-asian-gang-of-12-jailed-for-130-years-1-7722032
2 *The Times*, Andrew Norfolk and Sean O'Neill, 14 October 2016
3 http://www.dailymail.co.uk/news/article-3469732/Thugs-killed-
   Muslim-grandfather-jailed-46-years.html
   http://www.mirror.co.uk/news/uk-news/elderly-muslim-man-
   racially-abused-7340086

4   https://www.theguardian.com/uk-news/2016/nov/16/asian-men-
    far-right-rotherham-cleared-violent-disorder
    https://www.channel4.com/news/by/simon-israel/blogs/activists-
    bent-targeting-asians

5   www.yorkshirepost.co.uk/news/five-men-guilty-in-rotherham-
    asian-grooming-case-1-3024198

6   Drew Review http://www.southyorkshire-pcc.gov.uk/
    Document-Library/Publications/An-independent-review-of-
    South-Yorkshire-Police's-handling-of-child-sexual-exploitation-
    1997---2016.pdf

7   http://www.independent.co.uk/news/uk/crime/child-sex-
    grooming-the-asian-question-7729068.html

8   https://www.theguardian.com/world/2015/jun/13/godfather-of-
    british-jihadists-admits-we-opened-to-way-to-join-isis

9   The black American Muslim rapper Mos Def told Alim: 'The
    reason people are able to be hafiz is because the entire Koran
    rhymes. Bismillah Al-Rahman Al-Rahim. Al-hamdulillahi Rabb
    Al-Alameen . . . I mean, it's any surah that I could name. Qul huwa
    Allahu ahad, Allahu samad. Lam yalid wa lam yulad wa lam
    yakun lahu kufwan ahad . . . Like, there's a rhyme scheme in all of
    it. And then you start to have a deeper relationship with it on
    recitation . . . Hip-hop has the ability to do that on a poetic level.'
    Quoted in 'Fear of a Muslim Planet: Hip-Hop's Hidden History' by
    Naeem Mohaiemen, an essay in *Sound Unbound: Sampling Digital
    Music and Culture* by Paul D. Miller, MIT Press 2008

9 #NotinmyName

1   http://www.wnd.com/2015/02/no-go-zones-census-data-
    shows-100-in-britain/

2   https://abdulqadeerbaksh.wordpress.com/2013/05/27/salafis-
    remove-extremists-off-the-streets-of-luton/

3   http://www.independent.co.uk/voices/comment/we-need-the-
    help-of-non-violent-muslim-extremists-against-isis-10450646.html

4   http://www.bbc.co.uk/news/uk-england-beds-bucks-herts-
    27761075

5   https://www.youtube.com/watch?v=fA6XcyXsxXU
6   http://www.independent.co.uk/news/uk/crime/jayda-fransen-
    guilty-britain-first-deputy-leader-convicted-court-muslim-
    woman-hijab-a7395711.html
7   http://www.quilliamfoundation.org/press/ofcom-rules-against-
    islam-channel-following-quilliam-report/
8   http://5pillarsuk.com/2016/11/18/twenty-six-mosques-and-
    centres-in-luton-sign-statement-opposing-prevent/

10 Asians in Kilts

1   http://www.huffingtonpost.co.uk/2014/06/12/scotland-
    independence-referendum_n_5488582.html
2   http://www.dailyrecord.co.uk/news/scottish-news/police-
    launch-investigation-after-snp-6842380
3   https://www.youtube.com/watch?v=FCiRZXg5TzE
4   http://www.lutontoday.co.uk/news/education/challney-boys-
    denies-claims-student-was-referred-to-prevent-for-wearing-free-
    palestine-badge-1-7219114
5   http://www.bbc.co.uk/news/uk-36774358
6   For more details: http://www.dailymail.co.uk/news/article-
    3440506/Muslim-trio-face-jail-helping-17-year-old-jihadi-follow-
    big-brother-Cardiff-Syria-fight-ISIS.html

11 Another British Religion

1   https://www.theguardian.com/world/2016/jan/12/church-of-
    england-attendance-falls-below-million-first-time
    https://www.theguardian.com/world/2016/may/23/no-religion-
    outnumber-christians-england-wales-study
2   A survey by Faith Matters, conducted in 2010. See: http://www.
    economist.com/blogs/erasmus/2016/02/conversion-islam
3   'We were told on one visit to a northern town that all except one
    of the Asian councillors had married a wife from Pakistan. And
    in a cohort study at the Bradford Royal Infirmary, 80% of babies
    of Pakistani ethnicity in the area had at least one parent born

outside the UK.' https://www.gov.uk/government/uploads/
system/uploads/attachment_data/file/574566/The_Casey_
Review_Exec_Summary.pdf

My Ramadan Diary

1   Koran 2:185
2   Al Imran 3:120
3   Abu Dawud
4   http://www.inminds.co.uk/boycott-israeli-dates.php
5   *Medina in Birmingham, Najaf in Brent – Inside British Islam*, Innes
    Bowen
6   *Terror on the Pitch*, Adam Robinson, Mainstream Publishing 2002
7   Al Ma'ida 5:3 (Pickthall)
8   and 9   https://www.theguardian.com/uk-news/2016/
    may/20/police-study-radicalisation-mental-health-problems
10 http://www.mirror.co.uk/news/uk-news/jo-cox-dead-
    live-updates-8207676
    http://www.mirror.co.uk/news/uk-news/jo-cox-shooting-
    britain-first-8210521
11 Al-Hijr 15: 1–3 (Bewley)
12 A well-known *dua* from *Hisnulmuslim* (The Fortress of the
    Muslim), the most famous anthology of Muslim prayers compiled
    by Sa'ed Ibn'Ali Ibn Wahf Al-Qahtani, chapter 27, dua 84
13 http://www.theguardian.com/politics/commentisfree/2016/
    jun/24/divided-britain-brexit-money-class-inequality-westminster
14 http://www.telegraph.co.uk/news/uknews/terrorism-in-the-
    uk/11038871/British-jihadist-at-the-heart-of-terrorist-network-
    terror-in-Syria-and-Iraq.html
    https://www.theguardian.com/world/2016/feb/07/londoner-
    alexanda-kotey-identified-member-isis-group-jihadi-john
15 http://www.breitbart.com/london/2016/06/21/exclusive-anjem-
    choudary-says-uk-worse-off-outside-eu-muslim-perspective/
    https://www.thesun.co.uk/news/1321570/jihadist-preacher-anjem-
    choudary-backs-remain-because-eu-stops-unfair-deportations/
16 http://www.bbc.co.uk/programmes/b06gqr66

Bibliography

A note on the Koran

Islam cannot be understood without some reference to its central text, the Koran, which presents an immediate problem for non-Arabic speakers. Arabic words can have many meanings and connotations. The Koran, moreover, is written in elliptical, seventh-century prose-poetry that by its nature is subject to interpretation. The result is that no two translations are the same. I own five of them, and can attest that some renderings even flatly contradict one another in certain key passages. As the English convert Marmaduke Pickthall observed in the preface to his classic 1930 translation (which he humbly entitled 'The *Meaning* of the Glorious Koran'):

> The Koran cannot be translated ... The book is here rendered almost literally and every effort has been made to choose befitting language. But the result is not the Glorious Koran, that inimitable symphony, the very sounds of which move men to tears and ecstasy. It is only an attempt to present the meaning of the Koran – and peradventure something of the charm in English. It can never take the place of the Koran in Arabic, nor is it meant to do so ...

Which to choose, and which to trust? Everyone's tastes are different, but for its uncluttered language, and the accessibility and clarity of its presentation, I recommend the translation of Abdalhaqq and Aisha Bewley, in their revised edition (Ta-Ha Publishers Ltd 2011). Better than reading the Koran in English, however, is to listen to a recital recorded by a good qari, or, better still, to go to a mosque and hear it in person. Without learning to read Arabic, this is perhaps the only way to appreciate the 'inimitable symphony' that Pickthall describes, or to begin to grasp why so many millions believe the Koran to be the literal word of God.

Al-Britannia was also informed by the following more profane works:

Ahmed, Saira, *Disgraced – Forced to marry a stranger, Betrayed by own family, Sold my body to survive*, Headline Review 2008

Akhtar, Shabbir, *Be Careful with Muhammad! The Salman Rushdie Affair*, Bellew Publishing 1989

Athwal, Sarbjit Kaur, *Shamed – The honour killing that shocked Britain, by the sister who fought for justice*, Virgin Books 2013

Baggini, Julian, *Welcome to Everytown – A Journey into the English Mind*, Granta Books 2007

Baker, Abdul Haqq, *Extremists in our Midst – Confronting Terror*, Palgrave Macmillan 2011

Begg, Moazzam, *Enemy Combatant – The Terrifying True Story of a Briton in Guantanamo*, Free Press 2006

Bewley, Abdalhaqq, *The Natural Form of Man – The Basic Practices and Beliefs of Islam*, Ta-Ha 2016

Bowen, Innes, *Medina in Birmingham, Najaf in Brent – Inside British Islam*, C. Hurst & Co. 2014

Bunyan, Nigel (with 'Girl A'), *Girl A, My Story – The truth about the Rochdale sex ring by the victim who stopped them*, Ebury Press 2013

Clark, Malcolm, *Islam for Dummies*, John Wiley & Sons 2003

Engel, Matthew, *Engel's England – Thirty-nine Counties, One Capital and One Man*, Profile Books 2014

Fergusson, James, *Kandahar Cockney – A Tale of Two Worlds*, Harper Collins 2004

Fergusson, James, *The World's Most Dangerous Place – Inside the Outlaw State of Somalia*, Bantam Press 2013

Gilliat-Ray, Sophie, *Muslims in Britain – An Introduction*, Cambridge University Press 2010

Bibliography

Gove, Michael, *Celsius 7/7, How the West's policy of appeasement has provoked yet more fundamentalist terror – and what has to be done now*, Weidenfeld & Nicolson 2006

Griswold, Elizabeth, *The Tenth Parallel – Dispatches from the Faultline between Christianity and Islam*, Farrar, Straus & Giroux 2010

Halliday, Fred, *Britain's First Muslims – Portrait of an Arab Community*, I. B. Tauris 2010 (First published as *Arabs in Exile* in 1992)

Harkin, James, *Hunting Season – The Execution of James Foley, Islamic State, and the Real Story of the Kidnapping Campaign that Started a War*, Little, Brown 2015

Harris, Sam (with Maajid Nawaz), *Islam and the Future of Tolerance – A Dialogue*, Harvard University Press 2015

Husain, Ed, *The Islamist – Why I joined radical Islam in Britain, what I saw and why I left*, Penguin 2007

Kundnani, Arun, *The Muslims are Coming! Islamophobia, Extremism and the Domestic War on Terror*, Verso 2014

Lockwood, Danny, *The Islamic Republic of Dewsbury: 'Requiem'*, The Press News 2015

Malik, Ayisha, *Sofia Khan is Not Obliged*, Twenty7 Books 2015

Manzoor, Sarfraz, *Greetings from Bury Park – Race. Religion. Rock 'n' Roll*, Bloomsbury 2007

Mawdudi, Sayyid Abul A'la, *Let Us Be Muslims*, The Islamic Foundation 1982

McDonnell, Elizabeth, *You Can't Have My Daughter – A true story of a mother's fight to save her daughter from Oxford's sex traffickers*, Pan Books 2015

McDonnell, Lara, *Girl for Sale – The truth from the girl trafficked and abused by the Oxford sex ring*, Ebury Press 2015

Omaar, Rageh, *Only Half of Me – British and Muslim: The Conflict Within*, Viking 2006

Pantucci, Raffaello, *We Love Death as You Love Life – Britain's Suburban Terrorists*, C. Hurst & Co. 2015

Robinson, Tommy, *Enemy of the State*, The Press News 2015

Rosenthal, Eric, *From Drury Lane to Mecca – Being an Account of the strange Life and adventures of Hedley Churchward, also known as Mahmoud Mobarek Churchward, an English Convert to Islam*, Howard Timmins 1982

Salmond, Alex, *The Dream Shall Never Die – 100 Days that Changed Scotland Forever*, William Collins 2015

Saltman, Erin and Melanie Smith, *Till Martyrdom Do Us Part: Gender and the ISIS Phenomenon*, Institute for Strategic Dialogue 2015

Sanghera, Jasvinder, *Shame – Forced into marriage, rejected by those she loved*, Hodder & Stoughton 2007

Sanghera, Jasvinder, *Daughters of Shame*, Hodder & Stoughton 2009

Shah, Hannah, *The Imam's Daughter – Her father's slave . . . her family's shame . . . the true story of her escape to freedom*, Rider 2009

Sultan, Sohaib, *The Koran for Dummies*, John Wiley & Sons 2004

Verkaik, Robert, *Jihadi John – The Making of a Terrorist*, Oneworld 2016

Warrick, Joby, *Black Flags – The Rise of ISIS*, Bantam Press 2015

Werbner, Pnina, *Pilgrims of Love – The Anthropology of a Global Sufi Cult*, C. Hurst & Co. 2003

Williams, Rowan, *Writing in the Dust – Reflections on 11th September and its Aftermath*, Hodder & Stoughton 2002

Wilson, Sarah, *Violated – A Shocking and Harrowing Survival Story from the notorious Rotherham abuse scandal*, HarperElement 2015

Acknowledgements

I am deeply indebted to the trustees of the Airey Neave Trust, whose generous fellowship grant has once again made my research financially viable, and whose moral support and keen interest in this project have been equally sustaining. The trust exists to promote research that might 'help protect and/or enhance personal freedom under the rule of democratic law', and thus contribute in a practical way to the struggle against terrorism. As before, I hope that the trustees will agree that this book does that. The relevance of my topic, at least, cannot be in doubt in these strange and difficult times for British Muslims.

A great many people helped me on my travels around Al-Britannia, and I am grateful to all of you. Those not mentioned in the text – but who were no less kind and generous with their time and energy – include Shahab Adris, Riaz Ahmad (Oldham), Mohammed Alomgir Ahmed (Cardiff), Lord Nazir Ahmed, Sadiya Ahmed (everydaymuslim.org), Azad Ali, Shaista Aziz, Abdul Haqq Baker, Paul Bowen, Salih Brandt, Anna Croze, Simon Cornwall, Ahmad Al-Dubayan, Sam Eddis, Abdalhamid David Evans, Adam Fergusson, Lucy Fielding, Kamran Ghafoor, Henry Hainault, Liam Harron, Max Howarth, Deborah Hinton, Josie Hinton, Nojmul Hussein, Mohamed Ibrahim, Ishaq Kazi, Richard Kerbaj, Muadh Khan (Wifaq ul Ulama), Waheed Khan (Inverness), Zahra Khimji, Peter Kyle, David Loyn, Allan Little, Arshad Malik, Shona McAlpine, Idris Mears, Puru Miah, Ibrahim Mogra, Raheel

Mohammed, Sarah Montague, Annabel Mullion, Andrew Norfolk, Max Paradiso, Ismail Patel, Andy Pring, Geoff Petts, Rafaqat Rashid, Alex Renton, Kim Renton, Yusuf Rowland, Hajji Ali Ridwaan, Sarah Riddell, Mahera Ruby, Nadim Sawalha, Victoria Schofield, Jean Seaton, Jamil Sherif, Peter Tatchell, Shanaz Tayab, Charlie Taylor, Tom Tugendhat, Sayeeda Warsi, Doug Weeks, Andrew Wilson, Adam Wishart, Ahmed Versi, Miqdaad Versi, Simon Vivian, Sajaad Zamaan and Rahema Zaman.

I owe especial thanks to my agent, Julian Alexander, for his sage advice and encouragement; to my skilled and dedicated editors, Henry Vines and Mari Roberts, and to all the team at Transworld; but most of all to my wife Melou, without whose love, patience and steadfastness this book, like its predecessors, could never have been written.

Picture Acknowledgements

All photos courtesy of the author unless otherwise stated.

Page 1: Newspaper headlines courtesy of MEND. Page 2: Trump counter-protests © Vickie Flores/Alamy. Page 3: Anjem Choudary © Oli Scarff/Getty Images; The Evans family © PA/ PA Archive/PA Images. Page 4: Oldknow Academy © Christopher Furlong/Getty Images; Rossi's ice cream © Jamie Wiseman/ Solo Syndication; Cucumber drawing © BBC Asian Network. Page 5: Sadiq Khan © Toby Melville/REUTERS; Naz Shah © Paul Thompson/LNP/REX/Shutterstock. Page 6: Street gang © Christopher Furlong/Getty Images; Rotherham gang © South Yorkshire Police/PA Wire. Page 7: Luton shopkeeper © Tony Margiocchi/Barcroft Media/Barcroft Media via Getty Images; Traditionally submissive picture courtesy of Twitter; Oldham street prayers © Justin Jin. Page 8: Small Heath Park © Aaron Chown/SWNS.

Index

Index

Index

Index

Index

Index

Index

Index

Index

James Fergusson is a freelance journalist and foreign correspondent who has written for many publications, including the *Independent*, *The Times*, the *Daily Mail* and the *Economist*. A regular television and radio commentator on Africa and the Middle East, he is the author of four previous books, including the award-winning *A Million Bullets*. He is married with four children and lives in Edinburgh.

A MILLION BULLETS
The Real Story of the British Army in Afghanistan
James Fergusson

'If you read anything on Afghanistan this year, then read this
strong, intelligent book of crafted anger and insight'
Anthony Loyd, *The Times*

In April 2006 a small British peace-keeping force was sent
to Helmand province in southern Afghanistan. Within
weeks they were cut off and besieged by some of the world's
toughest fighters, the infamous Taliban, who had one goal: to
destroy the invaders. It was the beginning of an engagement
which has drawn the Army into the fiercest fighting it has
seen for fifty years.

This is the real heart of the modern battle zone: a dark,
violent, unforgiving place where young men and women
are pushed to their limits and beyond. Millions of bullets
and thousands of lives later, the British Army is still fighting
another apparently unwinnable war in Afghanistan.
Here, in the words of the participants, veterans, civilians
and Taliban, is the story of where it all began . . .

'Fascinating . . . Succeeds brilliantly in detailing the
emotional impact on soldiers killing for the first
time and seeing comrades killed'
Christina Lamb, *Sunday Times*

'The only thoughtful and informed book to come
out of the UK's venture into Helmand'
Frank Ledwidge, *Royal United Services Institute Journal*

'His account cannot be ignored by anyone seriously interested
in the future of the British armed forces'
Douglas Hurd, *Spectator*

THE WORLD'S MOST DANGEROUS PLACE
Inside the Outlaw State of Somalia
James Fergusson

'Fergusson has a talent for shedding light in dark places'
Observer

Award-winning journalist James Fergusson is among the few
to have witnessed at first hand the reality of life in Somalia.

This corner of the world has long been seen as a melting pot
of crime, corruption, poverty, famine and civil war. And in
recent years, whilst Somalia's lucrative piracy industry has
grabbed the headlines, a darker, much deeper threat has come
of age: the Al Qaida-linked militants Al Shabaab, and the
dawn of a new phase in the global war on terror.

Yet, as Fergusson discovers, Somalia's star is brightening, as
forms of business, law enforcement and local politics begin
to establish themselves, and members of the vast Somali
diaspora return to their homeland.

He takes us to the heart of this struggle, provides a unique
account of a country ravaged by war and considers what
the future might hold for a population who've grown up
knowing little else.

'Essential reading for those who seek to counter the menace'
Economist

'An elegant writer, with a scholarly understanding of history,
he brings to terrible light the catastrophe that is Somalia'
Spectator

'Coruscating reportage . . . truly brilliant'
Scotsman

TALIBAN
The True Story of the World's Most Feared Guerrilla Fighters
James Fergusson

'A brave book. Fergusson is prepared to
probe beyond the cliché'
Daily Telegraph

Fifteen years ago, southern Afghanistan was in even greater
chaos than it is now. The Russians, who had occupied the
country throughout the 1980s, were long gone. The famous
mujahideen were at each other's throats. For the rural
poor of Kandahar province, life was almost impossible.

Then, on 12 October 1994, a small group of religious students
decided to take matters into their own hands. Some 200 of
them surrounded and took Spin Boldak, a trucking stop on
the border with Pakistan. From this short and unremarkable
border skirmish a legend was born. The Taliban, as they now
called themselves, had a simple mission statement and they
fought with a religious zeal that the warring
mujahideen could not match.

On the night of 26 September, Kabul fell and the country was
effectively theirs. James Fergusson's fascinating account of
this extraordinary story is required reading for anyone
who wishes to understand the seemingly intractable
conflict in Afghanistan and its consequences for us all,
today and for the future.

'Excellent and very readable'
Time Out

'A useful primer'
Sunday Times